Praise for Glamour

'In her relish for brassy blondes, gutsy flamboyance and tinsel vulgarity, Dyhouse writes like a woman who knows her way around the lipstick counter and the flea market. She shows how a parade in the trappings of glamour expressed aspiration and assertion at odds with mousy, unobtrusive conformity. Glamour was a cynical business, but also a shriek of camp defiance. All fur coat and no knickers. Dyhouse has whipped the stopper from a vintage bottle of Evening in Paris and conjured a vanished world – cheap, a little tarty, but impossible to forget.'

Amanda Vickery, author of *Behind Closed Doors*

'In *Glamour: Women, History, Feminism*, Carol Dyhouse has written a study of the conception of glamour in the twentieth century that is sprightly, provocative, and penetrating. She adds greatly to our understanding of a phenomenon that has been central to women's attitudes toward themselves … This work will be interesting to both scholars and general readers alike.'

Lois Banner, author of *American Beauty*

'In her survey of changing ideas about "glamour" throughout the twentieth century and beyond, Carol Dyhouse has succeeded in fashioning scholarly empirical research into a clear, engaging and enthusiastic account.'

Elizabeth Wilson, author of *Adorned in Dreams*

'Rigorously researched and persuasively argued, *Glamour* represents an important contribution to the social history of fashion and of fabulousness.'

Caroline Weber, author of *Queen of Fashion*

'Riveting – from perfume to sexual politics and the precise definition of "It", Dyhouse gives us an entertaining and innovative analysis of a topic that, while hitherto underexplored, has a huge impact on all our lives.'

Sarah Gristwood, author of *Fabulous Frocks*

Glamour

Women, History, Feminism

Carol Dyhouse

Zed Books

London & New York

Glamour: Women, History, Feminism was first published in 2010
by Zed Books Ltd, 7 Cynthia Street, London N1 9JF, UK
and Room 400, 175 Fifth Avenue, New York, NY 10010, USA

www.zedbooks.co.uk

Text and cover designed by Safehouse Creative
Index by John Barker and Nick von Tunzelmann
Printed and bound in Great Britain by the MPG Books Group

Distributed in the USA exclusively by Palgrave Macmillan,
a division of St Martin's Press, LLC, 175 Fifth Avenue, New York,
NY 10010, USA

A catalogue record for this book is available from the British Library
Library of Congress Cataloging in Publication Data available

ISBN 978 1 84813 407 2

Contents

Illustrations

Acknowledgements

Many people were helpful while I was researching and writing this book. My family has been unstintingly generous and has put up with a great deal, so as always my first thanks go to Alex, Eugénie and Nick von Tunzelmann. Alex and Eugénie have always been willing to discuss ideas on glamour, feminism and fashion, and have shared with me a passion for perfumes and their history. Nick has patiently read through drafts, corrected proofs and encouraged me to persevere. I would particularly like to thank Claire Langhamer, Lucy Robinson, and other colleagues at the University of Sussex: Alex Shepard before she left for Cambridge and then Glasgow, Ian Gazeley, Michèle Harrison, Hester Barron, Eugene Michail, Naomi Tadmor, Paul Betts and Alun Howkins. Thanks also to Jenny Shaw, Marcia Pointon, Joyce Goodman, Stephanie Spencer, Ruth Watts, Jane Martin, Amanda Vickery, Sally Alexander, Penny Tinkler, Sylvie Zannier-Betts and Clarissa Campbell-Orr, all of whom were supportive in different ways. Elaine Uttley, Eleanor Thompson and Kate Rose helped me to explore collections at the Fashion Museum in Bath, Brighton Museum and Art Gallery, and Worthing Museum. Claire Smith guided me round the fashion and textiles collection at the Victoria and Albert Museum, in London. Daphne Hills at the Natural History Museum in London answered questions about musk pods and civet cats in relation to the history of perfume. My thanks go also to Irene MacGregor, Christine Clennell, Paula Sedgwick and the enthusiasts who contributed to the magazine *Common Scents*. Simon Brooke offered information about the history of Grossmiths. Mick Hamer was knowledgeable about Adelaide Hall. Gerry Webster shared his enthusiasm for pre-1960s cinema. I owe *Glamour of the Screen* to Frank Gloversmith. My thanks go to Norman Dombey for his keyword search on 'glamour' in *The Times*. I am grateful to the staff in the libraries at the University of Brighton and the University of Sussex, and in Special Collections at Sussex; also the staff in the British Library, and the University Library in Cambridge. Gen Carden, Maggie Hanbury and Tamsine O'Riordan were all encouraging at key points. The team at Zed Books and Jonathan Chapman at Safehouse Creative have all been a pleasure to work with.

Thanks to Pat Harper, who has been a sharp-eyed copyeditor; any remaining solecisms will be my own.

For help in identifying copyright holders and with picture credits generally my particular thanks go to Jakob Horstmann at Zed Books. I am grateful for the help and co-operation of Anne Ward, Tessa Lewis and Sarah Crowley. For permission to reproduce images I am indebted to the British Library, the Mary Evans Picture Library, the Advertising Archive, IPC+Syndication, V&A Images, Getty Images, Magnum Photos, John Bishop, Donald Hinds and Lambeth Archives, and David Tinworth of Martin and Savage. Material from Mass Observation is reproduced with the permission of Curtis Brown Group Ltd., London, on behalf of the Trustees of the Mass Observation Archive (© The Trustees of the Mass Observation Archive). Every effort has been made to trace and to acknowledge copyright holders of the images that appear in this book. The author and publishers apologise for any unintentional errors or omissions. If brought to their notice, any such errors will be corrected in future editions.

Introduction

When it was first used, in the nineteenth century, the word 'glamour' meant something akin to sorcery, or magical charm.[1] It became a buzz word in the twentieth century, its strongest associations being with American cinema between the 1930s and 1950s, the classic period of the Hollywood 'dream factory', and in particular the screen and still photography of its female stars.

Men as well as women can be described as glamorous, and the term can also be applied to things, places or lifestyles. Any judgement of what is and is not glamorous will be partly subjective: glamour (like beauty) can be judged to exist in the eye of the beholder rather than that which is beholden. Notions of what constitutes glamour have changed through time, and yet there are marked continuities. Glamour has almost always been linked with artifice and with performance, and is generally seen as constituting a form of sophisticated – and often sexual – allure. This book will focus on feminine glamour, the relationship between glamour and fashion, and what glamour has meant to women in modern social history.

'Glamour' as a term implying a form of sophisticated feminine allure has a history which is interwoven with changing constructions of femininity, consumerism, popular culture, fashion and celebrity. Few of those who have written on the subject have done so from a position of neutrality. Some feminist writers have adopted a critical stance towards what they have seen as the oppressive prescriptions for feminine attractiveness bolstered by capitalism and patriarchy.[2] A growing body of social critics and environmentalists deplore the ravages of unbridled consumption in the developed and developing worlds, highlighting the problems of affluence and its inability to ensure human contentment and happiness.[3] Women occupy uncertain positions in histories and critiques of consumerism: representations of the prudent and socially aware 'woman with the basket' of the early Co-operative Movement, the make-do-and-mend housewife of wartime austerity, changed radically after 1945. In the oft-quoted words of Mary Grieve, editor of the magazine *Woman*, in the 1950s 'it dawned upon the business men of the country that the Little Woman was now Big Business'.[4] Advertisers began to recognise more fully the importance of ordinary women as consumers, and as living standards rose, patterns of consumption expanded and changed. Concern about the shopping addictions of well-off women was nothing new.[5] However, household expenditure surveys in the early twentieth century showed that working-class women spent next to nothing on themselves, prioritising the needs of male breadwinners and children.[6] By the end of the century women's massively increased spending on fashion and beauty products had helped to reverse this image of self-sacrifice and to ensure their new representation as shoe obsessives and shopaholics, duped by the claims of manufacturers of beauty products and anti-ageing creams. Criticism of supermodels and celebrities can also foster a kind of misogyny, with regular media witch-hunts around the rich and brainless – particularly when glamorous and female.

Amongst the range of different ideals of femininity available to women over the past century, what did the image of the glamorous woman signify? Did – and does – it simply imply the objectification of woman, subject to the male gaze? Did – and does – it represent the seduction or subjection of women as consumer in capitalist society? John Berger memorably defined glamour as a form of envy.[7] Can ideals of glamour be blamed for feminine insecurities, body dysmorphia, eating disorders, addiction to cosmetic surgery, or a refusal to come to terms with old age? Or did glamour offer a kind of agency to women, even sometimes a way of getting their own back on patriarchy? If femininity can be seen as a form of belittlement, associated with the demure, the dainty and the unassuming, then glamour – it can be argued – could offer a route to a more assertive and powerful form of female identity.[8] Glamour was often linked to a dream of transformation, a desire for something out of the ordinary, a form of aspiration, a fiction of female becoming.

What is fashionable is not always glamorous, and glamour has not always been fashionable. In twentieth-century fashion, glamour had its clichés: glitter, fur and slinky dresses, hothouse flowers and a slash of bright red lips. Glamour was about luxury and excess. It spoke of power, sexuality and transgression. It could also be about pleasure, the sensuousness of fur, silk and rich fabrics, the heady sensuality and reveries of perfume. This book will suggest that in many contexts a desire for glamour represented an audacious refusal to be imprisoned by norms of class and gender, or by expectations of conventional femininity; it was defiance rather than compliance, a boldness which might be seen as unfeminine. Glamour could be seen as both risk and self-assertion, or as a resource which might be used by women, albeit on what was often dangerous territory, in a persistently unequal society.

Reflected from Hollywood cinema during the first half of the twentieth century, glamour allowed ordinary women to indulge in dreams of escape from everyday hardship and to express interest in sexual power, the exotic, presence and influence. The cinema exerted a strong influence on popular fashion and taste, although in the UK war, rationing and limited incomes exerted strong brakes on consumerism. For the upper and middle classes in Britain, American glamour had a more limited appeal. There was a longer tradition of associating class with breeding, elegance and restraint; for the middle classes, respectability and keeping up appearances were governing concerns in matters of dress and social comportment.

In 1950s Britain the idea of glamour became somewhat tarnished by its associations with cheesecake photography, pin-up nudes or scantily dressed models in naughty magazines. Women's magazines in the 1950s were leery about glamour. At the high end of the market, fashion editors emphasised class, elegance and refinement: models such as Barbara Goalen exuded an image of aristocratic, ladylike breeding, a somewhat mannered and haughty disdain. Lower down the social scale, representations of ideal femininity were associated with modesty, neatness and domestic respectability. Glamour might be viewed by the socially secure as brash and aspirational. For all of its associations with luxury and privilege, it was something middle-class England disapproved of, suggesting women on the make, who wanted too much, knew too much, wore too little or the wrong sort of clothes, and 'were no better than they looked'.

The style disruptions of the 1960s youthquake had a dramatic impact on images of feminine desirability. Fashion models from Jean Shrimpton to Twiggy adopted a wide-eyed, startled-and-innocent look: the glamorous sophisticate was out of fashion as swinging dolly birds and flower children took centre stage, and haute couture gave way to Carnaby Street. Glamour stayed somewhat out of fashion from the 1950s through to the 1970s: the word itself was much less frequently used by fashion editors and in women's magazines. There was less need for coded sexuality in a world of free love. With the rise of the women's liberation movement in the late 1960s (so-called second-wave feminism), glamour became something of a dirty word, associated with the sexual objectification of women's bodies, Miss World competitions and the cattle market. Fashion ideals began to emphasise the desirability of the natural look, with girls in long and floating floral dresses; advertisements for cosmetics depicted these women in hayfields and meadows. Fur and heavy perfumes went very much out of fashion.

But glamour was staging a comeback: in the pages of the magazine *Cosmopolitan,* confident, aspirational and sexually aware women took stock of their image and were emboldened to look anew at the old clichés. In the music world, 'glam rock', and the performances of exponents such as Marc Bolan, David Bowie and Alice Cooper, disrupted expectations about gender and style. Glamour in the 1980s drew upon diverse elements: traditions of stage and screen, American soap opera, a new affluence, public obsession with celebrity, and a heady and unapologetic consumerism. Glamour was more widely available than ever before: piled on and parodied, it ran to excess. There was more than an element of craziness and hysteria in the glamorous creations of designers such as Jean-Paul Gaultier and Gianni Versace, in the productions of *Dallas* and *Dynasty,* in the performances of Madonna and Elton John. Glamour was cranked up and camped up, less an escape from the humdrum than a clamour in popular culture from which it was difficult to find an exit.

In the first decade of the twenty-first century the word 'glamour' was so widely used that it came to dominate the discourse of magazines aimed at women, whatever their class, age or colour. Has the word lost edge and meaning? Has glamour been democratised and, if now accessible to the many, does this reflect a new confidence and self-assurance amongst women, or are they imprisoned and undermined by its dictates? Will global economic problems fuel interest in austerity, vintage and sustainable fashion, or intensify the desire for glamour as distraction and consolation? This is a history not a horoscope, but some of these issues are discussed in the final chapter of the book.

The organisation of the book is loosely chronological. It begins as the word 'glamour' itself started to come into general use, at the beginning of the twentieth century. Before that, the word was used sparingly. Lord Rosebery had a racehorse called Glamour, and scrutiny of the use of the word in *The Times* Digital Archive around the 1890s and 1900s shows that references to this animal accounted for much of its currency in these years. The first chapter of this book outlines the historical context in which the word 'glamour' rooted and took more of a hold, a context of widening horizons, new technologies, and shifting aspirations and assumptions: what contemporaries and subsequent historians have generally referred to as 'modernity'. The catalogue of the Newspaper Division of the British Library shows that a large number of magazines and newspapers founded in the 1920s and 1930s were given the prefix 'Modern': *Modern Home, Modern Marriage, Modern Woman, Miss Modern* and so forth. Representations of the 'modern girl' in her various incarnations in the 1920s – flapper, vamp or 'dancing daughter' – presaged the impact of the screen sirens and glamour icons of the 1930s. The *Oxford English Dictionary* records an early use of the term 'glamour girl' in a magazine published in 1940, which noted the emergence 'of the new glamour-girl, as one must call her nowadays, as thin and slender as a flake of silver leaf, as blanched as an almond, as "platinum" as a wedding ring'.[9]

This book has a broad focus because its aim has been to bring together a number of lines of enquiry, about the representation and construction of different femininities, about the shaping of aspiration and desire, and about the relationships between social conditions, fashion and material culture. When I first started out on this study, a few of my colleagues raised their eyebrows. As an academic social historian, most of my previous research had focused on gender, family and education. 'So it's out of the bluestockings and into the fishnets, is it?' quipped a friend in the corridor.[10] But the change of direction is not as radical as it might first appear: education is also about dreams and aspirations (not just the targets and skills of contemporary policymakers), and fashion, cinema and magazines, like educational institutions, offer glimpses of different worlds, different models and different cultural understandings about ways of being female.

This book stems in part from a fascination with material and visual culture, clothes, cosmetics, popular fashions and inexpensive jewellery. Flea markets, junk shops and car boot sales have always distracted me, offering a rich source of social history. Piles of moth-eaten old furs, shoe boxes of paste clips, strands of fake pearls, and pretty, empty scent bottles speak about women's dreams in the past and are highly evocative: *especially* the scent bottles. I am a pharmacist's daughter, and one of my earliest pleasures was playing with the discarded perfume display bottles and cosmetic samples which my father would bring home. I particularly remember a set of Chanel No. 5, Cuir de Russie, Bois des Iles and Gardenia, magical names and haunting fragrances in elegant bottles, each with a ground glass stopper.

Perfume, as is well known, triggers memory, and sometimes a profound sense of loss and desire. Glamour has been usefully defined as a *visual* language of seduction but it also includes a dimension of sensuality and magic through touch, texture and scent.[11] There are a number of published histories and celebrations of classic perfumes, but less has been written of the cheaper and popular scents worn by women since the early 1900s. In 2003 Newcastle Public Library hosted a display celebrating the history of popular scents, perfume bottles and related products arranged by an enthusiastic local collector. Visitors were greeted by a large display of Evening in Paris, a scent created by the famous Russian *parfumier* Ernest Beaux (who also came up with Chanel No. 5). Evening in Paris, marketed by Bourjois and widely available from 1929 to 1939 and through the postwar years, is remembered by almost every woman over the age of fifty, and even the empty blue and silver bottles are now eagerly sought by collectors. The exhibition in Newcastle was enormously popular and moved many visitors to muse on the dreams they had cherished in girlhood and to share their memories of growing up in the last century.[12]

Much of women's social history is embedded in clothes, cosmetics and material culture. Dress history is now an important area of study in its own right, and there are many invaluable studies of the history of fashion and clothing.[13] There are also numerous magazines and books addressed to collectors of such artefacts as powder compacts, jewellery, scent bottles and the like. This book is obviously not simply a history of fashion nor is it a collectors' book, but I have found the focused collectors' guides very useful. Indeed the breadth of my own focus, and a synthetic approach, has meant a considerable reliance on the work of other scholars, which I hope is fully reflected in the bibliography.

The origins of glamour:
demi-monde, modernity, 'It'

The word 'glamour' was obscure before 1900. It meant a delusive charm, and was used in association with witchery and the occult. Sir Walter Scott is generally credited with having introduced the word into literary language in the early 1800s.[1] In Victorian times the word was often used in cautionary tales. In a poem called 'A Victim to Glamour' (1874) by a long-forgotten versifier, Annie the mill girl turns her back on the trusty blacksmith who is courting her after she is seduced by the darkly handsome son of her wealthy employer. Shame and ruin follow as the two men fight it out, and an ill-aimed shot nearly kills Annie. After a long and painful convalescence she sees the light and is reconciled with the distinctly *un*glamorous, humble but reliable Walter.[2] Texts of this kind warned against glamour as dangerously alluring, leading innocents astray from virtue, and emphasised the perils in store for anyone with social aspirations above their lot in life.

The period from 1900 to 1929 saw the beginnings of the modern idea of glamour, in the opulence and display of the theatre and demi-monde, in Orientalism and the exotic, and in a conscious espousal of modernity and show of sexual sophistication.[3] During this period, the word's meaning expanded to describe the magic of new technologies: the advent of moving pictures on the silver screen, new forms of transport through air, on vast, luxurious ocean liners and in fast cars; travel to distant and exotic places. Glamour could attach to both people and objects, and its connotations were by no means exclusively feminine. Pilots and rally drivers could be described as glamorous, especially the former. Later, in the 1930s, dashing young officers of the RAF in their grey-blue uniforms stitched with silver wings would become stereotypes of the glamorous male.[4] Even so, the term 'glamour' came to be associated more commonly with women and with a type of feminine allure.

Stars of the stage could be glamorous: actresses, or singers in opera and the music hall. The designer and photographer Cecil Beaton recorded his childhood passion for the music-hall artiste Gaby Deslys, 'the first creature of artificial glamour I ever knew about', whose 'taste ran amok in a jungle of feathers, diamonds and chiffon and furs'.[5] The young fashion designer Norman Hartnell confessed to a similar infatuation, recalling Deslys looking 'like a humming bird aquiver with feathers and aglitter with jewels' setting off 'her custard blonde hair'.[6] Her staggering toilettes were legendary; even her pet chihuahua was observed to sport a pair of pearl-drop earrings. Beaton identified Deslys as a transitional figure, her style and demeanour deriving partly from the demi-monde of courtesans and cocottes of the 1890s, but in her theatrical performances the precursor of a whole school of glamour that was to be exemplified later by Marlene Dietrich, Rita Hayworth and the other screen goddesses of Hollywood.[7] Glamour, for Beaton as for many others at the time and since, conveyed sophistication, artifice and sexual allure. Extravagant displays of femininity were common in the Edwardian demi-monde of actresses, courtesans and music-hall artistes. The actress Sarah Bernhardt staged most of her public appearances as major performances, swathed in satins, lace and chinchilla. Beaton's representation of Deslys as standing out from other female performers of her day, and as distinctly *glamorous*, stemmed not least from an appreciation of the *outré*: the sexiness, confidence and air of indifference to convention that this particular star exuded throughout her career. Norman Hartnell had similar thoughts: at one point in his autobiography he suggested that the word 'glamour' had become so vulgarised by over-use that it was no more than 'the small-change of advertising currency'. For him, though, glamour remained inextricably connected with *naughtiness*.[8]

By the 1900s the prolonged proprieties of the Victorian period were giving way to more open, though still highly coded, discussions of feminine sexual allure. Elinor Glyn's sensational novel *Three Weeks* (1907) was a watershed, thrilling readers with its purple-prose descriptions of a mysterious Slav Lady arrayed in rich materials of the same colour, viewed through silk curtains of 'the palest orchid mauve', squirming seductively on a tiger skin.[9] Here were all the stock props of Edwardian glamour: heady Oriental perfumes pumped through Cupid fountains drugging the senses of her young lover, couches of roses, ropes of pearls and rich jewels twined through luxuriant, unbound hair. Above all, there were the tiger skins themselves, replete with references to carnality, primitive instincts, hunter and prey. Glyn herself owned a number of tiger skins. She bought one with an early royalty cheque, and subsequently acquired another eight, naming each after a man in her life: either fictional or flesh and blood.[10] 'Would you like to sin with Elinor Glyn on a tiger-skin?' asked the doggerel verse of the day, 'Or would you prefer to err with her on some other fur?' Elinor revelled in the sensuousness of animal furs whether dead or alive: she once made a dramatic entrance at a literary lunch party in London with her marmalade-coloured pet cat curled around her shoulders.[11]

As a writer of best-selling popular fiction in Britain, and later as a successful screenwriter in Hollywood, Elinor Glyn was even more than Gaby Deslys a transitional figure, her colourful life spanning the worlds of Edwardian luxury (country house parties, old aristocracy and new wealth) and the new glamour of cinema. Glyn further bridged the worlds of the kept woman and the celebrity writer and public figure. Her marriage to the financially incompetent and emotionally unreliable Clayton Glyn failed to provide the security and privileged lifestyle she had expected.[12] As her husband's debts mounted she relied on wit, talent and sheer hard work to bail them out of ruin. Like her sister, the dress designer 'Lucile' (Lady Duff Gordon), she combined elements of a romantic, rather elitist social vision with entrepreneurship and a very modern resourcefulness.[13] In spite of her insistence on an exaggerated, conventional version of sexual difference (man the hunter, woman his alluring prey), she was a staunchly independent woman, carefully constructing her public image and very much the author of her own life. Many of her fictional heroines exhibit this same autonomy and independence. They refuse definition by birth, fate or fortune and make what they can of themselves and their lives. The best example is the uncompromising Katherine in *The Career of Katherine Bush* (1917). Of low birth (she is the grand daughter of a pork butcher and the daughter of a Brixton auctioneer), Katherine sets herself on a mission to rise up the social scale, acquiring classy manners and accumulating what we might now call cultural capital in a process of self-transformation. She is not shy of using her sexual powers to the full to attract an aristocratic husband.[14] There are echoes in this of Glyn's own love life – Katherine's goal is the distinguished Duke of Mordryn, loosely modelled on Glyn's own *amour* of the 1900s, a former Viceroy of India, Lord Curzon. Curzon eventually deserted Elinor and married someone else. Elinor named one of her tiger skins Curzon.

Glyn's romantic fiction, together with her pronouncements on the nature of love, romance and attraction – famously referred to as the 'It quality' – were eagerly devoured by an attentive public. 'It' was much discussed, especially after Clara Bow was immortalised as the 'It' girl in the 1927 film *It*, based on Elinor's story and screenplay. According to Glyn, 'It' could attach to both men and women: a quality *not* merely sexual, but 'a potent romantic magnetism'. In the animal world, she declared, 'It' was most potently demonstrated in tigers and cats, both animals being 'fascinating and mysterious, and quite unbiddable'.[15] The public read 'It'– like 'oomph'– to mean basic sex appeal.

The glamour of early, silent screen cinema drew upon a heavy exoticism. Invited to Hollywood in 1920 to try her hand at script writing, the 56-year-old Glyn was in her element. Vamps, mysterious Slavs, doomed queens and gypsies were her stock in trade. Glyn's first script, for *The Great Moment*, starring Gloria Swanson, met with considerable success, the producer (Sam Goldwyn) announcing that Elinor Glyn's name was synonymous with the discovery of sex appeal for the cinema.[16] *Beyond the Rocks*, which paired Swanson with Rudolph Valentino, followed in 1922. The feminine aesthetic of these years combined a touch of the harem with the Cleopatra look: women were kitted out in unlikely slave-girl costumes, wreathed in beads, with serpent-of-the-Nile arm and ankle bracelets and kohl-rimmed eyes. This vampish Arab princess look, associated with Theda Bara, Nita Naldi and Pola Negri, gave way in turn to the image of the flapper, the fun-loving, pleasure-seeking modern girl.[17]

As many historians have emphasised, the new freedoms of work and the vote were seen as having revolutionised the role of women in the years following the First World War, and the state of modern girlhood became a cultural obsession.[18] Probably a more enduring stereotype than that of the 'bright young things' of the 1920s, 'the modern girl' was associated with much more than just hectic partying, jazz and the dance crazes of the decade.[19] Representations of both stereotypes owed something to the literature of Scott Fitzgerald and Evelyn Waugh, and also to the impact of screen performances by Clara Bow in *The Plastic Age* (1925), *Mantrap* (1926) and *It* (1927), by Louise Brooks (*Pandora's Box* and *The Canary Murder Case*, both 1929, *Prix de Beauté*, 1930) and Joan Crawford, especially in *Our Dancing Daughters* (1928). What was distinctively modern about these performances becomes clear when they are contrasted with earlier silent-screen heroines of rustic simplicity and doomed innocence such as some of the roles played by 'America's sweetheart' Mary Pickford, or by Lillian Gish (*Broken Blossoms*, 1919, or *Way Down East*, 1920). Whereas these earlier heroines embodied the traditional virtues and values perceived as under threat from the city and modernity, the shop girls, beauticians and husband hunters played by Brooks, Bow and Crawford were modern, metropolitan, and in their element; defying convention and revelling in a new freedom. British film-makers similarly featured a new form of intrepid female: cinema historian Jenny Hammerton has shown how the cinemagazines of the 1920s and early 1930s, particularly *Eve's Film Review*, featured a carnival parade of women aviators, stunt drivers, lion tamers and martial arts experts in a celebration of modernity and of widening opportunities for girls after the war.[20]

Emancipation was sometimes more apparent than real. Women over the age of thirty gained the vote in 1918, but fears of the consequences of 'a flapper vote' (and of women voters outnumbering men) delayed full female suffrage until ten years later. There was much unease around the new freedoms. Both in literature and in film the heroines depicted as enjoying them were often made to suffer for their self-assertion. Today, A. S. M. Hutchinson's 1922 novel *This Freedom* reads as a maudlin anti-feminist tract, but it was a best-seller in the USA and Britain when first published. It depicts a woman involved in career ambitions as bringing death and destruction to her children.[21] The original, silent version of

the film, which became *Prix de Beauté* or elsewhere *Miss Europe,* was made
in 1922, starring Louise Brooks. It was later dubbed and appeared in
France in 1930.[22] Brooks plays Lucienne, a typist bored by her conventional boyfriend's aspirations for her and his possessiveness. In search
of adventure, she enters a beauty contest; her success, together with the
attention she gets from other men, drives the boyfriend wild. In the end,
she leaves him, but he seeks her out in a murderous passion of jealousy,
killing her as she sits with a new lover, watching her own performance
on a cinema screen. Iris Storm, the undeniably glamorous heroine of
Michael Arlen's cult best-seller of 1926, *The Green Hat,* flaunts all the signs
of modernity: she has attitude, sexy clothes, red lipstick and a fast car.[23]
The car is a yellow Hispano-Suiza: driving it is a metaphor for agency and
sexual self-possession. But Iris is doomed, for precisely these qualities.
The somewhat complicated narrative ends with a confusing mix of self-
sacrifice and social vengeance: Iris engineers her own suicide by hurtling
her car into an ancient ash tree, which stands for tradition, in all its
obduracy. There was a stage version of *The Green Hat,* and in 1928 a film
based on the novel, entitled *A Woman of Affairs,* starring Greta Garbo.

The glamorous woman of the 1920s might still wear clothes inspired
by Orientalism, which had become fashionable under the influence of
set and costume designer Leon Bakst, the Ballets Russes and couturier
Paul Poiret before the war. Rich, embroidered fabrics, encrusted with
beads and glitter, were part of this look. A new, boyish figure increasingly
replaced the Edwardian pouter-pigeon shape and, alongside bobbed or
shingled hair, came to epitomise the modern girl. Bias-cut gowns, introduced by Madeleine Vionnet in the 1920s, emphasised slender curves
unrestrained by corsets, with crêpe and satin flowing down the body.
An advertisement in *The Times,* in 1922, for an exhibition of Japanese
kimonos in Harrods aptly illustrates the connotations of exoticism
carried by the word 'glamour' at this time: a graceful line drawing of
a woman in a silk kimono is set against a stylised oriental background,
and the text invokes 'the witchery of the Far East' and 'the glamour of
blue-skyed Nippon'.[24]

These fashions involved a reworking of traditional ideas of femininity. In the eyes of many observers the modern girl embodied a kind
of androgyny: her boyish look went along with boyish habits, she was
not afraid to drink or smoke or drive a car. Nor was she slow to exploit

new and highly controversial opportunities for mixed bathing, sporting increasingly revealing bathing suits. The rising popularity of sunbathing and swimming as leisure pursuits after the 1914–18 war both represented and reflected new freedoms for women.[25] Bathing beauty contests may have offended some, but proved enduringly popular: they were often filmed, and the archives of British Pathé and the British Film Institute preserve much footage of 'aquatic frolics' and beauty line-ups from the 1920s.[26] Cinemagazines such as the already mentioned *Eve's Film Review* and *Topical Budget* are a particularly rich source of images of the fashions and styles of the 1920s. Wearing pyjamas – in bed, if not on the beach as well – was considered daring but almost de rigueur for stylish young women. In her autobiography, *This Great Journey* (1942), the politician Jennie Lee recalls how her mother scrimped and saved in order to equip her daughter to go off to university in Edinburgh in the 1920s. Collecting a suitable set of clothes was akin to, if not a substitute for, assembling a trousseau. Alongside more serviceable items her mother proudly produced a voluminous white nightgown, elaborately embroidered and adorned with frills and pale blue ribbons. Jennie was aghast:

> *The stuff must have cost a fortune. And this was 1922, the very height of the pyjama age. I would rather have died than be caught by my fellow-students floating around in an outfit of that kind. I was staggered, and didn't know whether to laugh or cry. My mother's face was the last straw …* [27]

A key sign of modernity in women was the wearing of cosmetics, particularly lipstick, probably the most significant issue marking the generation gap between mothers and daughters in the 1920s. Iris Storm in *The Green Hat* applies lipstick to a mouth described by her author as a drooping red-silk flower.[28] Tallulah Bankhead, who played the role of Iris in the stage version of the book, used cosmetics freely. Cecil Beaton likened her cheeks to 'huge acid pink peonies', adding that 'her eyelashes are built out with hot liquid paint to look like burnt matches, and her sullen, discontented rather evil rosebud of a mouth is painted the brightest scarlet and is as shiny as Tiptree's strawberry jam'.[29]

Bankhead quoted this description in her autobiography, but left out the words 'rather evil'.[30] Greta Garbo, playing the part of the siren Felicitas in *Flesh and the Devil* (1926), touched up her lipstick in church

Valaze for Beauty

Beauty will not Evade You
IF
the aids to your toilet bear the above
"Hallmark of Beauty"

Twenty-five years have passed since Madame Helena Rub'nstein first introduced her marvellous Beauty Treatments and Preparations. Since then, these have mounted from success to still greater success, gathering to themselves the staunch faith and lasting gratitude of many thousands of women throughout the world, and necessitating the opening of Salons in London, Paris, New York, Melbourne, Sydney, Chicago, San Francisco, and other resorts of beauty and fashion.

During the Autumn Season, Madame Rubinstein will be happy to give to clients, personally, the benefit of her vast experience and most recent researches.

Those whose complexion has suffered through exposure during the exceptional Summer weather will be particularly interested in the special preparations, new and unique, for the removal of sunburn and freckles; also the latest methods of removing wrinkles—face lifting in advanced cases of relaxation, etc., etc.

VALAZE BEAUTIFYING SKIN FOOD. You will not gain complexion beauty by *covering up* defects with inferior cosmetics and powders. The clogged, distended pores need "Valaze," the inimitable acne Beautifying Skinfood to clear and cleanse them, *to remove* sallowness, *discoloration and freckles,* and to safeguard the skin against attacks of sun, wind and weather. Price **5/-, 9/6** and **22/6**

VALAZE SUN AND WIND-PROOF CREAM protects the skin from ill-effects of exposure to sun, cold or wind, entirely *preventing* sunburn, freckles and tan. Excellent foundation for powder. Price from **3/9**

VALAZE CREME DE LILAS. A beautifying day cream of unique fragrance. Price **3/3**; sample size **1/9**

SPECIAL REDUCTION.

VALAZE FRECKLE AND SUNBURN CREAM for *removing* freckles and brown patches, sunburn and tan, and whitening the skin of face, throat or arms. A **6/-** jar for **3/10** post free.

VALAZE WHITENER. Invaluable for whitening the hands, arms and throat. *It will not rub off.* Quite unique. Will not soil dancing partner's clothes. Price **3/6**

NOVENA CERATE. A unique skin cleansing cream, indispensable for dry harsh complexions. Price from **2/9**

VALAZE ROMAN JELLY has a remarkably bracing tonic effect on loose skin on face or throat. Price from **4/6**

VALAZE COMPRESSED POWDER. Of highest quality, in usual shades; put up in dainty little boxes with puff. Price **2/-**

For two months only.

VALAZE BEAUTY GRAINS incomparably cleanse and clear the pores of the skin, prevent and remedy blackheads — beautify the complexion. To be used when washing. A **5/-** box for **2/10** post free.

Private consultations daily. Advice and brochure sent on application.

There is no complexion so bad that it will not yield to the "Valaze" treatment—no contour so blurred but it can be given again the line of youth. Every facial defect can be successfully *and safely* treated at the "Valaze" Salons including: Sunken eyes, "crow's feet" - Deep facial lines (completely *eradicated in 2 or 3 sittings*)—Sunburn, Freckles—Blackheads—Open Pores—Rashes and Spots—Scars and Birthmarks—Warts and Moles, "Broken Veins"—Falling Hair (scalp treatment)—Loss of Contour—Double Chin—Red Nose—Superfluous Hairs—Facial Relaxation. Special treatments also given for beautifying the Arms, Hands and Throat - improving the shape and removing discoloration. All treatments are given by, or under the personal supervision of a qualified Lady Doctor.

MADAME HELENA RUBINSTEIN,
24 Grafton Street (Opposite Hay Hill), Bond Street, LONDON, W.1.

New York: 46, West 57th St. Paris: 126, Faubourg St. Honore. Melbourne: 274, Collins St., &c. Harrogate Agency: Miss Morton, 92, Station Parade. Wholesale Agents for India: E. Kemble & Co., 1, Mission Row, Calcutta.

Advertisement
for Helena
Rubinstein's
Valaze skin
creams, 1920s.

while the priest inveighed against her wicked ways as a woman. To women raised in the Victorian tradition of ladylike modesty, the wearing of cosmetics was unacceptable. But in the 1920s they became fashionable. According to Graves and Hodge in *The Long Weekend*, the fashion spread 'from brothel to stage, then on to Bohemia, to Society to Society's maids, to the mill girl, and lastly, to the suburban woman'.[31] But it was the influence of the stars of early cinema, Clara Bow, Gloria Swanson, Joan Crawford and their like, which encouraged so many young women to start wearing make-up. Helena Rubinstein and Elizabeth Arden were among those who began to capitalise on this new trend.

By the end of the First World War Arden and Rubinstein were already rivals.[32] Both came from necessitous backgrounds, and they shared qualities of social ambition, commercial imagination and a steely determination that underlay their separate global success as entrepreneurs. They were not the first women to succeed in the beauty industry: two equally rivalrous black American women, Annie Turnbo Malone and Madame C. J. Walker, had earlier amassed fortunes from hair treatment products, and Harriet Hubbard Ayer, whose *Book of Health and Beauty* was published in New York in 1899, had enjoyed considerable success with her Luxuria face-cream, manufactured by Recamier and Company.[33] 'Beauty is Power' asserted an early advertisement for Rubinstein's Valaze skin cream: by 1914 she had salons in Australia, France, England and America and her products gained an international following.[34] Elizabeth Arden (born Florence Graham) had salons in New York and Washington, marketing her 'Venetian' creams 'with the perfume of delicate May flowers', and a new trademark Ardena Skin Tonic. From 1916 she set about manufacturing her own range (her products were originally made up by Stillwell and Gladding), adding a bevy of products to deal with wrinkles and spots as well as Velva Cream and Ardena Orange Skin Food. In *War Paint*, a study of the lives and rivalry of Arden and Rubinstein, Lindy Woodhead observes that, 'Charting the growth of the beauty business in the twentieth century is following history "moving like lightning".'[35] But although creams and lotions for the care of the skin sold well in the early 1900s, it was a while before either Arden or Rubinstein felt confident about the market for pigmented cosmetics. Most of Helena Rubinstein's advice on feminine beauty focused on diet, exercise and skincare: there was a strong element of homeliness mixed in with her self-conscious emphasis

GROSSMITH'S
PHŪL-NĀNĀ
The Fascinating Indian
PERFUME
An Exquisite and Lasting Fragrance.

DELIGHTFULLY REFRESHING and lasting, this perfume possesses a quite unique Eastern character. The most fastidious lady will be charmed with the many dainty accessories, which provide for every requirement of her toilet. Particularly attractive is the

PHŪL-NĀNĀ FACE POWDER

Adherent and unobtrusive, it is not merely non-injurious, but actually beneficial to the most sensitive complexion. This superlatively soft and fine powder is supplied in various shades to suit all skins.

Perfume, 4/9, 9/6 and 19/- per bottle; Face Powder, 9½d. and 1/2 per box; Powder Leaf Books, 7d. each; Toilet Soap, 10½d. and 1/7 per tablet; Toilet Cream, 1/3; Dental Cream, 1/3; Bath Crystals, 2/9 and 5/3; Hair Lotion, 10/-; Toilet Water, 8/6; Shampoo Powders, 3d. each; Brilliantine (Liquid), 2/-; (Solid), 1/4; Talcum Powder, 1/3; Sachets, 9d.; Cachous, 6d.

Other Perfumes in Grossmith's Oriental Series are as under:

SHEM-EL-NESSIM. The Scent of Araby.

WANA-RANEE. The Perfume of Ceylon.

HASU-NO-HANA. The Scent of the Japanese Lotus Lily.

Of all Chemists and Dealers in Perfumery, and from the Sole Proprietors:

J. GROSSMITH & SON, Ltd.,
Distillers of Perfumes and
Fine Soap Makers,
Newgate Street, LONDON.

Helen Jacobs

on science and professionalism. *The Art of Feminine Beauty*, for instance, published in 1930, recommended a face mask made of raw meat:

> *Fresh beef is cut into very thin slices, according to a pattern which you should make at home … Give your pattern to the butcher, who will cut the meat accordingly … Pack the meat over your skin and secure it with a strip of muslin … Leave it on for one or two hours or overnight if possible.*[36]

There were rather more appetising suggestions for masks made of egg whites or pulverised water lilies. Rubinstein packaging could be elegant; Helena had modernist tastes and her original products were labelled in black and gold. Elizabeth Arden had a lifelong fixation with pink. Arden products were advertised around 1930 with images of soft-focus romanticism: Fragonard-type ladies with basketfuls of pale pink roses rather than representations of screen sirens or vamps such as Theda Bara, let alone the modern girl.

Powder and paint continued to attract censure from moralists, who condemned both the artifice with which fashionably exotic appearances were cultivated, and the deliberate loucheness of 'It' as attributed to the modern girl. Such outcries did little but add to the appeal of the exotic. Controversy also surrounded the use of scent. Single-note floral perfumes were considered respectable – one writer has described Yardley's lavender water as the 'only admissible perfume for a lady' before the Great War.[37] In England, 'Zenobia' flower waters sold well: there were thirty different fragrances to choose from.[38] But the 1910s and 1920s saw a growing demand for complex oriental compositions that evoked the harem-girl fantasies filling the pages of women's weeklies, and the dusky charms of Valentino in the desert. Grossmith's four mass-market orientals – Phul-Nana, Shem-el-Nessim, Wana-Ranee and Hasu-no-Hana – were sometimes stigmatised as 'servant girls' scent' but proved immensely popular. In 1923 they added a fifth fragrance, Tsang-Ihang, to this exotic-sounding range.[39] Boots the Chemists added Nirvana and Bouquet d'Orient to the floral scents of its successful Madame Girard et Cie collection. The more up-market perfumers joined in. The French perfume house Guerlain's Mitsouko was a complex modern aldehydic scent introduced in 1919. The name was from the Japanese word for mystery, inspired by the heroine of a novel *La Bataille* by Claude Farrère, which told the

Perfume card advertising Shem-el-Nessim (Scent of Araby), another of Grossmith's mass-market oriental fragrances from the 1920s.

(Author's collection)

story of a romance between a young British naval officer and the wife of a Japanese admiral.[40] Guerlain's Shalimar, launched in 1925, was named after the gardens laid out by the Mughal Emperor Shah Jahan, its romance deriving from his love affair with Mumtaz Mahal.[41] Even the name Shalimar was hotly competed for: in England, the Dubarry Perfume Company produced Shalimar Complexion Creams from its fashionable new Art Deco manufactory in Hove.[42] Both the Shalimar and Mitsouko perfumes were great successes and remain big sellers today, reminding us of the long association between sensuality and the exotic. Turkish and amber perfumed cigarettes were also fashionable in the 1920s: advertisements represented these as signifying a mysterious, seductive quality in the daring sophisticates who smoked them.[43] Perfumes such as Caron's Tabac Blond (by Ernest Daltroff, 1917) and Chanel's Cuir de Russie (Ernest Beaux, 1924) played on associations between femininity, tobacco and leather. Another facet of modernism was apparent with the introduction of Chanel No. 5 in 1921. There were no overt references to flowers here: Chanel herself dismissed any idea that women should smell of roses. The composition (by Ernest Beaux) was aldehydic, complex, abstract: the packaging square, spare and modern.[44]

During the 1920s, then, the idea of glamour evolved from its associations with Orientalism and the exotic into something approaching a distinctly modern, feminine style. It was a style that continued to connote artifice, luxury and sensuousness, signalled particularly through the wearing of feathers and fur. Despite Victorian campaigns against the slaughter of birds for millinery, feathers had become intensely fashionable in the 1890s and they remained desirable. The *Punch* cartoonist Linley Sambourne had been horrified by the sight of cheap, exotically plumaged dead birds piled in baskets in London markets:

> *I saw trays and baskets full of tropical birds exposed – tanagers, orioles, kingfishers, trogons, humming birds etc., from twopence to 4 and a half pence per bird. They were indeed cheap – so cheap that even the ragged girl from the neighbouring slums could decorate her battered hat, like any fine lady, with some bright-winged bird of the tropics.*[45]

The use of whole humming-birds and kingfishers on hats deplored by campaigners such as the Reverend Hudson in England at the turn of the century might have declined, but bird-of-paradise and egret feathers

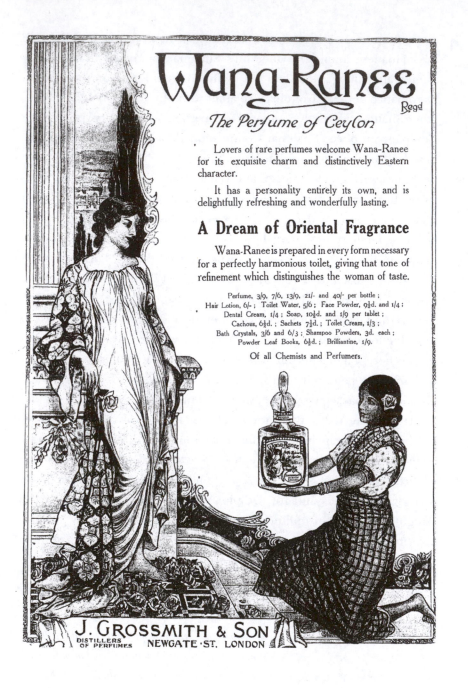

Wana-Ranee Regd

The Perfume of Ceylon

Lovers of rare perfumes welcome Wana-Ranee for its exquisite charm and distinctively Eastern character.

It has a personality entirely its own, and is delightfully refreshing and wonderfully lasting.

A Dream of Oriental Fragrance

Wana-Ranee is prepared in every form necessary for a perfectly harmonious toilet, giving that tone of refinement which distinguishes the woman of taste.

Perfume, 3/9, 7/6, 13/9, 21/- and 40/- per bottle ;
Hair Lotion, 6/- ; Toilet Water, 5/6 ; Face Powder, 9½d. and 1/4 ;
Dental Cream, 1/4 ; Soap, 10½d. and 1/9 per tablet ;
Cachous, 6½d. ; Sachets 7½d. ; Toilet Cream, 1/3 ;
Bath Crystals, 3/6 and 6/3 ; Shampoo Powders, 3d. each ;
Powder Leaf Books, 6½d. ; Brilliantine, 1/9.

Of all Chemists and Perfumers.

J. GROSSMITH & SON
DISTILLERS OF PERFUMES   NEWGATE·ST. LONDON

remained in demand, with up to 200 million egrets killed annually for

their plumage before 1921.[46] A collection of clothes owned by Emily Tinne, a well-off married woman living in Liverpool between the First and Second World Wars, contains many examples of headwear and hair ornaments decorated with egret feathers.[47] Fashion advice offered to working girls in the first issue of the paper *Girls' Cinema*, in 1920, included the suggestion that home dressmakers could 'liven up a black evening frock with a bunch of ostrich feather fronts in cherry red or jade green at the corsage'.[48] There was a steady demand for feathers from farmed and non-endangered species such as ostrich and marabou, for use in stoles and boas. But during the 1920s the demand for fur rose rapidly, completely eclipsing that for feathers.

The fur coat, worn from Victorian times with the fur on the outside rather than as a lining, became an object of unbridled desire and a hallmark of the glamorous woman. Fur had always carried status, being associated with aristocracy and royalty. In the nineteenth century its use spread amongst the prosperous bourgeoisie.[49] Edwardian furriers used pelts in large quantities to produce enormous muffs and stoles, ankle-length coats with heavy bands of fur around the hemline. But affordable at first only to the upper and middle classes, fur was soon much sought after lower down the social scale. By the beginning of the 1920s, the fur craze in the United States was so frenzied that writers were comparing it to the Dutch tulip fever of the seventeenth century.[50] In England, the first issue of a new publication, *The British Fur Trade*, in 1923, attested to the huge and growing popularity of fur: a large number of furriers' trade papers and journals appeared regularly through the 1920s and 1930s. The editor of the *British Fur Trade* noted that furs long sought by 'Madam and My Lady' now had a popular appeal, suggesting that from recent observations two thirds of women of all classes were wearing fur or fur-trimmed garments.[51] Costume collections are not always representative of the extent to which fur was worn, not least because conservation poses challenges: furs become bug-infested and moth-eaten. Women who could afford it kept them in the cold storage facilities offered by many big department stores and furriers. Emily Tinne owned many furs, including a full-length coat of red Kolinsky sable worked in a chevron pattern and lined with olive green sateen.[52] There were many cheaper pelts such as moleskin, squirrel or rabbit fur. During

8193/5

and after the First World War it was common for munitions and factory workers to be censured for wearing fur coats while their husbands were away fighting, or later unemployed.[53]

The frenzy for fur and feathers attracted censure from a small but vocal animal protection movement. In England, a guild called Our Animal Brothers published a periodical of the same name edited by the prolific animal rights author Edith Carrington. Carrington's long list of titles included *The Dog: His Rights and Wrongs, Peeps into Birdland* and *Grandmother Pussy*.[54] An illustrated booklet published in Bristol in 1911, entitled *Fashionable Furs – How They Are Obtained*, contained harrowing detail under subtitles such as 'The Kindly Little Musquash' and 'A Dying Creature's Reproach'.[55] But there was little evidence of any squeamishness about the use of fur. Indeed, the last decades of the nineteenth century had witnessed a gruesome fashion for using stuffed baby animals – baby squirrels and kittens' heads – on muffs and trimmings.[56] Even in the 1920s, studio photographs often showed young women posed in a way designed to make them look appealing, wearing broad scarves edged with rows of tiny heads and paws and tails. Miss Carrington and her colleagues had been taking on a booming industry. Adverts in fur trade journals in the 1920s and 1930s from dressers and cleaners show them boasting about working on pelts of just about everything once living, 'from a mole to a buffalo'.[57] Reports from the fur auctions of the period show the scale and extent of the industry: enormous numbers of pelts were sold. At the Hudson's Bay Company winter sale in 1933, over 20,000 beaver skins, some 227,344 ermines and 40,280 fox pelts were offered for sale.[58] The range of species skinned was mind-boggling, including badger, fisher, skunk, wolf, polecat, squirrel, musk ox, monkey, nutria, raccoon, wombat and wallaby. Even hamsters and house-cats were skinned for their fur. In the 1920s, advertisements in *Vogue* for the upmarket French fur house Revillon Frères promised that women would literally weep with gratitude to men who indulged them with furs ('A Revillon fur is a gift to win tears of thanks-giving from the most pampered of her sex').[59] But gender politics were changing, and the films of the following decade featured more than a few self-reliant heroines who were perfectly able to acquire furs for themselves.

A search through *The Times* Digital Archive suggests that the word 'glamour' was fairly widely used in the 1920s, but it was much more likely to be used in connection with features on travel, and particularly

Authentic Furs

The possessor of a Revillon fur and the other woman may
be sisters under their skin. All the same, it is the first sister's
skin that makes the second feel anything but sisterly.

Revillon Frères

180 REGENT STREET, LONDON

PARIS   *NEW Y(*

Authentic Furs

*A Revillon fur is a gift to win tears of thanks-
giving from the most pampered of her sex.*

Revillon Frères

180 REGENT STREET LONDON

ARIS   *NEW YORK*

to connote the exoticism of the Orient, than to describe a kind of feminine allure. Glamour attached to places rather than persons. Gradually, items of clothing came to be described as glamorous, especially rich silks and embroideries from India, China and Japan. But the interest in the foreign and the exotic encompassed most distant lands, from the snowy steppes of Siberia and the Canadian North to the Tropics, to Arabia, Egypt and the Sudan. A particular glamour and romance attached to furs brought from faraway places, resonant with gendered associations of intrepid male hunters and trappers, securing trophies for favoured females.[60] In the 1930s the meaning of the word 'glamour' shifted, and it became widely used to describe fashions and a particular kind of feminine appeal. The catalyst here was the cinema. The edgy modernity of the dancing daughters and 'It' girls of silent movies was about to give way to the glamour of the iconic screen goddesses of classic Hollywood.

▲

Adverts for Revillon Frères in the 1920s comment both textually and graphically on the association between fur and femininity which was taken for granted by many contemporaries.

(From British Vogue, September and October 1928, courtesy of the British Library)

Hollywood glamour

The 1929 Wall Street Crash knocked the confidence of the rich, and the material hardship and instability that followed impacted on all sections of society. Young women had been entering the labour market in increasing numbers after the First World War: many of them had few opportunities for marriage and had to depend upon their own efforts for support.[1] Well-paid jobs were hard to get, and girls were advised to work hard to exploit whatever talent they had. 'Beauty is a very tangible asset in these days of fluctuating values,' noted an Elizabeth Arden advert in 1932. 'If your face isn't your fortune today, who knows that it may not be tomorrow – and what kind of fortune is it going to amount to?'[2]

The explicit suggestion that allure was the key to a woman's economic potential, combined with the powerful need for escapism during the Great Depression, set the scene for the golden age of glamour. Hollywood delivered the performance. The booming American film industry built up a new type of heroine, or anti-heroine: the glamorous woman on the make. Its costumiers dressed her in a fashion heavy with sexual imagery, which showed up well in black and white: glitter (especially the sparkle of diamonds), thick, lustrous furs, slinky dresses over curvaceous but slim figures, exotic flowers, and stark red lips. Combined with a witty, risqué, devil-may-care confidence, these elements codified glamour, and coincided with an explosion in the use of the word 'glamour' in popular literature, women's magazines and fashion journals.

Light, glitter, sheen

The black-and-white photography of cinema emphasised light, texture and sparkle. In her book *Seeing Through Clothes* (1978), art historian Anne Hollander notes that as ideas of luxury were derived increasingly from cinema in the 1930s, 'colour drained out of elegance', bringing a new importance to materials such as white gold, platinum, sequins and lamé:

> *draped lamé and sequined satin offered rivulets of light to the eye as they flowed and slithered over the shifting flanks and thighs of Garbo, Dietrich, Harlow and Lombard … For women's clothes, sequins, marabou, white net and black lace developed a fresh intensity of sexual meaning in the world of colourless fantasy.*[3]

The black-and-white still portraiture of George Hurrell and Clarence Sinclair Bull in 1930s Hollywood depended upon consummate skill in lighting. Light plays across skin, satin, the surface of fur and hair, and it is in large part this quality, along with careful posing and retouching, that gives the well-known stills of screen goddesses their extraordinary seductiveness. These portraits address the viewer's senses 'through surface qualities, shadow, lustre, sparkle, gleam and glow'.[4] Mark Vieira, a portrait artist inspired by Hurrell, and who has made a special study of his methods, comments that Hurrell's photographs from the 1930s looked 'as if he were thinking of light as a solid substance, something akin to gold spray paint'.[5] The qualities of light could even be used to *suggest* colour. In *The Bride Wore Red* (1937), for instance, a *Pygmalion*-type story with Joan Crawford playing a poor singer (Anni) trying to better herself by passing as rich, Anni fantasises about a red dress. The heavily beaded red dress – reflecting too much glamour and self-assertion to indicate real class – was designed by MGM's costume artist, Adrian, cut on the bias and covered in bugle beads, carefully shaded to emphasise the curves of Crawford's body. The wearing of a red dress conventionally signifies *unconventionality*, or passion and rebellious sexuality in its wearer: in this black-and-white film, Anni's dark gown contrasts dramatically with

▲

Gloria Swanson
looking exotic,
lolling on a tiger
skin.

*(Photograph
by Clarence
Sinclair Bull,
early 1930s.
© John Kobal
Foundation/
Getty Images)*

the full-skirted pastel evening gowns worn by women with the confidence and status of a more privileged background.[6]

The connection between glitter and wealth was obvious. The fashion editor Diana Vreeland described costume designer Travis Banton's beaded dress for Marlene Dietrich in *Angel* (1937) as being 'like a million grains of golden caviar'.[7] The showgirl played by Ginger Rogers in *Gold Diggers of 1933* wore a costume seemingly made entirely of gold coins. Marlene Dietrich covered her legs in gold paint for the film *Kismet* in 1944. A few years earlier, in 1938, Norma Shearer upstaged the real Marie Antoinette in a film performance based on the French queen's life, sporting a wig allegedly frosted with real diamonds.[8]

Jewels of all kinds were important. Dietrich was famous for a legendary collection of emeralds, including one particular cabochon emerald 'the size of a small avocado'.[9] Pearls were more modest, associated tradition-ally with virtue, and with class. Wearing *real* pearls could indicate a quiet distinction. Diamonds were more flash: the most expensive form of sparkle, and the most significant. In the 1930s, they began to acquire new layers of meaning in consequence of a highly successful marketing campaign run by diamond monopolists De Beers. In 1938, the advertising firm N. W. Ayer had reported that sales of diamonds had been declining in the United States since the end of the First World War. De Beers and N. W. Ayer set out to reverse this trend by emphasising the link between diamonds and romance.[10] They began a campaign to persuade movie stars to wear ostentatious jewellery in public.[11] Jeweller Harry Winston set up a shop in Hollywood, and lent diamonds to the famous free of charge. The campaign was strong and many-sided, including lectures to girls in college and high school on choosing their diamond engagement ring – a tradition which, while not exactly invented by N. W. Ayer and De Beers, was greatly boosted by them.[12] With the 1948 slogan 'a diamond is forever', N. W. Ayer suggested an association between the permanence and value of a diamond, and true love and commitment. Identifying the gift of a diamond as the ultimate tribute a man could pay to a woman, it had no qualms about emphasising the link with masculine status and success.[13] The modern idea that it was reasonable for a man to spend the equivalent of two months' salary on his fiancée's engagement ring had roots in this connection.

Diamonds carried a double or even contradictory message: enduring love, purity and simplicity on the one hand, enormous material success on the other. A diamond solitaire encapsulated the love of one man for one woman. But its significance as a token of female romantic triumph did not end there. Too many diamonds could indicate that too many men had paid their ultimate tribute to the woman wearing them. 'Diamonds Are a Girl's Best Friend' became the best-known song from the Broadway musical *Gentlemen Prefer Blondes*, based on the novel by Anita Loos, first filmed in 1928, and later (1953) made into a film starring Marilyn Monroe.[14] In this later production, Monroe was to be dressed by costumier William Travilla in nothing but bands of black velvet and masses of rhinestones, appearing in effect as a woman-sized diamond necklace. The studio eventually censored this outfit in favour of something more modest.[15] Women who flaunted large diamonds were often described as doing so shamelessly. In *Night after Night* (1932), Mae West's glitter caused a cloakroom attendant to exclaim, 'Goodness, what lovely diamonds,' prompting the famous retort from West that '*Goodness* had nothing to do with it.'

Fur and feathers

Searching for a definition of the term 'camp', Susan Sontag suggested that it approximated to 'a woman walking around in a dress made of three million feathers'.[16] Some of the most spectacular costumes worn in movies of the interwar years, and even later, sported extravagant displays of plumage. Theda Bara was decked out in peacock feathers for her role as Cleopatra in the 1917 film of that name. Cecil B. De Mille was alleged to have harvested feathers from peacocks on his own ranch for Hedy Lamarr's costume in *Samson and Delilah* (1949), designer Edith Head attaching them individually so that they cascaded down Lamarr's back as she walked.[17]

Late Victorian campaigners against the destruction of birds ('nature's living gems') for millinery had hoped that the fashion for feathers – and the 'slaughter of songsters' that it entailed – would soon pass.[18] One letter writer to *The Times* suggested optimistically that women in the twentieth century would probably come to look upon the wearing of feathers as akin to 'the idea of a Mexican lady decorating herself with a necklace of human ears'.[19]

But feathers were to prove rather more than a passing fashion. Colin McDowell has suggested that their lasting allure, 'as in Edwardian times, is sexual. They quiver orgasmically with the slightest movement or puff of wind' and are widely assumed to exert an irresistible seductive power.[20] This was certainly the case in early-twentieth-century cinema. Fashion editor Diana Vreeland recalled that for her, one of the most magical moments in early Hollywood was Mae Murray waltzing with John Gilbert in von Stroheim's silent film *The Merry Widow* (1925), when the dancers 'took that famous dip and her bird-of-paradise feathers almost swept the floor'.[21] Mae West's costumes for vaudeville and cinema performances were almost always finished with extravagant cascades of plumage.

beauté exotique

Miss
ADÉLAÏDE HALL,
des Black-Birds.
Photo Walery

— 119 —

Adelaide Hall, an American-born jazz singer, made her name on Broadway with the revue *Blackbirds* in 1928. From 1938 she lived in Britain. Like her contemporary Josephine Baker, Hall was known in her youth for a glamorous, feathery exoticism. Later, she shed the feathers but retained the glamour: in 1941 she was named as Britain's highest paid female entertainer.

(Mary Evans Picture Library)

Garbo's famous 'Eugénie' hat in *Romance* (1930) featured a dramatic plume of black ostrich. In Marlene Dietrich's legendary performances for von Sternberg's films of the period the actress wears feathers: black coq feathers in *Shanghai Express* (1932), and in *The Scarlet Empress* (1934) a feathery négligée of soft quills and delicate fronds which almost appear to pullulate on screen. Dietrich herself was alleged to have a collection of illicit, smuggled bird-of-paradise feathers, some of which were confiscated on one occasion by an agent of the US federal government.[22] Much

Marlene Dietrich as Shanghai Lily in Paramount's film *Shanghai Express* (1932), directed by Josef von Sternberg. Costume by Travis Banton. Dietrich's black veil and jagged coq feathers warred with her creamy pearls, exuding glamour with a disreputable, menacing edge.

(Photograph © Eugene Robert Richee/Hulton Archive/Getty Images)

later in her career, she would appear on stage in a coat of white swans-down with an eight-foot circular train; the coat was said to be culled from over two thousand individual swans.[23]

Even more than feathers, in the 1930s animal fur epitomised glamour. You could writhe on it, sit on it, or drape it on and around your body. In a number of films, women show just how rich they are by walking on it.[24] Gloria Swanson drove in a leopard-skin-upholstered Lancia.[25] To quote Colin McDowell again, 'a fur coat arouses fear and loathing, lust and

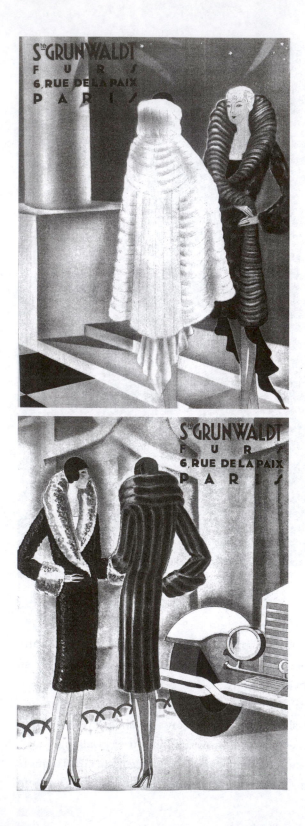

desire as no other garment can'.[26] But fear and loathing were less evident

reactions than lust and desire to the use of fur in the 1930s. Hollywood idols wore masses of it, especially fox, the most fashionable fur of the decade. Marlene Dietrich, Carole Lombard and Loretta Young posed for stills literally swathed in red fox; floor-length coats were constructed entirely of pelts, even négligées were edged at sleeve and hem with prodigal bands of the fur. Twenty-three red fox skins were lavished on the trim of one beige velvet evening wrap worn by Dietrich for a series of publicity stills in the 1930s.[27] The costume designer Adrian, working on outfits for the film *Faithless* (1932), is said to have remarked that Tallulah Bankhead could wear more silver fox than almost any other woman and still look underdressed.[28] Dietrich in *Blonde Venus* (1932) was memorably described as 'a Venus fur-trap'.[29] It has been suggested that the designer Travis Banton was instructed by Paramount head Adolph Zukor, a former furrier, to use as much fur as possible in costumes for *The Scarlet Empress* in order to boost the fur trade at the time.[30] If so, he certainly took the hint: in the film Dietrich flaunts a coat edged with the tails of what appear to be several dozen small creatures, and carries a fur muff the size of a beer barrel.

Women drift through the foyer of *Grand Hotel* (1932) cushioned in luxury and protected against the outside world by rich cloaks and towering collars of fur. In the film, Garbo's success as a performer is signified in full-length fox and sable. If fox was the most fashionable fur of the decade, sable was still the most expensive and luxurious. In the 1937 film *Easy Living*, a sable coat is thrown from a penthouse and lands on the head of a working-class woman, literally transforming her life.

The fur trade boomed. In 1914, it was estimated that around 2,000 silver fox pelts were auctioned in London: by 1934, the number had risen to 350,000, and demand was still rising.[31] But as fox became commonplace, Hollywood stars sought more unusual trappings. Carole Lombard wore a black 'simian' coat in *Love before Breakfast*, Irene Dunne what looks like hairy black gorilla in *Theodora Goes Wild* (1936). A cape of stranded black monkey designed by Schiaparelli for Gertrude Lawrence was featured proudly in a 1936 issue of the *Furriers' Journal*.[32] By the close of the 1930s, fox was losing popularity; the fashionable fur of the new decade was mink. Later in the century a long parade of actresses, including Crawford and Dietrich, would pose for the Great Lakes Mink

Association's Blackglama mink advertising campaign's slogan 'What Becomes a Legend Most?', emphasising the link between fur, glamour and Hollywood legend.[33]

Slinky shapes and figures

'Slinky' was an adjective much used in the 1920s and 1930s to describe the way that bias-cut gowns made of lustrous satins, silks and velvets accentuated the silhouette. Underneath her fur coat, the glamorous woman wore touch-inviting fabrics in figure-hugging shapes. Glamour was curvaceous. Not too fat, nor too thin. Victorian and Edwardian women had resorted to all manner of expedients to accentuate their curves according to the fashion of the day: props and scaffolding of whalebone and steel, tight-lacing, hoops, stuffing and pads of horsehair. Twentieth-century corsetry relied increasingly on rubber and elastic. During the 1920s, 'It' girls with boyish, slender figures had rejected constraining Edwardian undergarments in favour of the free flow of silk over uninhibited skin. The 1930s saw a return to a more womanly shape, though the ultimate goal was to achieve this look without corsetry. The glamorous ideal was slenderness, but with three sets of twin heart-shaped curves: lips, bosom, behind. The lift provided by shoes with high heels accentuated the illusion.

Though in their prime some screen heroines had bodies that allowed them to wear Adrian's bias-cut evening gowns without underwear, in order not to spoil the line, most had to battle with their shape through diet, exercise and the careful cut of clothes. Mae West tended to the pouter-pigeon shape beloved of the Edwardians – she wore platform soles for height and dresses with darker side panels both to accentuate her curvaceousness and also to give the impression of a somewhat slimmer figure. Dietrich was allegedly sewn into some of Jean Louis's flesh-coloured silk gowns in the course of lengthy 'fitting' sessions in which they were effectively constructed around her. As she aged she struggled, eventually having recourse to structural supports, surgical tape and even body suits of net, wire and rubber.[34] Dietary specialists, masseuses and 'physical culturists' such as Gaylord Hauser and Madame Sylvia at Pathé advised actresses on slimming regimes and techniques of figure restoration. Salons set out to capitalise on the desire for trimness. Maine Chance, a health-and-beauty sanctuary run by Elizabeth Arden,

▶

West Bromwich-born Madeleine Carroll looking slinky in bias-cut satin. A graduate in French and former schoolteacher, she achieved fame as a film star notably for her performance in Alfred Hitchcock's *The 39 Steps* (1935). In the mid 1930s she contributed tips on cosmetics and glamour in the magazine *Miss Modern*.

(Sasha/Hulton Archive/Getty Images)

had a battery of exercise machines, one operator boasting that 'we've got an instrument of torture here to suit the fancy of every fat ass in the world'.[35] For those who couldn't afford salons, the women's magazines of the 1930s sported a variety of advertisements for dodgy-sounding slimming panaceas: Español Solvent which allowed fat women to shed up to eight stone, or Marmola Gland Food tablets, which would 'feed your fat away'.[36] Marmola was based on a combination of desiccated animal thyroid gland and laxatives: it was allegedly very damaging, and after the

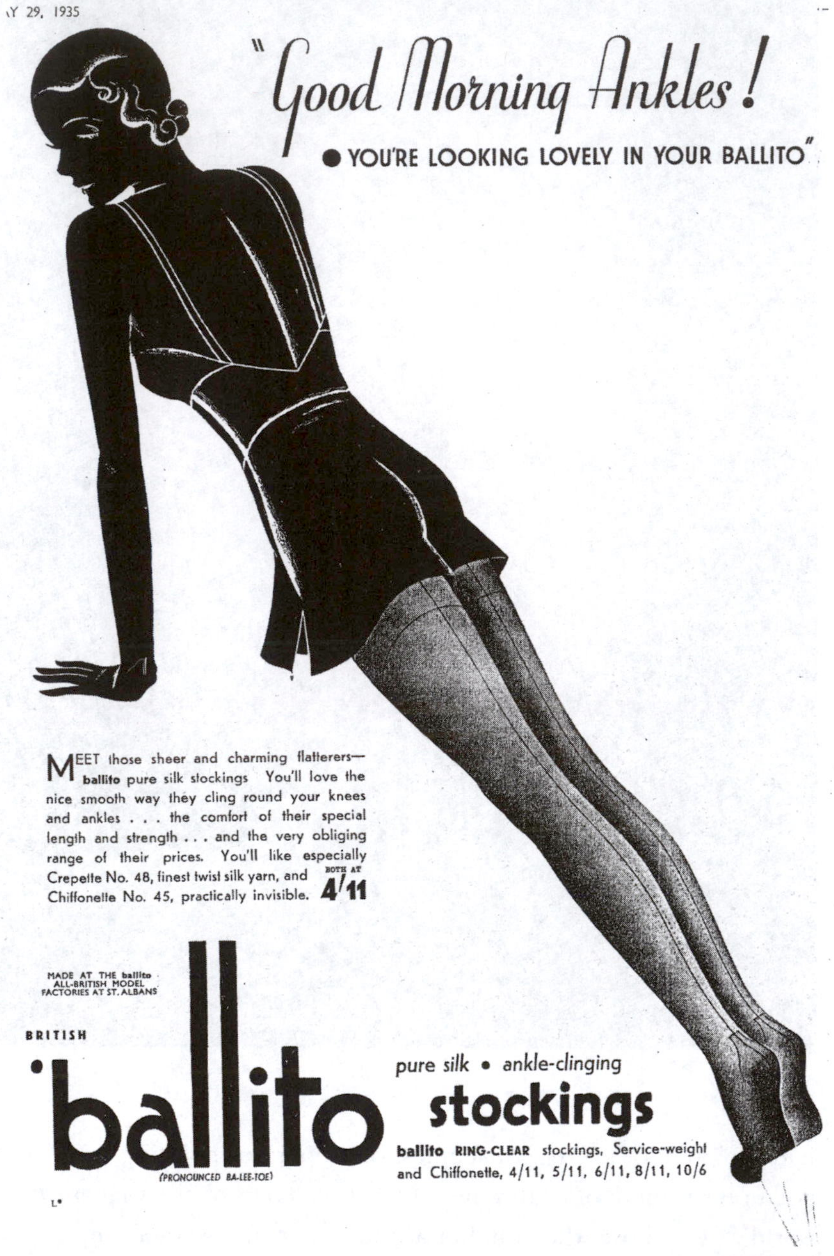

Y 29, 1935

"*Good Morning Ankles!*

● YOU'RE LOOKING LOVELY IN YOUR BALLITO"

MEET those sheer and charming flatterers— **ballito** pure silk stockings You'll love the nice smooth way they cling round your knees and ankles . . . the comfort of their special length and strength . . . and the very obliging range of their prices. You'll like especially Crepette No. 48, finest twist silk yarn, and Chiffonette No. 45, practically invisible.

BOTH AT **4/11**

MADE AT THE **ballito** ALL-BRITISH MODEL FACTORIES AT ST. ALBANS

BRITISH

'ballito stockings

(PRONOUNCED BA-LEE-TOE)

pure silk ● *ankle-clinging*

ballito RING-CLEAR stockings, Service-weight and Chiffonette, 4/11, 5/11, 6/11, 8/11, 10/6

1938 Food and Drug and Cosmetics Act in the USA it was banished from the market.[37]

Figure-hugging beachwear became extremely desirable in the 1930s, with a vogue for poolside glamour associated with both California and Biarritz. The popularity of swimming and sunbathing and their association with luxury lifestyles on the one hand, health and fitness on the other, stimulated the building of outside lidos even in the less reliable climates of Britain and Northern Europe.[38] Bathing beauty contests, already popular in the 1920s, fuelled increasing concern with body shape. Knitted swimming costumes did little for the silhouette, but carefully cut fabric and boning gave a better look until the discovery of Lastex in the 1930s revolutionised the appearance of the swimming costume.[39] The impact of Busby Berkeley dance routine spectaculars in movies such as *42nd Street* and *Gold Diggers of 1933* familiarised the public with skimpy costumes: in *42nd Street* the dancers wear leotards covered with white fox furs, complete with heads, tails and paws. The costumes worn by the city girls and young mothers who rushed to join the Women's League of Health and Beauty in Britain in the 1930s were rather less glamorous – they practised in inexpensive white blouses and black satin knickers – but the ordered and synchronised movements and formations of the final performances had something in common with Busby Berkeley fantasies.[40]

Cosmetics

A glamorous image required careful construction, depending on artifice and illusion. Gloria Swanson is said to have resisted the suggestion that she have cosmetic surgery on her nose early in her career.[41] Crawford and Garbo both had serious work done on their teeth.[42] Dietrich had wisdom teeth extracted to hollow her cheeks, and is said to have had two full facelifts by the early 1960s and a third soon after.[43] Photographs of Garbo when she first arrived in the USA in the mid 1920s show a fairly unprepossessing face; there is little to indicate the beauty with which she was later to grace the screen.[44] In the 1930s, all four of these women, like most nascent female stars, were given serious makeovers by Hollywood cosmeticians and glamour experts. Joan Crawford's mouth was constantly reshaped through the use of cosmetics, as were her – and Dietrich's – eyebrows through crayon and depilation.[45] Dietrich's eyebrows were ever-changing: delicate crescents, sometimes arched, sometimes pencilled into lines with an upward lilt like butterfly wings. Crawford and Dietrich became expert cosmeticians in their own right: Dietrich to the extent that she was even admitted to the film make-up and hairdressers' professional union.[46]

When Dietrich contrived her own make-up in the early years of her career she used as eyeliner the soot deposited by a lighted match on a saucer.[47] According to Helena Rubinstein, writing in 1930, this was a common practice amongst French women in the 1920s.[48] But with the development of cinema, cosmetic techniques and products became ever more sophisticated. Dorothy Ponedel established herself as a gifted make-up artist, first for Paramount and after 1940 for MGM, developing close friendships with Dietrich, Mae West, and later Judy Garland. Max Factor, of course, was the best-known name in Hollywood make-up artistry, both his salon and his products achieving world renown. Max Factor originally used Leichner theatrical make-up, and then began to manufacture his own cosmetics. The perfect matte finish his Pancake foundation (1938) gave to skin was legendary. Max Factor was further credited with inventing lip gloss and certain kinds of mascara. Also famous for their make-up artistry were George Westmore and his five sons, all of whom followed in their father's footsteps as cosmeticians to the stars. It was the Westmore dynasty who were responsible for the dramatic change in the appearance of Bette Davis's mouth in the 1930s – straightening the line of her upper lip from Cupid's bow to an unbroken line.[49] The House of Westmore, famed for its luxury, was patronised by actresses and rich women from all over the world, including the Duchess of Windsor, Barbara Hutton and Madame Chiang Kai Shek.[50]

Capitalising on his reputation in Hollywood, Max Factor marketed his cosmetics worldwide. Like the products manufactured by Elizabeth Arden and Helena Rubinstein, they were widely advertised in newspapers and women's magazines and could be purchased in pharmacies and department stores. News of innovatory products spread fast. In 1938, Antonia White reported excitedly in Britain's *Picture Post* that

> *The most sensational new make-up is Max Factor's Pancake, a new panchromatic base originally evolved for colour films which doesn't get caked and mask-like when exposed to a hot atmosphere. You can even*

put your pancaked face into a bucket of water and come up smiling
with your beautiful matt bloom unblemished.[51]

Cakes of this water-soluble make-up foundation sold like wildfire: more
than ten million cakes were said to have been bought by 1953.[52]

The gospel of Max Factor and the Westmores was that glamour
could be achieved by any woman who put her mind to it. On the eve
of the Second World War in Britain, Ern and Bud Westmore took up a
challenge offered by *Picture Post*'s editor, and set out to prove that they
could turn a charlady into a glamour girl.[53] Charlady Mrs Nichols was
chosen for this early attempt at a complete makeover. Her hair was
'baked with electric conductors' into curls and she was given full 'correc-
tive' make-up. The article was illustrated and bore captions such as 'Mrs
Nichols gets a new mouth' and 'Her features have been redistributed'.
'After three and a half hours Mrs Nichols rose from her chair to examine
£3 15s. 6d. worth of glamour in the mirror … She thought the experts
had done very well.' Then she washed it all off and went back to her
husband and work.[54]

Flowers and perfume

In her autobiography, Mary Pickford described how, aged five or six, she
took a fading rose from the florist and ate it. 'It had tasted very bitter
at first', she wrote, 'but I thought that if I were to eat it, the beauty and
colour and the perfume would somehow get inside me.'[55] There was
nothing new in the association of flowers with femininity. Women had
always been compared with flowers, and flowers had always been named
after women: the long-stemmed American Beauty rose was said to be
named after the buxom American Lilian Russell.[56] But while early screen
heroines like Mary Pickford and Lilian Gish had evoked rosebuds and
the frail blossoms of innocence, glamorous women were associated with
the sexual symbolism of hothouse exotics. Carole Lombard was sold by
Paramount as 'the Orchid Lady'.[57] Hedy Lamarr wore gigantic orchids
on her bust, hip and head to perform 'Minnie from Trinidad' in 1941's
Ziegfeld Girl. Greta Garbo, once likened by Cecil Beaton to 'a rare white
convolvulus', was also described by him as 'the most glamorous figure
in the whole world'; he noted that 'huge boxes of orchids are sent to

her daily by dozens of complete strangers'.[58] Compounding the exoticism, Garbo's character is romanced by a prince who compares her 'cold
enchantment' with Javanese women and the flowers of the film's title
in *Wild Orchids* (1929). The Duchess of Windsor's hairdresser, Antoine,
remembered her talking admiringly of the New York designer and
socialite Elsie de Wolfe (Lady Mendl), who had so much vitality that she
could shop all day and still be as fresh as a daisy – the duchess suddenly
correcting herself, 'No, she's not in the least like a daisy, she's as fresh as
a crisp orchid.' [59]

Marlene Dietrich's famous line in 1932's *Shanghai Express* summed
up glamour's challenge to respectability: 'It took more than one man
to call me Shanghai Lily.' Any reference to the purity of white flowers
is heavily controverted by the sheen of black coq feathers in her outfit,
the uncompromising glitter of jet. The same effect is there in stills of
Swanson from *Queen Kelly* (1929), where white orchids and pearls are
muffled in black marabou. The scene at the beginning of *Morocco* in
which Dietrich takes a rose and tosses it to Gary Cooper produces a
frisson based on the ambiguity of gender assumptions: the gesture has
masculine agency and confidence, it suggests the casual courting of a
woman. The language of flowers was every bit as complex as in Victorian
times. An early publicity photograph of Joan Crawford was a montage
showing the actress's face set in the whorled petals of a gardenia.[60]
Crawford declared herself obsessed with the heady scent of gardenias,
filling her house with bowls of them and wearing them with every outfit.
But unfortunately she would have to throw them away about an hour
after she put them on, she confessed. 'They just turned brown. Nothing
you can do about it. I just have too much body-heat.'[61]

This language of flowers continued into scent. The single-note, ladylike florals of the late Victorians, such as lavender or lily-of-the-valley,
lacked the sophistication that went with real glamour. Again, the hothouse
blooms were better. Mae Murray drenched herself in gardenia perfume
and was known as 'the gardenia of the screen'.[62] Pungent Orientalism
gave out similar messages. In 1937 Schiaparelli's Shocking (a heady
oriental fragrance rumoured to be based on the smell of a woman's sex
organs and sold in a bottle inspired by Mae West's curves) was marketed
on the basis of luxury and voluptuousness. Manufacturers had long
advertised perfumes through their association with opera singers and

actresses. Rigaud had named its scents after opera stars (Mary Garden, Geraldine Farrar and Emma Trentini). The tradition continued through stories of the signature scents of stage personalities and Hollywood stars. Gertrude Lawrence was said to have sprayed each room of her London apartment in Portland Place until it was impregnated with a different scent, her favourites being Chanel (Cuir de Russie and No. 5) and Dans La Nuit (Worth, 1924).[63] Buoyed by the success of No. 5, in 1933 Chanel introduced another new perfume called Glamour, although this seems to have been short-lived, and to have disappeared with the outbreak of war.[64] The film-star lifestyle depended on using perfume unapologetically and lavishly. In *Ziegfeld Girl* (1941), Sheila (Lana Turner) is woken from slumber in satin sheets by a maid spraying her with perfume. The late Victorian dressing table, frilled and flounced like a Victorian bride, gave way to more jagged, angular, Art Deco lines and peach-coloured mirror-glass. Often adorned with expensive crystal perfume bottles decorated with spray-bulbs and silken tassels, together with swansdown powder puffs, the new dressing table came to signify the glamorous lifestyle.[65] Edwardian actresses had often been photographed at the mirror in their dressing rooms: this convention of portraiture continued, and just about every screen siren of the twenties and thirties at one time or another posed for a photograph by gazing at her reflection in the mirror while applying perfume or cosmetics at her dressing table.

Attitude

Glamour was in part an expression of attitude. Margaret Thorp reflected on the quality in her study of *America at the Movies* (1945). Glamour didn't depend on exceptional beauty, she argued, partly because fans needed to identify with movie stars and 'glamour should never be so bright that it dims hope'.[66] What a glamorous female star needed above all else, she decided, was *personality*: she needed 'to dare to be herself'.[67] Glamour involved confidence and self-possession: it didn't sit easily with more traditional feminine virtues of innocence and modesty.

The glamorous siren might come close to the seductive vamp of the 1920s, though Thorp contended that 'the fatal tigress fashion' had waned with the Great War.[68] A study of screen stills of the 1930s and even after suggests rather more continuity: there are endless photographs of female stars posing with magnetically come-hither looks on tiger or bear skins. Clarence Bull's portrayal of Gloria Swanson, head upside down against a tiger's head for instance, was echoed in Hurrell's photo of Jean Harlow leaning seductively on the head of a polar bear.[69] The charge of sexual confidence is there. 'I dress for the men in the audience', asserted Mae West, 'I'm not afraid to give them what they want.'[70] A woman in some kind of masculine clothing could be glamorous: Garbo in trench coats, Dietrich in casual slacks, or camped up in tuxedo with top hat and fishnet tights. These women had no doubt about their own desirability, and they were desiring subjects, not just objects of the male gaze. The androgyny of Garbo, and particularly Marlene Dietrich, afforded far more agency than conventionally feminine roles. 'She has sex, but no particular gender,' Kenneth Tynan memorably remarked of Dietrich.[71]

Sexual confidence went along with a delight in worldly luxury and a go-getting attitude to enjoying it. Again, there is continuity here with the 1920s: the stars of the films made in Hollywood in the early 1930s are girls on the make with few illusions about romance or the realities of the social world. The spaces they inhabit – as for modern girls working in department stores, offices or the entertainment industries – afford all kinds of 'entrepreneurial' opportunities which they seize with alacrity. A publicity poster for Warner Brothers' *Baby Face* (1930) featured an image of Barbara Stanwyck in a sexually challenging pose over the legend, 'She had "It" and made "It" pay!'; alongside was printed a warning, 'Parents, please do not bring your children!' In this film, Stanwyck played the part of Lily Powers, a girl from a deprived, abusive background allegedly inspired by a reference to Nietzsche to avoid slavery at the hands of men and to take control of her own fate by exploiting the exploiters. Lily befriends her black maid (Chico, played by Theresa Harris) and they escape together, ill-gotten earnings spent on glamorous clothing: Lily wears a dark fox fur, Chico an arctic white. Lily sleeps her way to the top of the company she works for, before finally falling in love. Another example of the genre, *Red Headed Woman* (1932), featured Jean Harlow as the central character (another 'Lil'), who sleeps with rich men for social position whilst ensuring her own gratification in the arms of a sexy chauffeur. Even worse, in the eyes of the moralists, was that she got away with this. The film was banned in Britain. Glamour and go-getting were regularly contrasted with breeding and refinement in women, and shown to be vulgar. 'Don't you think all the glamorous women in your life have all been a little common – a little Tenth Avenue?' asks the doctor's wife Lucy, in the film *Dinner at Eight?* (1933). But the proprieties of social class don't stand a chance, pitted against the quick wit, slinky white satin and steady ambition of Harlow's Kitty Packard.

The rise of the star system in Hollywood depended upon elaborate systems of image construction, publicity management and media manipulation. Stars were packaged and produced, and for some actresses the distinction between their private and public selves was inevitably a source of tension and confusion. 'I'm a goddam image, not a person,' moaned Crawford at a low point in her career.[72] Some women were uneasy about the carefully contrived process of glamorisation. The designer Travis Banton allegedly found it hard to work with Clara Bow because of Bow's impatience with her appearance; she insisted on wearing high heels with ankle socks and junk jewellery.[73] Bette Davis objected to the careful make-up that would turn her 'into a piece of shiny wax fruit' and protested, 'I want to be known as a serious actress, nothing else … I don't want some glamour girl stuff.'[74] Her biographer quotes Davis as having commented that on the set of *Whatever Happened to Baby Jane?* 'Miss Crawford wanted to look as nice as she could; I wanted to look as terrible as I could. Miss Crawford was a glamour puss. I was an actress.'[75]

Margaret Thorp observed that the popularity of stars often rested on their conveying of the impression that though fabulously rich, they were basically people of simple tastes, that underneath the glamour they were much like you or me. Reports of personal suffering or misfortune could sometimes add to a star's popularity, she observed: there seemed to be a touch of sadism in the fans' reaction, a desire to bring glamour down to earth.[76] Whilst legends of upward social mobility brought hope, moral narratives of decline might reassure fans that fabulous riches were no guarantee of happiness, thus diminishing envy and making it easier to be content with what one had. But the incontrovertible legacy of Hollywood glamour in the 1930s was that it demonstrated new ways of looking, being and living as a woman: in the words of film historian Annette Kuhn, it 'extended imaginings of what a woman could be'.[77]

Dreams, desires
and spending

The go-getting heroines of Hollywood disturbed guardians of public morality on both sides of the Atlantic. In the United States, those who deplored the looser morals associated with modernity fought for the Motion Picture Production Code, which was adopted in 1930 and effectively enforced from 1934. Popularly known as the Hays Code (after its advocate Will H. Hays, President of the Motion Picture Producers and Distributors of America), the code aimed to curtail the supposedly malign influence of film on public morals through stringent censorship. In Britain, there was anxiety both about morals and about the impact of American consumerism. Would the young be seduced and unsettled by the images of luxury and sophistication they enjoyed in the cinema palaces? A number of studies set out to investigate the impact of cinema-going on the British public.

The concern centred particularly on women. A large proportion of regular cinema-goers in Britain in the 1930s were working-class women under the age of forty.[1] For these women, going to the pictures represented a major leisure activity, and an avenue of escape from the hardships of everyday life. Part of the pleasure came from the picture palaces themselves: often warm and comfortable, and, in the larger cities, elegant, opulently furnished spaces which suggested a world very different from

Pulp novelette
from Gramol
Publications,
1935, warning
of false values.
The story is
a potent mix
of glamour
and crime
in which the
heroine comes
to realise that
'stardom' is
nothing more
than 'stardust'
in the face of
True Love.

that of the working-class home.[2] Some of these cinemas were got up like oriental pleasure domes or Moorish palaces. Others hinted at the clean lines and chromium finish of Art Deco villas and luxury cruisers. Most important, cinema attendance offered a space for and a stimulus to daydreaming, a fact recognised by most contemporary observers.[3] In *The Cinema Today* (1939), for instance, D. A. Spencer and H. D. Waley pointed out that: 'For the average human being, there yawns a considerable gap between what he or she would like to get out of life and what life actually offers. This gap can be partly bridged by daydreaming, and it is as aids to daydreaming that we must regard most fiction films.'[4] Recreative fiction, they suggested, acted as an important safety valve for pent-up ambitions: in this sense, cinema-going had a stabilising effect on society.[5] But others were less convinced.

In a later study, J. P. Mayer found that many British women confessed that films made them critical and dissatisfied with their own lives. One fifteen-year-old schoolgirl confided that: 'after a film that I have enjoyed very much, that has many beautiful glamour girls in it, I feel irritable and want something better out of life'.[6] A 26-year-old housewife asked by Mayer whether films made her dissatisfied, responded emphatically, 'Definitely they do! I find myself comparing my home, my clothes, even my husband. I get extremely restless and have a longing to explore uncharted lands.'[7]

In spite of their youth, some of Mayer's respondents were philosophical about the feelings of envy they had experienced through cinema-going, or their dreams of escape. Moreover, the 'impossible dreams' confessed by some of the respondents seem modest by today's standards. They included the desire to travel and to experience different lifestyles, and a longing for education as much as affluence. For instance, a seventeen-year-old typist wrote that:

> *films have made me discontented with being poor, and I am not ashamed to say so because it is the truth and you asked for that. I have always had ambitions to play the piano, perhaps this doesn't amount to much, but I haven't been able to realise this ambition just as I haven't been able to realise so many others.*[8]

Another young woman confessed that:

During the past few years films have made me want to be smart and glamorous. After seeing beautiful creatures displaying the latest and most expensive creations all evening, I go home, gaze at myself in the mirror and give up all hope. I have often thought like many other silly adolescents that it would be marvellous if some famous producer from Hollywood, or even Elstree, would discover me – as if I had ever been lost! Seeing films has made me want to go to America and see for myself how the Americans live – probably half the population live in penthouses and the rest wallow in dirt in filthy tenements ... Most of all, I think, films have made me dissatisfied with my life.[9]

▶

Cover of the first issue of *Girls' Cinema*, October 1920.

(Image courtesy of the British Library)

Whatever the effect on general attitudes and aspirations, the glamour of cinema had an enormous impact on popular fashion. Stars became style leaders, their hairstyles, make-up and clothes emulated by thousands.[10] Fan magazines proliferated as a source of information on these subjects between the world wars. In Britain, *Girl's Cinema, Women's Filmfair, Film Fashionland* and *Picturegoer* were carefully studied for fashion details, gossip about goings-on in Hollywood, and insights into the lives lived in luxury mansions in a different part of the world.

Girls' Cinema ran weekly from 1920 to 1932 and was one of the earliest examples of the genre. Printed on cheap, absorbent paper mainly in black-and-white, it cost tuppence, and its format didn't change much in the course of some six hundred issues. The paper bridged the gap between Victorian and Edwardian girlhood and a new interest in the silent screen, and the tone tended towards sentimentalism rather than sensationalism, with heavy authorial interventions. There was a lot of girly chat and the advice on fashion was homespun: 'Violet Hobson's Fashion Fancies' featured the art of smocking and how to contrive sprays of artificial flowers from old stockings. 'Fay Filmer' offered counsel to 'the up-to-date girl', and readers were encouraged to swoon over Famous Love Scenes involving Lilian Gish and Mary Pickford. There were few advertisements, and those that did appear sometimes adopted a terrifyingly hectoring tone. An advert for a hair removal product in 1932, for instance, warned that no man would ever want a fiancée 'with ugly and disfiguring growths of hair', and that 'even a trace of hair showing through fine silk stockings will repel and disgust a man'.[11] There were many strident references to body odour and bad teeth.

"HER WEDDING DAY"—COLOURED PICTURE INSIDE

Mary Pickford in the frock in which she was married to Doug

GIRLS' CINEMA

2d

NO. 1. VOL. 1.
OCT. 16. 1920.

No. 1 of the NEW Paper for Girls!

(Paramount)

12 FAMOUS LOVE SCENES No. 1. "The Kiss" W. S. HART & ANN LITTLE in "Square Deal Sanderson."

◀

Sally Alexander has described some of the ways in which modern, cropped hairstyles and cosmetics, or 'the cheap trappings of glamour' were seized on by many young working-class women in London between the world wars, with no prospect of further education and keen to escape the hardship and struggle of their mothers' lives.[12] A glamorous appearance might signify rebellion, a spirited independence or defiance. Even in the poorest parts of Britain young girls might contrive to acquire a fashionably sophisticated appearance: in the 1950s, Jane Walsh, who had grown up in a poor Catholic family in Lancashire, reflected upon the fact that like many women, she was inclined to date things by the clothes she had worn at the time. In the 1920s, she remembered, 'I made myself a blue coat-frock, the first I'd ever made for myself … It was of cheap, coarse serge, but I'd spent hours and hours embroidering it with tiny beads. At this period, beaded trimmings were considered the last word in smartness.'[13] Men had looked at the general effect, she recalled, not at the quality of the garment: the coat had attracted many admiring glances and allowed her to swagger a little at the success of all the effort taken.

Compared with *Girls' Cinema*, the film and fan magazines of the 1930s purveyed much more glamorous images of femininity. The long-running *Picturegoer* (weekly), *Film Fashionland* (monthly, 1934–5), and *Woman's Filmfair* (after 1935, *Woman's Fair and Filmfair Fashions*) featured many advertisements for cosmetic and beauty products, showing women in slinky dresses, satin pyjama suits, swansdown-trimmed boudoir wraps and négligées. Clothes were modelled directly on the costumes worn by actresses and film stars, and a special pattern service was provided to enable the clothes to be made up at home. These proved enormously popular. Worthing Museum's costume collection contains many examples of frocks made at home to this kind of pattern: the prints and fabrics (eau-de-nil silk or crêpe, oyster-coloured satin) are close to those recommended in the pages of the magazines and highly evocative of the period. Silky wraps and dressing gowns were universally popular – Vera Brittain presented her friend Winifred Holtby with a dressing gown of thin, peach-coloured satin as a birthday gift in 1932.[14] But such sophisticated *déshabillé* would have been chilly in an unheated bathroom or most working-class homes, and for many women the clothes featured in the fashion magazines must have been the stuff of dreams rather than having any real practicality: in 1934 *Film Fashionland* ran a feature, for

instance, on clothes for the cruise.[15] *Filmfair Fashions* offered a pattern service but readers could also order clothes by post or from big department stores like Lewis's in Birmingham, which displayed a 'Margaret Sullavan picture frock' in 1934.[16]

Investigating sixty years later the role of cinema in women's lives during the 1930s, the film historian Annette Kuhn found plenty of elderly women who testified to the ways in which they copied fashions in hairstyles, make-up and clothing from the screen.[17] Ginger Rogers was a favourite role model for hair and make-up, as was Kay Francis. It was cheaper to imitate details than whole outfits: one woman remembered her aunt copying a lace collar worn by Ginger Rogers.[18] Similarly, many of the women who contributed to Mayer's study of cinema audiences described how they would copy hair and dress styles from screen heroines in the films of the early 1940s. The frustrated would-be piano player mentioned above described how: 'When I saw "Marriage is a Private Affair" I certainly came under the heading "did you ever imitate a star", I put my hair in the page bob like Lana Turner and I kept it like that until I saw "Thirty Seconds over Tokyo" when I changed it to the way Phyllis Thaxter had hers.'[19]

Humour and realism were threaded through these stories of emulation. Kuhn's informants fell about laughing as they remembered imitating hairstyles, attempting blonde streaks with hydrogen peroxide and sugar-watered kiss curls.[20] In Mayer's study, a 22-year-old female clerk who described how she had copied Deanna Durbin's hairstyle remembered that 'As I gradually grew up, my hairstyles changed according to the latest screen fashion, often to the vast amusement of my friends. But there the influence of the latest glamorous fashions had to stay. My mother's slender purse could not stretch to new dresses as they took my eye.'[21]

Mass-market versions of clothes and accessories worn on screen were very popular – examples included versions of Joan Crawford's dress with ruffled sleeves worn in *Letty Lynton* (1932), and Garbo's Eugénie hat from *Romance* (1930). In *The Power of Glamour*, Annette Tapert points out that Garbo (whose first job was modelling hats) had a huge influence on the millinery of the decade: the various turbans, skullcaps, peaked hats and other headwear she wore on screen were widely copied.[22]

Fur, already popular in the 1920s, became even more sought after in

▲
Designs from *Film Fashionland*, mid 1930s, which were modelled on outfits worn by leading cinema actresses. The dress with the crossover back, for instance, claimed to be based on a Travis Banton design for Carole Lombard. Readers were encouraged to write for cutouts in various coloured fabrics and to make the garments up at home.

Britain in the 1930s. Those who couldn't afford a full fur coat might aspire to a huge fur collar: fashion illustrations from the period show these collars towering around necklines like furry ramparts. Furriers cashed in on the vogue with all manner of promotions, such as 'Empire Fur Week' in 1934. In October 1934, the *Morning Post* featured an illustrated Fur Supplement. Department stores such as Debenham and Freebody or Marshall and Snelgrove had opulent fur showrooms, some offering cold storage facilities for furs in the warmer months. The demand for fox pelts in all colours, but particularly silver, continued to soar, reaching a height of popularity around 1936. Some one hundred and fifty silver fox fur breeders were listed in Britain in the *British Fur Trade Yearbook* for 1933.[23] An article in the *British Fur Trade* suggested that the farming of fox was an industry for which women were particularly suited, although the actual killing of the animals would be 'revolting to the delicately nurtured woman' and would be better left to men.[24] Hutchinson's *Woman's Who's Who* for 1934 listed twenty-one women specialist silver fox fur breeders.[25] *Eve's Film Review* produced interesting footage on fur farming, with voice-over commentary which was clearly deemed witty at the time, although now it might be regarded as in questionable taste. In one film clip of 1931, for instance, a bright voice announces that 'It's tough luck to be a soft, silky fox – even though you might finish as a caressing necklet around some ravishing young lady's shoulders!'[26] In Evelyn Waugh's novel *A Handful of Dust* (1934), Tony Last's rambling Victorian-Gothic mansion is threatened first by a fashionable modernism, in the shape of his unfaithful wife Brenda's penchant for a white suede and chromium-plated décor; it finally falls into the hands of relatives who turn it into a silver fox farm.[27] Every large town in the country at this time could boast several fur retailers; Brighton, for instance, had around thirty, Glasgow near one hundred.[28] The trade journals were well aware of the importance of film star example, and regularly featured photographs of fur-swaddled actresses, such as Mary Taylor in a three-quarter fox fur cape in Paramount's comedy *Soak the Rich* in 1936.[29]

As the trade expanded, fur became accessible to a much wider section of the female public. Adverts for Imperial Fur Traders in the trade press from the mid 1930s show that it was the cheaper furs – coats made of mole or white coney (rabbit), for instance – that were the real profit makers, available from five guineas or so upwards. Everyone could

ANOTHER SEASON HAS STARTED~

MAKE IT A BUMPER SUCCESS WITH
IMPERIAL FUR TRADERS' VALUES

Let us help you with your Press Publicity, Catalogues, etc.

Publicity Experts will be only too pleased to help you free of charge.

STRANDED MINK MARMOT

Mink Marmot is one of our speciality lines. The model shown is designed in a smart yet practical style, and is one of this season's finest sellers. The pelts are wonderfully silky and supple. The fine quality and finish are all that could be desired in a coat at anywhere near this price **10** GNS.

NATURAL GREY SQUIRREL

Made from selected choice Siberian pelts of blue-grey colour and superfine texture, furriered to that high standard that stamps all I.F.T. productions **18** GNS.

MUSQUASH CONEY   *(Illustrated in centre)*

I.F.T. first again with the new MUSQUASH CONEY NOW PERFECTED. Why not call and see these excellent models?—no obligation and no charge! From **55'-**

IMPERIAL FUR TRADERS, 16 OLD BAILEY, LONDON, E.C.4

afford a fur coat at these prices, they declared.[30] Towards the end of the decade, an uncertain political situation precipitated a fall in the price of furs. In October 1938, a front-page spread in the *Daily Herald* announced that Swears and Wells were mounting what they claimed to be the world's biggest ever fur sale.[31] Stoles made of skunk were priced at a mere two guineas a piece. Bargains were snapped up after war broke out in 1939: researchers from Mass Observation set out to record events at the closing-down sale of the exclusive Revillon fur outlet in London's Regent Street.[32] Arriving just after nine a.m. they found the store packed. In an article in the *Evening Standard* the store's manager noted that over five hundred women had rushed to the sale, and that mink and ermine had been selling like hot cakes.[33] By this time mink was beginning to usurp the popularity of silver fox. This had little impact on the cheaper lines of fur: draper's representative Elizabeth Wray, interviewed by Mass Observation in 1939, commented that in spite of the fur trade's efforts to promote Australian wallaby in recent years, it was over-shaggy and rabbit remained the most popular pelt for factory girls' coats.[34]

Fur was far too popular – warm and practical, as well as glamorous – to disappear with wartime austerity. It was seen by many as an investment worth saving up coupons for: furs could be remodelled and reconditioned and were expected to last. Not all of them did. The manageress of Samuel Soden (a Regent Street furrier), interviewed by Mass Observation in 1940, commented that although some people were buying hard-wearing, sensible furs like Russian lamb, which would last for years, many fell for baby seal or baby squirrel, which looked lovely but didn't last and tended 'to look like rat after a time'.[35] She clearly knew her market, adding that

> We've got some very good coats made of cat-fur, which looks really just like squirrel– they're £30, and very good for wear. We've sold lots of them. Of course there is still quite a good sale for these short jackets – I'll tell you the sort of girl who buys them: the girl who has more money than she ever had before, the factory girl and so on; she feels awfully glamorous in one of these (opossum), and it doesn't take so many coupons, it's twelve for a jacket.[36]

The continuing demand for fur in wartime Britain was reflected in the

▲

Advertisements from the *British Fur Trade*, 1937.

(Courtesy of the British Library)

▶

Advert for Snowfire vanishing cream and face powder from the mid 1930s. As was the case with Max Factor, Tangee lipstick and many other cosmetic products, consumers were lured by the promise of looking like film stars.

Film-star Glamour

1. *Always use a vanishing cream before you powder to avoid ugly roughness and blackheads.*

2. *Try several shades of face powder to find the one that suits you best.*

WHEN YOU wish so wistfully that you were half as glamorous as your favourite film star, hasn't it occurred to you that you could be if you only set about it in the proper way?

One of the most glamorous things about a lovely woman is a perfect complexion and that is easy to acquire with the right care. The first aid to a flawless skin is a good vanishing cream like Snowfire—good because it is the perfect non-shining powder-base you must use before powdering to save you from clogged pores and roughness : good because it is a real beautifier. Snowfire Cream smooths your skin to satin softness, banishes blemishes, and restores radiant appealing clearness. The second aid is extra-soft Snowfire Powder. It puts a real peach-bloom on your cheeks that *stays* 'matt' because of its secret ingredient, temperature-proof ' Mattex ' which checks excessive greasiness as well. There

are five wonderfully becoming shades to choose from—Naturelle, Peach, Rachelle, Deep Rachelle and Sun-Tan.

Snowfire Cream and Powder are sold everywhere. Snowfire Vanishing Cream costs 3d. for handbag cases, 6d. for tubes and jars, and 1/3 for opal jars. Snowfire Powder is in 3d. cases and attractive 6d. boxes for the dressing table. (*These prices do not apply in I.F.S.*)

ADVICE ON YOUR BEAUTY PROBLEMS.
If there are any beauty problems worrying you, write to the Snowfire Beauty expert, ANNE ARLEN, 39, Sunnydale, Derby, and remember to enclose a stamped, addressed envelope for her reply.

Snowfire

decision to produce Utility fur coats conforming to government rationing regulations for the clothing industry after 1941. These can be seen in a Pathé news feature made and screened in 1944, and an example is preserved in Brighton Museum's clothing collection.[37]

The use of cosmetics became more widespread in Britain in the 1930s: the rise of the Woolworths chain stores with their specialist make-up counters played an important role here. Cosmetics historian Maggie Angeloglou observes that 'assistants in "Woollies" were advisors and confederates to the girl with little money and immense ambition'.[38] Actresses and titled ladies, and home-grown film stars, advocated the (discreet) use of Pond's vanishing cream and light powder to remove the shine from noses. In March 1930, the magazine *Home Chat* distributed free samples of Gladys Cooper's Face Powder and her own blush rouge.[39] Angela Rodaway, who grew up in Islington between the world wars, recalled girls' experimental use of cosmetics in these years: pencilled eyebrows plucked to a thin arch, tints of orange, purple and emerald green.[40] She remembered how as an adolescent she would drift round shops after school, seeking 'food for dreams' that would make her rather impoverished life more tolerable.[41] Department stores served as art galleries and museums, a stimulus to her imagination. She once shoplifted some nail varnish and a manicure set in a pretty white and gold box:

> *I had always been vain about my hands. I varnished my nails at night and lay on my bed, watching them twinkle. They looked like wet shells tossed by spray into the sunshine. My hands might have belonged to the most privileged woman in the world. But I had to take off the varnish before morning.*[42]

Rodaway's contemporary Joan Wyndham was from a much more affluent background: living in Chelsea on the eve of the Second World War she too described how she used to study her appearance, and experiment with make-up. Joan curled her hair in pipe cleaners, slanting her parting, before carefully applying the new Max Factor pancake foundation with a sponge, and rouging her lips with two layers of the new cyclamen lipstick she had bought in Woolworths.[43] Even very young girls would experiment with cosmetics: Mass Observers in the East End of London reported that girls there would start using lipstick around thirteen years of age.[44]

Younger British women in work had disposable income to spend on their appearance and much of it went on make-up. The very smart might get fashion tips from *Miss Modern*, a magazine launched in October 1930 (it ran for ten years, until 1940). The first issue of *Miss Modern* featured a piece by Elinor Glyn pontificating about 'It' and what would arouse the hunting instinct in men.[45] *Miss Modern* incorporated the usual mix of Hollywood glamour, pattern services, fiction and advertising in a particularly attractive format. Readers were wooed with 'little fur capes', and knitting patterns such as that offered in October 1936 for an 'adorable, feather-trimmed' dressing gown. From 1935 the British film star Madeleine Carroll (well known before her appearance in Hitchcock's *The 39 Steps* of that year) offered a regular column, 'Beauty Talks': her earlier background as a teacher in West Bromwich may have been assumed to have given her the right touch to communicate with the office girl. The March 1935 issue of *Miss Modern* carried an advertisement for Miss Carroll addressing 'Poise and personality' alongside a brightly coloured image of a stylish blonde in black hat and black gloves, looking very like the actress, applying bright red lipstick. The June issue of that year offered free powder puffs to its readers; its cover featured a woman powdering her nose.

'Is the Modern Girl a Gold-Digger?' asked a headline in *Woman's Filmfair* in December 1934. Two contributors slugged it out. Joan Gardner contested the view that women were becoming coldly calculating in their attitude to men and defended the new economic freedoms enjoyed by many young girls:

> *Your really modern woman is essentially independent, from the tips of her painted finger-nails to the last curl of her perm. Her most devastating weapon today lies in the jingle of her weekly salary, which tells her boyfriend that he cannot keep her quite at his personal beck and call as in the old days.*[46]

Modernity, independence and lipstick continued to go together in the minds of many contemporaries. There was something of a generation gap still, reflected in some of the cosmetics advertisements featured in *Miss Modern*, which were addressed to 'all the mothers of all the daughters who do not use make-up – yet', warning that 'they soon will', and advising mothers that their best course of action was to try to control

the quality of the products that their daughters would use rather than to try to obstruct the inevitable. But wives and mothers were increasingly likely to turn to the same products. In January 1931, *Woman and Beauty* magazine presented a short story, 'The Lipstick Mood' to its readers with the tagline: 'How a LIPSTICK made a husband REALISE that his wife was a DESIRABLE woman and that OTHER men thought so, too.' The heroine puts on lipstick of a pomegranate hue, prompting a change in her personality:

> She held her lips open just a little and began carefully to destroy the line which seemed so characteristic of acceptance and reserve. It changed from the mouth which marriage and life with Frank had been forming. It became a free-lance mouth, red, confident and just a little insolent.[47]

Another character observes that husbands only like lipstick on other men's wives. 'When I want the entire love of one good man – the one I'm married to – I don't bother to use it,' she says. 'But when I'm not so single-minded, out comes the old lipstick.'[48]

The reddened mouth had become what Angela Carter defined as one of the great glamour conventions of the twentieth century, and the very act of putting on lipstick had acquired multiple meanings, from self-assurance through provocation to defiance.[49] The Imperial War Museum has a well-known photograph of an ambulance worker in Kennington bolstering her courage through the application of lipstick; in the 1931 film *Dishonoured*, Dietrich's last act in facing a firing squad is to paint her mouth, nonchalantly checking her appearance as reflected in the blade of a young officer's – and executioner's – sword.[50] During the Second World War, a supply of lipstick was deemed essential to women war workers' morale, and in view of the need for escapism during these years the advertising copy for cosmetics became ever more extravagant. The hype continued after the war. *Picture Post* in April 1947 carried a full-colour advert for Tattoo lipsticks, 'provocative … ultra vivid … glamour-laden … and lastingly, reassuringly, serenely unmoved by time, teacups, cocktails, kisses'. The formula was said to provide a stain rather than a greasy coating, the colours as enchanting as lagoonside flowers, black magic, orchid, and pagan red.[51]

British women saw red nails, like red lips, as glamorous in the interwar years, but they also attracted censure. The Duke of Windsor described his father, King George V, as an arch-conservative, who 'disapproved of Soviet Russia, painted fingernails, women who smoked in public, cocktails, frivolous hats, American jazz, and the growing habit of going away for week-ends'.[52] A Mass Observation report from 1939 reveals that the king was not alone: many men claimed to dislike or even be disgusted by painted fingernails. One respondent claimed that nail polish reminded him of 'Egyptian whores', another thought of the blood-stained talons of a bird of prey. An insurance clerk considered some colours positively murderous, bringing to mind images of the wicked queen in Walt Disney's 1937 film *Snow White and the Seven Dwarfs*.[53] Some women shared these views. The wearing of pale pearl pink or colourless nail varnish was often deemed feminine and acceptable – deep dark red said something more dodgy and defiant.

Perfume and scent were marketed as luxuries and alongside cosmetics their use spread in Britain in the interwar period. Traditional English floral scents such as apple blossom, lavender and violet remained widely available, but lacked the allure of poppies, which were intensely fashionable in the 1920s and 1930s. Roger and Gallet had success in the late 1920s with Pavots d'Argent. Expensive new scents by Chanel and other French producers were eagerly welcomed in the more up-market department stores all over Britain, even during the Depression. In Newcastle in the 1930s, advertisements for Fenwick's in the local press regularly announced new arrivals, such as Chanel's Glamour and Schiaparelli's Shocking.[54] Cheaper glamour was epitomised by Atkinson's Californian Poppy, aimed at working-class British women during the 1930s and 1940s: 'As teasing as a stolen kiss … As heady as champagne … As wilful as a shower … As haunting as an old refrain … As mysterious as the East itself.'[55] In other adverts, Californian Poppy was compared to a first kiss, a flirt, the languor of Hawaiian guitars, and the glamour of orchids. The illustration invariably showed a man and a woman in a clinch. Unlikely flowers might suggest a rare appeal, as had been the case with Guerlain's Narcisse Noir (1919). There were also relatively inexpensive 'exotic' florals such as Yardley's Orchis or Goya's Black Rose. But many middle-class women remained conservative about scent. Fashion writer Alison Settle warned the woman of taste to avoid anything cloying or seductive,

▶

Atkinson's popular scent, Californian Poppy; advert from the 1940s.

As tantalising as a flirt . . .
as tender as a southern
breeze . . .

as naughty as a sparkling
wine . . . .
as lingering as twilight . . .

as stirring as a bugle call . . .

Californian Poppy
PERFUME

adding sternly that 'Hyacinth is about the line, there.'[56]

Advertisements for Orchis emphasised the exciting glamour of life in a rich setting.[57] Like adverts for Saville's Mischief perfume, the lure was aspirational. Mischief was described as 'the most frightfully swagger perfume that's causing a flutter in the Mayfair dovecotes', the copy suggesting that it would help its user to attract upper-class males.[58] ('Mischief makes a girl "super". No wonder her pretty green telephone rings and rings, and the orchid shop declares a bonus.'[59]) Probably the most successful of all perfumes in this period was Bourjois's Evening in Paris. The composition was by Ernest Beaux, who had created Chanel's No. 5, and the perfume was packaged imaginatively in blue and silver; tiny, inexpensive bottles of the stuff could be bought in Woolworths, although it was also available in large, crystal-stoppered flasks in up-market department stores. Goya scents, marketed by the young and highly entrepreneurial Douglas Collins, also began to break new ground when they were sold as 'precious, costly' perfumes in tiny inexpensive bottles. Collins's first scent, Jaeger Bracken, was sold in simple phials wrapped in amber-coloured cellophane from the counters of Jaeger dress shops: the retail price was just one shilling.[60] In November 1938 Collins brought off an advertising coup, persuading Jean Cleland, the beauty editor of *Woman's Journal*, to distribute free phials of Goya Gardenia scent with every copy of the magazine.[61] The name Gardenia suggested luxury, Collins asserted, a flower bought by millionairesses to pin on their dresses before going out to dinner at eight.[62] Oriental perfumes, however, retained their appeal. In one striking advert for Coty's Chypre that appeared in 1938, a woman veiled with a black yashmak looms phallus-like from between two large speckled petals. 'Warm, dark and dangerous as an Egyptian night', reads the copy: 'Chypre surely was the throbbing fragrance which delivered great Anthony captive to regal Cleopatra on the banks of Old Nile. This languorous perfume is not for the ingénue or the outdoor woman in tweeds. Chypre is for the woman of moods and mystery – for the Cleopatra of today.'[63]

There were different kinds of femininity then, just as there were different kinds of scent and mood. Women's magazines of the period between the world wars and after commonly featured articles dividing women into types. Much of this writing is banal, of the 'fair English rose', 'sultry brunette' and 'fiery redhead', or match-your-perfume-to-your-

▶ Coty's Chypre was described as 'a throbbing fragrance' appealing to the woman of moods and mystery; advert from 1938.

FOR THE MODERN CLEOPATRA

WARM dark and dangerous as an Egyptian night—*Chypre* surely was the throbbing fragrance which delivered great Anthony captive to regal Cleopatra on the banks of Old Nile. This languorous perfume is not for the ingénue or the outdoor woman in tweeds. *Chypre* is for the woman of moods and mystery— for the Cleopatra of today.

Chypre, created by Coty, the world's master parfumeurs, costs from £11.10.0 down. We recommend the size at one guinea.

PARFUMS

personality genre. A series of articles in *Film Fashionland*, for instance, asked readers 'Are you the Sylvia Sidney/Elissa Landi/etc. type?'[64] But the representation of so many different styles of being female was essentially part of modernity. The confident glamour girl was no shrinking violet. The word 'dainty' was probably one of the most overused adjectives in women's magazines of the early twentieth century. 'Daintiness', a quality which had also been much appreciated by the late Victorians, signified on old-fashioned form of femininity, and was altogether different from glamour. A woman could increasingly make choices: as a wage earner, a cinema-goer and a consumer of magazines, she might browse, dream and reflect upon her own identity.

Jackie Stacey's study of female film spectatorship in the 1940s and 1950s shows how Hollywood cinema helped to reshape British ideas about femininity.[65] It can be argued that this process began in the 1920s and was well under way in the following decade. Contemporary social observers such as J. B. Priestley, who in the 1930s described factory girls as looking like actresses, or George Orwell, who noted that the production of cheap smart clothes since the Great War had allowed working-class girls to indulge in daydreams of themselves as Greta Garbo, picked up on the new tendencies in emulation and mass-market fashion.[66] The changes struck some as obscuring traditional class divisions. Thomas Burke, for instance, commented that in public spaces it was now difficult to place girls socially from their dress:

> In the past, you could immediately recognise the social girl, the middle-class girl, the City girl and the factory-girl. Each had its own tone, its own dress and its own bearing ... In these times, while the higher and lower ranks are still distinguishable, the intermediate rank, and all the little ranks within ranks, have fused, and only fine and closely observed shades mark the difference between the shop assistant and the actress.[67]

Some girls studied more than the dress, hair and make-up of their favourite stars, and took inspiration from or emulated their screen personalities. J. B. Mayer found that Deanna Durbin was very popular with some of the women in his sample, for instance – she tended to model a sweetly healthy, teenage brand of femininity that went down well with British audiences.[68] This preference for the fresh and natural, represented as an absence of affectation and artificiality, somewhat in keeping with the perceived national character, underlay the appeal of Gracie Fields and Jessie Matthews, both of whom had the added appeal that they had achieved startling success in spite of being born poor.[69] Jessie Matthews was one of eleven children, her father had been a costermonger in Soho, and her plummy accent came from elocution lessons. Her involvement in the break-up of the marriage between Sonnie Hale and Evelyn Laye dented her reputation early in her career, but she recovered to become one of Britain's greatest stars in the 1930s. Many women who had been keen cinema fans in the 1930s, interviewed decades later by film historian Annette Kuhn, admitted ambivalence towards the more robust glamour of Ginger Rogers, whose brashness they had found slightly vulgar at the time.[70] Some film-goers professed to find American glamour altogether too much. Jackie Stacey quotes a correspondent who wrote to *Picturegoer* in 1945 asserting that

> Our girls don't need glamour, Mr and Mrs America; they've got
> something far more real and precious – charm and natural refreshing
> beauty. I've always looked upon British film stars with relief from the
> tinsel and painted 'angels' of Hollywood. English beauty and talent is
> here in plenty, it merely wants publicity, not a cloak of glamour.[71]

But many felt differently. One of Stacey's respondents remembered that in the 1940s she had hugely preferred Hollywood stars to their British equivalents:

> It had mostly to do with glamour. No matter what our girls did, they
> just couldn't hold a candle to the American girls. I remember I went
> to see a British musical called London Town – the attempt at glamour
> was so awful it just made us giggle.[72]

It was the confidence, sophistication and self-assurance of some of the screen heroines that many of the fans in Stacey's research had found inspirational. Bette Davis, Joan Crawford and Katharine Hepburn were remembered as powerful, confident figures, and herein lay a major source of their attraction.[73] Jeanine Basinger has emphasised that films that appealed to women in the period 1930–60 sent out highly ambiguous messages: even though independent and go-getting women might eventually suffer for their insubordination, they were shown in the mean-time as enjoying worldly success, sexual pleasure and the good things in life.[74] The morality tale embedded in a patriarchal narrative might not be the lesson learned.

It was scarcely surprising that some detected a process of cultural invasion. In October 1946, *Picture Post* carried an article on Goldwyn's 'glamour missionaries', a troupe of would-be starlets and cover girls sent to Britain to cement the wartime *entente*.[75] By the 1940s the lure of Hollywood as seen as potent enough to sell even sanitary wear ('Holly-Pax from Hollywood; Modern insertion-type sanitary protec-tion from the City of Stars').[76] For all those who dismissed American glamour as tinsel or illusion, there were plenty of cinema-goers who couldn't get enough of it and continued to scrutinise the appearance and demeanour of actresses for tips and information. The film maga-zines knew their market and responded with helpful articles, such as one by Tony Sforzia, 'the make-up wizard of London film', in *Woman's Filmfair* on 'Glamourizing the English Girl'. His line was a familiar one by now. Glamour was not just prettiness, he asserted, but a combina-tion of slickness, smartness, perfection of detail, and personality. Anyone could look glamorous if they chose to make the effort, and British girls were fast catching up with the United States in this respect.[77] Everyone wanted in on such a desirable and saleable commodity as glamour. An advert in *Picturegoer and Film Weekly* in January 1941 asking 'What Is the Secret of Glamour?' (defined as a lovely skin, bright eyes, slenderness and personal magnetism) turns out to be for the then well-known laxa-tive Bile Beans.[78]

If the glamour of the cinema exerted a potent influence on the aspirations and appearance of young working-class women in Britain during the 1930s, its impact on their middle-class equivalents was less clear. Catherine Horwood's study of dress codes between the world wars has emphasised the premium placed on respectability, decorous-ness and keeping up appearances amongst the British middle classes.[79] In Liverpool, the well-to-do shopaholic Emily Tinne purchased at least two black satin-backed crêpe evening dresses cut on the bias around 1935–36. But they managed to combine an almost Edwardian matronly respectability with the merest touches of fashionable glamour: wing-shaped shoulder drapes and a diamanté-paste belt clasp.[80] The fashion writer Alison Settle, between 1929 and 1936 editor of British *Vogue,* urged that the well-dressed woman of good taste should avoid looking anything like an imitation of a film star.[81] An unshowy chic should be her goal. Younger middle-class girls were still expected to dress neatly and tidily and not to draw too much attention to themselves. Grooming and daintiness (often a code for personal hygiene) were vital. White collars and trim costumes were seemly wear for typists and office girls; flashy red nails or low-cut blouses were distinctly inappropriate. In 1932 the Bank of England even banned its female employees from wearing make-up. Godfrey Winn objected to this ruling in the pages of the magazine *Miss Modern,* asserting that the majority of businessmen delighted in 'the pretty, varied clothes and the lovely (though artificial) complexions of the women members of staff ... they introduce glamour and romance into our humdrum routine'.[82] But leaving aside glamour, in these years even looking smart might position someone as overdressed and pushy. The cultural historian Janice Winship has suggested that the overarching expectation about lower-middle-class girls between the world wars was that they should look 'nice and neat', orderly and controlled: cleanliness and unobtrusiveness were what was expected by teachers and employers.[83] Dressing for special occasions – such as a first dance – allowed the middle-class girl space for more fantasy in dress.[84] But evening wear, too, was expected to be 'suitable' and not too sexy or revealing, with evening make-up limited to discreet powder and a little lipstick at most: the 'cheap', painted look was anathema.

The writer Vera Brittain was a middle-class woman who took a pronounced interest in her appearance and often looked glamorous, but this was frequently viewed negatively, as she herself was ruefully aware. Lunching at the University Women's Club early in 1939 she noticed that she alone amongst the English women in her party had painted her lips and varnished her nails, while taking care to wear clothes that 'didn't look as if they'd been put on after hanging in a cupboard for 5 years'. 'Why, why must social reform and political intelligence in the women of this country be associated with shiny noses & unwaved hair?' she asked, somewhat melodramatically, in her diary.[85] Middle-class women could be cutting critics of other women's dress, demeanour and hygiene. Virginia Woolf, for instance, found Katherine Mansfield a bit too modern and self-assertive for her liking, describing her in a diary entry for 1917 as rather common and 'cheap': 'She stinks like a – well civet cat that had taken to streetwalking.'[86] Discretion mattered in most middle-class circles, up to and beyond the Second World War, and too-obvious use of perfume could draw censure. When Douglas Collins, grown over-confident by his success in selling inexpensive perfume and dreams to ordinary women in the 1930s, took a big gamble and in March 1939 purchased the whole front page of the *Daily Mail* for an advertisement, he overreached himself.[87] The space was used to show a blonde siren in a white fur wrap lying on a chaise longue with the headline announcing: 'Now you can afford luxury perfume.' The advertisement was a disastrous flop: not only was the timing wrong, but the message was patronising and insulting, and the image was way beyond anything that readers could or wanted to identify with – even in their wildest dreams.

An interest in fashion, personal appearance and social change underlay a series of investigations by Mass Observation between 1938 and 1954. Mass Observers spied on young girls hanging round the 'toilet counter' in Woolworth's, or wistfully gazing at fur coats and trims in shop windows in Paddington. In 1940, one observer noted that:

> *The East End women are rather distinctive in their style of hairdressing, jewellery and in fact, general appearance. 'Glamour' is the keynote, and the Hollywood influence is much in evidence. Make-up is heavy, hair is dyed often, styles are not intended to appear natural, jewellery flashes from nearly every girl.*[88]

Mass Observers reported differences between women of different generations. They dutifully catalogued the contents of a girl's handbag in Stepney, and recorded that cosmetics were the last thing that young girls would economise on, whereas they were rarely used by women over the age of forty-five or so.[89] Straight hair, they noticed, was almost non-existent among younger women: the fashion was for curls and waves, the curls being massed up over the forehead.[90] Oral history has recorded reminiscences containing the phrase 'Friday night is Amami night' (a reference to a then current advertisement for a popular brand of setting lotion), about girls getting together to set their hair for the weekend, in preparation for dancing on a Saturday night.[91] Mass Observers in London described girls' hair as often bleached or dyed bronze, adorned with decorative clips, red or diamanté and shaped like ribbons or bows.[92]

There is a huge amount of detail in these MO surveys, and some of the concerns of the investigators today seem bizarre. A good deal of effort went into comparing the appearance of 'Cockneys' and 'Jewesses', for example: a much higher proportion of the Jewesses were deemed to be smartly dressed, defined by observers as wearing fur coats and high-heeled shoes.[93] Some items of glamour wear were not surprisingly seen as an irrelevance, particularly in wartime: in a conversation overheard by an observer in Fulham Road in 1940, girls examining high-heeled pink feathered bedroom slippers admitted wistfully that they were very pretty but 'you couldn't wear them'.[94] Others felt glamour was not for them: one woman in what Mass Observation dubbed 'Worktown' (Bolton/ Blackpool) averred, 'I don't want to look like a kitten or a vamp. Everybody would laugh if I tried to.'[95]

Researchers at Mass Observation were interested in the way Hollywood was influencing British fashion and also in the speed with which trends in the West End spread to the poorer parts of London. In a press release issued in 1939, the organisation's founder, Tom Harrisson, announced that the fashion leaders that housewives were following at that moment were, first, the Duchess of Kent, second, the Queen and, third, Joan Crawford.[96] MO asked women where they thought the latest fashions came from: 23 per cent answered Paris, 21 per cent Hollywood, 9 per cent Royalty, 6 per cent 'the Jews', 3 per cent magazines and 2 per cent the West End. Interestingly a sizeable 36 per cent were recorded as having answered that they didn't know or care.[97] Observers conscientiously carried out studies of the headwear worn by women in the street to explore diffusion trends. There were detailed 'hat counts'.[98] Harrisson estimated that Mrs Everywoman bought an average of 2.7 hats per year. Up-to-the-minute fashions in millinery were available in the East End within days of their arrival in Oxford Street, and at a fraction of the price.

At the beginning of the Second World War, little hats were glamorous and fanciful. Fashion journalist Ailsa Garland remembered that in the 1930s and 1940s all the editors at *Vogue* wore hats in the office at all times.[99] In 1939 the fashion was for jaunty little confections with the strap at the back, velvet-flecked veils and lots of flowers. Elizabeth Wray was interviewed by Mass Observation in that year wearing a black pillbox hat with a chenille fishnet snood and two roses at the back. Mrs Garland of *Vogue*, who was also interviewed, wore a round black pillbox hat with fishnet snood and a tuft of fur to one side.[100] As Tom Harrisson realised, the fact that hats were cheap relative to other items of clothing increased their appeal: especially to the large class of women who he estimated as having around one shilling and sixpence per week to spend on clothes. Harrisson drafted an article entitled 'Mad Hattery', and fashions in hats certainly reflected a note of flippancy and playfulness, if not outright lunacy, during the war.[101] The *Daily Mirror* commented on an endless array of freak hats; for instance: 'Bang goes the housekeeping money … (on) the latest in military modes … a gold felt cannon hat with a puff of smoke veil and peacock blue chenille cannon wheel.'[102] A cutting from the *Daily Telegraph* in the MO file illustrates a hat sporting a twig of different-coloured plums; there were toques made entirely of white hyacinths and flowerpot hats with long-stemmed blooms.[103] The excesses probably reflected a need to keep spirits up in wartime, and glamour wasn't really the point any more. The *Daily Mirror* failed to summon any enthusiasm for a 1940 creation that was said to look like a cross between a warden's helmet and a dinner bell, and which it tersely judged 'would kill Dietrich stone dead'.[104]

In her autobiography, professor of fashion Janey Ironside observed that fashion came to a full stop during the war.[105] But in spite of the disruption to the luxury trades a need for glamour was often deemed central to

▼
Wedding photo of a young working- class couple in wartime Leeds. The bride's hat, with its distinctive crown, ostrich feather and veil at the back, represented the height of fashion in 1941–2. Her appearance is carefully crafted. Note the plucked eyebrows, skilful make-up and tiny corkscrew curls. The romantic hairstyle echoes that of Garbo in *Camille* (1936).

morale. Cosmetics were advertised as necessary to the war effort: 'Beauty goes hand in hand with service to King and country', primly announced *Miss Modern* in 1940.[106] 'War has put lipstick on fashion's front-page news', announced *Picture Post* in October 1939, suggesting that shades of 'Burnt Sugar' and 'Sporting Pink' went well with khaki, whilst 'Redwood' looked good with airforce blue.[107] In November 1939, Mass Observers recorded a display of cosmetics by Helena Rubinstein in the windows of D. H. Evans featuring a 'thrilling' new colour called 'Regimental Red'.[108] Later shortages of cosmetic ingredients forced women to make do with what they could get: stories of ingenuity and contrivance using gravy browning and burnt matches abound. Even a simple twisted scarf worn round the head with a roll of hair at the front was known as a 'glamour band', according to fashion historians Elizabeth Wilson and Lou Taylor, although this was predominantly a working-class fashion originating in the need to protect hair from machinery in factory work.[109] For a while, uniforms – with their hints of androgyny – were considered glamorous. Margaret Sweeney (later Duchess of Argyll) had her Red Cross uniform made by Molyneux and accessorised it with her trademark pearls until told in no uncertain terms to take them off.[110] The historian Penny Summerfield has described how some women enjoyed the liberty of battledress and trousers whilst making a point of wearing silk cami-knickers next to their skin as a statement about feminine identity, or for reassurance.[111] But glamour, once conscripted, developed a tacky edge, represented by the calendar pin-ups supplied to servicemen, and the cone-breasted women painted on the sides of aeroplanes, generally referred to as 'nose art'. The distinctions between empowering images of glamorous women, 'cheesecake' and soft pornography were sometimes fairly obvious, sometimes finely drawn.

Princesses, tarts and cheesecake

After the Second World War ended, and as the need for rationing receded, the spirit of liberation triggered an appetite – in part nostalgic – for half-forgotten forms of femininity, for luxury and for cheap glitter. Manifestations of this included a buoyant demand for costume jewellery, and the impact of Dior's New Look. Fashion – like material culture generally – reflected and embodied the contradictory social position of British women in the 1950s. Where were women supposed to be? At work or in the home? It was often argued that housekeeping and motherhood were a full-time job if women attended to these tasks properly, but given that paid employment was a necessity for many, and that some women even enjoyed the independence that went with it, there was a good deal of conflict.[1] There were of course class dimensions to this, as well as issues of race. Middle-class women could no longer reckon on a supply of cheap domestic servants. Some of the lowest-paid jobs available in postwar Britain went to migrant women, particularly black women from the Caribbean.[2] Adverts in women's magazines could reflect a general assertiveness about 'whiteness': an issue of *Woman's Own* in 1957 carried an advert for Kestos underwear showing a white, very middle-class-looking woman being attended to by a black woman dressed as a servant.[3] As traditional social markers of gentility shifted and gender roles came

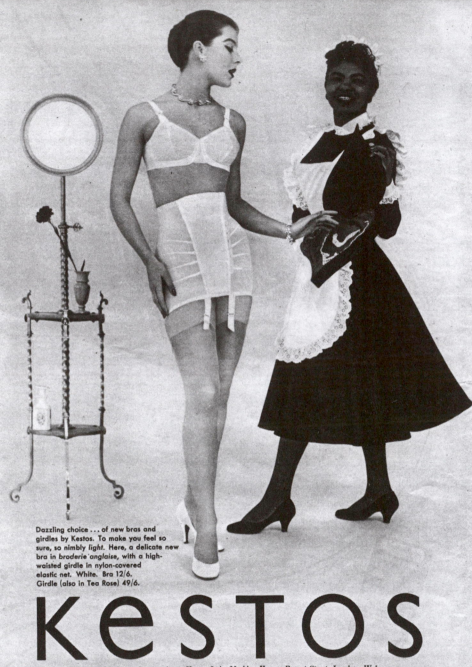

Dazzling choice . . . of new bras and
girdles by Kestos. To make you feel so
sure, so nimbly *light*. Here, a delicate new
bra in *broderie anglaise*, with a high-
waisted girdle in nylon-covered
elastic net. White. Bra 12/6.
Girdle (also in Tea Rose) 49/6.

KESTOS

for free brochure please write to Kestos Ltd., Maddox House, Regent Street, London, W.1.

under strain, the establishment of social respectability became a matter of pressing concern. This was a context in which glamour came to look increasingly vulgar in the eyes of the middle class. The New Look was not so much a new version of glamour, but more a nostalgic statement about a world in which gender identities and the hierarchies of class and race were part of a common understanding.

The New Look was not as new as it looked anyway. Something like it had been emerging in the USA before the war. A Mass Observation report for 1939–40 quoted 'the editress of a leading trade paper':

> *I have been following American fashion pages pretty closely and they read like a foreign language now. They are all talking about wasp waists and corsets, and this season is supposed to be striking for its glitter and masses of jewellery and bustles and things. It's supposed to be the most extravagant season for a long time. While here you don't even get people bothering about cheap frocks – factory girls go to work in slacks.[4]*

Like many observers and later historians, Madge Garland (then editor of *Vogue*) judged that the New Look was really a last look at a vanishing conception of femininity. The fashion writer Alison Settle saw it as the return of the feminine repressed.[5] Dior himself submitted, 'I design clothes for flowerlike women, with rounded shoulders, full, feminine busts and hand-span waists above enormous spreading skirts', he added that he saw himself as having brought back 'the art of pleasing'.[6] His Ligne Corolle, literally 'corolla line', was designed to make women look like flowers: 'femmes-fleurs'.[7] Getting the right shape could entail struggle: fashion editor Ailsa Garland remembered buying a waist-cincher, which used to make her feel so sick after lunch or dinner that she had to disappear and remove it.[8] A former model, Cherry Marshall, similarly recalled the waspies needed to constrict the waist in order to fit into New Look dresses, and how the constriction had prevented her from eating because it wouldn't let food get as far as her stomach. Her mother had demurred that she looked in need of a good meal, but Cherry did well professionally, becoming well known as Miss Susan Small: she was reputed to have the smallest waist in London.[9]

TO THE SMALLER
SMART WOMAN...

...it's a
SUSAN
Small
world!

◄

Model Cherry
Marshall in
an advert for
Susan Small,
1949.

High-heeled shoes might lift and tilt the body, but as Alison Settle wrote in the *Observer* in 1956, the new lines demanded the most firm-minded figure control.[10] Many women had to diet. Diet pills based on thyroid extract may have been dealt a blow by legislative controls, but these were nonetheless years in which diet fads proliferated, focusing on various gimmicks and wonder foods such as molasses, yoghurt and liquorice.[11] There was a vogue, for example, for fruit diets, with slogans like 'Apples fight Amplitude.'[12] Eve Merriam noted that the new desire in the USA to look both busty and thin was contributing to the success of a wave of Slenderella reducing salons with 'vibrating tables' promising trimness.[13] The Elizabeth Arden salon in London advertised a 'giant roller', 'which whirls round in a semi-circular threshing movement, wearing down your redundant flesh'.[14] In England, the 1950s were the decade of the Stephanie Bowman Slimming Garment, regularly depicted in the small ads, a kind of boil-in-the-bodybag for sweating it out in and, its users hoped, losing inches round the middle.

Not everyone took to the New Look: many were critical of what they saw as a wasteful, expensive and retrograde style. It wasn't easy to go to work in, and not only because tight waisting made breathing and eating difficult: Merriam commented that full skirts with high heels made it impossible to walk up and down steps 'without risking an unladylike pratfall'.[15] Others found the New Look simply unappealing. Flowery feminine skirts were not seen as sexy or glamorous enough by Marilyn Monroe in *How to Marry a Millionaire* (1953); she preferred a figure-hugging line.[16] But Mass Observers watching the trend noticed that most women soon came round to the style of almost caricatured femininity, commenting that 'the masculine, capable, efficient, strong-willed female is, so it seems, about to be *out of fashion*'.[17] The New Look soon dominated the pages of the fashion magazines, even the domestically oriented *Woman's Own*, which ran a series of exclusive articles on and interviews with Dior and instructed readers how to make a hat like that worn by Princess Margaret to complement a cutting-edge New Look ensemble.[18] Hats, gloves and slender umbrellas were as much a part of the look as nipped-in waists and long full skirts. The historian Carolyn Steedman has written of her mother, in the 1950s longing for a New Look skirt, despairing and resentful because, in spite of all her hard work, as the barely supported mother of two young children she simply couldn't see how to afford it.[19]

Inspired by flowerlike women, the New Look often went hand in hand
with a range of floriferous accessories. Writing from Paris shortly after
the war, Alison Settle reported 'a flowering, seen in hats'.[20] Hats were
scattered with rosebuds, petals and violets, huge corsages of purple
velvet Parma violets, popular for daytime as well as evening wear. All
this was very much in keeping with the postwar celebration of fresh
and often girlish femininity. Manufacturers of perfume, cosmetics and
fabrics followed the trend, advertising rose-tinted, rose-scented and rose-
decorated products, such as Morny's June Roses scent. Norman Hartnell
introduced a new scent called In Love (1950), based on white flowers.
He hadn't liked the strong perfumes of the interwar years, he explained,
and had gone for 'a clear and lingering loveliness that should become

the light-complexioned women of England'.[21] Cosmetics and make-up were sold in gimmicky packaging, often featuring extravagantly feminine Milady figures in crinolines. Christmas 1952 saw Elizabeth Arden offering My Love or Blue Grass in a sparkling bell, and Coty selling L'Aimant in a Cinderella slipper. Softer fabrics replaced clingy silks and satins, as fashionable women dressed in structured wools by day, gauzy crêpe de Chine, chiffon, mousseline and charmeuse in the evening. 'The gentle look is in', announced Alison Settle in the *Observer*, 'our girls will have none of the Michael Arlen influence.' The edgy, exotic glamour of Iris March was now profoundly unfashionable; instead, the entire trend was based on roses, fragility, and serenity.[22]

Chunky and showy jewellery became immensely popular in Britain in the 1950s. As Jane Mulvagh comments in her book on the history of costume jewellery, after years of hardship, buyers were 'hungry for expensive-looking glitz'.[23] Inspiration came from pieces by designers such as Jacques Fath and Dior. Chanel, who staged a comeback after the Second World War, also had an impact on the fashion for costume jewellery through her signature gilt chains and ropes of pearls. Writing in 1955, Alison Settle gushed enthusiasm for Dior designs which were made up in Wales by Mitchell Maer: 'the jewellery falls in little cascades, even bracelets cascading down the arm, in freshwater pearls, agates, moonstones tinted pale green and pink'.[24] There were brooches, earrings and heavy necklaces by Trifari gilded in three different shades. Diamanté bracelets were worn over black, elbow-length gloves; outsize brooches were sometimes worn on the hipbone.[25] Adrian Mann, a London-based wholesaler who had contacts with manufacturers in Czechoslovakia, was one of the first to attract the popular market, selling jewellery from counters in department stores alongside cosmetics. Approaching Christmas in 1956, Alison Settle noted that Mitchell Maer's 'triple stringed necklet of near-pearls fronted with a quivering near-diamond Christmas rose' for Dior, sold in Debenham and Freebody stores, was a best-seller.[26]

In the trade press, jewellery manufacturers in Hatton Garden and the Midlands celebrated rocketing demand. 'The Business Girl Means Big Business' announced one such article in 1956, commenting on the new city landscape populated by girls who went out to work with cash to spare and an interest in looking good.[27] Magazines, films and television had given these girls an eager interest in changing fashions, the

Sixteen-year-old hairdresser Betty Burden, living in a 'back-to-back' area of housing in Birmingham, photographed by Bert Hardy for an article written by Hilde Marchant for Picture Post *in 1951. The article, 'Millions Like Her', described the modest hopes and home-loving nature of the postwar respectable working class. Several of Hardy's shots focused on Betty applying lipstick at her dressing table.*

(© Bert Hardy/ Picture Post/ Hulton Archive/ Getty Images)

writer observed, and 'they spend all they can on prettying themselves.' But fashion writers warned that though 'a little that glitters can make all the difference', too much of it looked cheap and vulgar. Jewels could make a woman, but they could also mark her, warned one such voice.[28] Some of the British fashion crazes of the 1950s were watched sniffily by observers such as Alison Settle, who complained that women choosing spectacles or sunglasses were often more interested in the glamour effect of twinkling mock-jewels set into wing-shaped frames than in the quality of lenses.[29] There were also the ubiquitous 'poppets': cheap plastic beads which one could join together at will, available in just about every size and colour, including a pearlised finish.[30] Their novelty value soon wore off: just about everybody could afford these.

Fur remained glamorous, in Britain as elsewhere, though fashions in fur had changed. The furrier J. G. Links, writing in the mid 1950s, lamented the fall from grace of silver – and indeed all hues of – fox: pelts that would have fetched a fine price before the war were now virtually unsellable.[31] The trade was now almost completely driven by the demand for mink. 'Every woman hankers after a mink coat and regards it as her withheld birthright. Every woman cannot have one,' Alison Settle had pontificated in 1937.[32] The cachet of mink carried over into the postwar years. Stoles of white mink were the most desirable accessory amongst those who had the means and opportunities for elaborate evening dressing. Settle also extolled the charms of ocelot fur as used by Balenciaga and other designers, recording that at a dress show she had attended one woman had her own hair flecked all over with patches, dark and light, exactly to imitate her ocelot coat.[33] Settle was particularly enthusiastic about a new collection of furs advertised by Bradley's in 1955 which featured creamy ivory beaver pelts and minks, white ermine stoles and boleros, and Chinese lamb in biscuit beige.[34]

Fur was still a sign of wealth and luxury. But it was also becoming increasingly available to British women, even in the years shortly after the war. As well as Utility fur coats, there was a steady trade in second-hand fur; following demobilisation, precious coupons might be blown on a coveted fur coat. Beaver lamb and mink may have been sought after, but there were cheaper options. Alison Settle, writing from Paris, noted that 'Pussies had obviously contributed their skins to fur linings for autumn and winter.'[35] Cheap furs, sometimes purchasable by instalments, were advertised in magazines aimed at working-class girls. The February 1948 issue of *Glamour and Peg's Paper* offered an ocelot-patterned coney (rabbit) coat at £9 18s.6d., plus eighteen clothing coupons.[36] In 1955 the paper *Marilyn* ran regular competitions offering readers the chance to win a fur coat. For those whose budgets couldn't stretch to a whole mink coat, there was always the mink stole, the mink brooch, or even mink earrings. Artificial roses or clusters of fake pearls set in little nests of fur were widely available as brooches in the 1950s: there is an example in Worthing Museum's costume collection, and they can still be found in junk shops and at car boot sales. Settle's column in the *Observer* in October 1954 was illustrated with a sketch by the artist Fromenti showing a furry mink gypsy earring.[37]

Even mink, now widely farmed, had come down in price dramatically, Links commented, and indeed was not much more expensive than it had been in his father's day.[38] In the late 1950s Leslie Durbar, writing in the *British Fur Trade*, argued that the cost of a mink fur coat was governed more by manufacturing cost than the cost of the pelts themselves: mink was becoming so cheap that its exclusiveness was going and there was a danger of it falling out of fashion.[39] Improvements in the quality of fake furs, and their widening availability in the 1950s, chipped away still further at the exclusivity of fur generally. As early as July 1952, even the upmarket *Vogue* was running regular advertisements for 'Furleen', 'Minkaleen', 'Pershnelle' and other imaginatively named fur substitutes, which together featured in a 'Fabulous Furleen Coronation Collection'.[40] Settle in the *Observer* recommended bed jackets of white 'erminette', with the joins herring-boned exactly in the manner of the working of real fur.[41] However, even Settle was getting uneasy about the ubiquity of fur, comparing fashions in the USA with British restraint, and observing rather sniffily that 'Our dolls do not yet, I am glad to say, have mink coats.'[42] The potency of fur as a symbol may have been further diluted by the way it was constantly hijacked by other products: there were cosmetics in the shade of 'mutation mink' by Gala, for instance, and there was Steiner's White Mink perfume.

Along with fur, glamour itself was suddenly becoming both much more affordable and accessible. Not surprisingly, this fuelled fears about cheapness and vulgarity. Anxieties about social class and women's role in the postwar world encouraged women to censure each other for looking 'tarty' or 'common'. The line between glamour and vulgarity had always been blurry, but the fashion industry and the media did their best to erase it entirely during the 1950s. The New Look contradicted much that had been associated with Hollywood glamour. Where glamour had allowed women to test the barriers of gender and class, the New Look reinvented traditional femininity with all its class-based, hierarchical associations. It was a style replete with limitations, its celebration of well-bred, ladylike containment making it much easier to stigmatise the vulgar and down-market. 'Gentlemen Prefer Ladies', announced the cover of *Time* magazine in January 1955 alongside a glowing photograph of Grace Kelly, allegedly heralding a new kind of movie star.[43] 'The new word for beauty is Grace', announced *Woman's Own*.[44] In the public mind Grace Kelly radiated purity and class, never more so than when she walked towards the altar to marry Prince Rainier, clutching her lace-embroidered and seed-pearl-encrusted prayerbook. Just as the dichotomy between madonna and whore had haunted the Victorians, the postwar years were haunted by the distinction between fine ladies, 'real princesses', and the less pure kinds of pin-up girl, roll-in-the-hay glamour models, and other forms of 'cheesecake'.

The *Oxford English Dictionary* suggests that the use of the word 'cheesecake', as slang for female sexual attractiveness and display, originated in the United States in the 1930s. An early reference in *Time* magazine defined cheesecake as 'leg pictures of sporty females'.[45] Cheesecake implied feminine passivity, rather than agency: women represented for the purpose of male consumption. In spite of the fact that the same magazine heralded Marlene Dietrich as 'the supreme Empress of Cheesecake' in 1942, the word was often from the outset associated with the tacky and the vulgar, as evinced by the adjective 'cheesy', used around the same time to suggest the tawdry and the second-rate.[46] Referring to a woman as a 'tart' also carried double meanings. Although the *OED* cites usages from the 1860s through to the 1960s where 'tart' carried no implication of disrespect or loose morals, the adjective 'tarty' almost always meant gaudy or cheap. Generations of girls brought up in the twentieth century were warned by their mothers not to look tarty, lest they signal an unseemly – and unladylike – interest in sex. 'Fast' women, tarts and 'floozies' were all unrespectable, outside the pale of the home-loving middle classes. Girls had to tread carefully and to watch their reputations.

References to 'pin-up' girls date from the 1940s.[47] *Life* magazine described Dorothy Lamour as the 'No. 1 pin-up girl of the US Army' in 1941, but hardly surprisingly there were many contenders. Betty Grable was famous for a poster widely displayed in GI locker rooms during the war: the image showed her in a swimsuit, coyly looking backwards over her shoulder, her legs, famously insured by Lloyds of London for some $2,000,000, showing to their full advantage. Pin-ups as a genre had roots in Edwardian bathing beauty postcards or cigarette cards, but were of course much more publicly displayed. To quote Richard Hoggart, they were 'and still are, standard decoration for servicemen's billets and the cabs of lorries'.[48] The boundaries around what became known as 'glamour photography' were somewhat unclear. It expanded massively in the 1940s and 1950s, encompassing pin-ups, cheesecake calendars, up-market men's magazines, down-market 'girlie' magazines, soft porn, comic strips and 'art' photography of all kinds.

The magazine *Esquire* met with huge success in the United States in the 1930s. Illustrations by George Petty of the rather innocent 'pouting cutie' variety were popular, but were soon eclipsed by the flawless, gleaming finish of Vargas girls.[49] Vargas glamour girls – the artwork of the Peruvian-born Alberto Vargas y Chavez – have been seen by some feminists as representations of a new and powerful form of female sexuality, of a particularly untouchable or 'don't mess with me' kind. Maria Elena Buszek has argued that they need to be seen in the context of wartime conditions.[50] Images of Vargas girls painted on the walls of tanks and planes, or used as 'nose art' by bomber squadrons, she points out, reflect an idea of the female sex as powerful and aggressive, reversing 'normal' male/protector, female/protected role expectations.[51]

In 1944, *Picture Post* featured an article headed 'An Experiment in Taste – What Is a Pin-Up Girl?' In it, British servicemen were presented with a series of photographs of women, including photographs of paintings of women by old masters, and they were asked to vote for those they found the most attractive.[52] It was thumbs down for the old masters. The most popular image was an 'art' photo by Horace Roye of a nude slithering down a rock. (Roye specialised in photographs of comparatively innocent, healthy outdoor types, and published a number of books of such images, such as *Perfect Womanhood*, in 1938.[53]) In second place was a photograph of the American film star Dorothy McGuire, in a kind of unspoiled sister-sweetheart pose. Third place went to an image of Jane – the popular cartoon ditzy blonde from the *Daily Mirror*.[54]

According to Mark Gabor, author of *The Pin-Up: A Modest History* (1972), Britain lagged well behind the United States in the development of the genre.[55] In the USA, the success of *Esquire* was followed by that of *Playboy*, founded in 1953. *Esquire* went up-market in the 1950s, integrating images of well-known movie stars in fashion settings: Hollywood photographer George Hurrell contributed a series to the magazine at this time. *Playboy* built on the pin-up tradition with centrefolds and the 'Playmate of the Month' series: Marilyn Monroe appeared in the first issue, photographed by Tom Keeley.[56] Britain had little to compare. 'Art' photography not dissimilar from Roye's was available through the small ads in the form of Jean Straker's 'photonudes'.[57] There were also a large number of cheap pin-up magazines aimed at working men, with titles that included *Spick, Span, Fiesta, Funfair, Fanfare, Beautiful Britons, Knave* and *Parade*.[58] These tended to contain lots of images of girls up trees with wind blowing their skirts up, of an 'ooh la la!' and comparatively innocent variety. Richard Hoggart turned his attention to this kind of literature, and to what he dubbed 'technicolor "cheesecake" in 3D', complaining that 'we are a democracy whose working-people are exchanging their birthright for a mass of pin-ups'.[59] Much of this imagery was, as he conceded, fairly homely; the 'pleasantly English-looking chorus-girl from Scunthorpe, tricked out unconvincingly in silky pants and brassiere, with a few beads'.[60] Even posters advertising racy serials tended to feature the smiling faces of nice girls from Leeds, he continued. The girl ostensibly trapped and bound by pagan savages, for instance,

> *will have the face and the attractively-waved auburn hair of the girl who smiles from the fourpenny patterns for knitting jumpers. It is clear that the moment she is released she will hide that not-altogether-nice bathing costume masquerading as a wild animal's pelt beneath the cable-stitch cardigan she made for twelve-and-six and the rather fashionable skirt she got half-price at the C & A sale.[61]*

These descriptions – rich as they are with social nuance and domestic sentiment – probably tell us more about Hoggart than the images themselves. But the images were certainly not classy, and had a decidedly 'cheesy' quality about them.

The glamorous wartime pin-up girls popular in both the United States and Britain had showed their mettle by contributing to the war effort. Nevertheless, in postwar Britain, such glamour girls were firmly sidelined by high fashion, which instead associated itself with the icy aloofness of models such as Barbara Goalen, Dovima and Fiona Campbell-Walter. Films and the popular imagination focused on princesses in love. The Cinderella story exerted a potent appeal. Disney's *Cinderella* (1950), *Roman Holiday* (1953) and *The Glass Slipper* (1954) enshrined innocence, the gamine look, pearl chokers and ballet slippers. Grace Kelly's real-life story did the same. In *Roman Holiday*, Hepburn proves she is 'a real princess'. Drugged up and out at night on the pavements of Rome without any money, she still hangs on to her spotless white gloves. As Rachel Moseley has contended, Hepburn's appeal was grounded in class rather than sexuality.[62] Even as the amoral Holly Golightly in *Breakfast at Tiffany's* (1961), she wears jewels in her hair reminiscent of a coronet or tiara. In the 1950s class and social deference were woven through advertisements and marketing: Aristoc, a popular brand of stockings, had been manufactured since the 1920s. The autumn issue of *Vanity Fair* in 1956 carried an advert for 'English Rose Nylons': the range included a variety called Hunt Ball.[63] The image showed a woman in evening dress looking rapturously over a balcony flanked by two attentive gentlemen in equestrian gear.

This fairytale fashion represented a late flowering of traditional femininity, enshrined in narratives in which quiet and submissive patterns of behaviour – sitting and spinning – attracted the attention of princes. Unlike glamour girls, who got up and went for what they wanted, fairy princesses stayed submissive in the face of adversity: or, at the very least, they were clever enough to act like ladies and not to look pushy. Obedience might be rewarded by marriage to a prince. Again, real life was held to bear this out. Grace Kelly's marriage to Prince Rainier of Monaco was the best-known example, but far from isolated. Both Helena Rubinstein and Elizabeth Arden netted princes. Rubinstein's marriage, in 1938, to Prince Artchil Gourielli-Tchkonia, a Russian émigré twenty years younger than her, lasted fairly amicably until his death; she launched a line of cosmetics for men using his name.[64] Her rival Arden's marriage to Prince Michael Evlonoff in 1942 proved more ephemeral.[65] Movie star Rita Hayworth – who managed to keep her

reputation in spite of her pin-up status – married Prince Aly Khan, son and heir to the Aga Khan, hereditary leader of Shia Ismaili Muslims, in 1948. This marriage did not last. Hayworth returned to the United States in 1951 to a highly successful resumption of her film career. *Woman's Own* published a feature on her life, billed as 'the fabulous story of a modern-day Cinderella who rose from obscurity to marry her millionaire Prince Charming', even though this 'emotional, exotic star … has failed to find happiness'.[66] The magazine gleefully retailed rumours about the glamour of Hayworth's lifestyle: it had been said that when she married, the swimming pool at Chateau L'Horizon on the French Riviera would be filled with expensive perfume, and that turtles would float around with lighted candles on their backs; her engagement ring would boast a 32-carat diamond as big as a belt buckle and heavy enough to tire a weightlifter. But readers would be reassured to learn that riches were no substitute for married bliss.[67] Hayworth, like Marilyn Monroe, bridged the gap between glamour and a less assertive kind of femininity.

Successful models too sometimes married princes, strengthening the hold of the Cinderella story on the feminine imagination in the 1950s. In *How I Became a Fashion Model* (1958), former model Jean Dawnay described her life as just like a fairy tale – even though it had been hard work.[68] She eventually married Prince George Galitzine. A modelling life was not all glamour, she warned her readers, although most women dreamed of dressing up and finding a Prince Charming. The frontispiece of her book was a photograph of Dawnay resplendent in white ballgown, a white fur over her bare shoulders, set off by glittering diamond-cluster earrings. What Colin McDowell called the 'icy perfection' of model Barbara Goalen was similarly exemplified in a photograph by John French of the same period, Goalen looking like a snow princess in Dior white chiffon, white fur stole, white flower at the (tiny) waist, long white gloves, and diamond earrings.[69] Goalen was described by model-school manager Lucie Clayton as always looking 'groomed, suave, sophisticated, cold'; Clayton added that 'She embodied the England of stately homes, Bond Street, Harrods and the younger Hartnell.'[70] Her look was less about glamour than about class and *Country Life*. Successful models might marry into this world in the 1950s: Fiona Campbell-Walter married Baron von Thyssen; Bronwen Pugh, Lord Astor; Jane McNeil, the Earl of Dalkeith.[71]

Princesses who were born to the title were of course the real thing. When the girlish Elizabeth II came to the throne in Britain, the public revelled in what the historian David Cannadine has called 'a pageant of history, empire and inequality'.[72] Press and television coverage was riddled through with social deference and respect for aristocracy and old Britain. Norman Hartnell pinpointed the turning point in his career to the occasion when he had been asked to design dresses for Lady Alice Scott's wedding in 1935.[73] In dressing the youngest bridesmaids – the princesses Elizabeth and Margaret Rose – he had gone for palest pink satin, made into girlish short dresses with graduating bands of ruched pink tulle. In his autobiography, Hartnell describes how the new King introduced him to the Winterhalter portraits in Buckingham Palace, which inspired his enthusiasm for the romantic crinoline and many of his clothes for the Queen and the two young princesses.[74] Hartnell had shelved his sequinned sheaths and dazzle and applied himself to embroidered leeks and coronets for the royal wedding in 1947. In January 1953 *Picture Post* ran a leading article on Hartnell and the Coronation, detailing the designer's concern with the niceties of sartorial differentiation between viscountesses, baronesses and countesses.[75] It was no coincidence that the same magazine showed a particular interest in debutantes that year. The March issue pointed out that in normal years around 500 debs made their debut annually: this year would see 2,000 of them presented at court, many of them preparing for this by going to curtseying classes at the Monkey Club in Kensington.[76]

The young Queen's sister, Princess Margaret Rose, became a template for feminine fashion at this time. Margaret took naturally to Dior and the New Look, and photographs from the early 1950s show her glorying in fairytale dresses with full skirts of spangled chiffon. Dior himself described her as 'a real fairy princess, delicate, graceful, exquisite'.[77] *Woman's Own* loved her. In 1952 the magazine published a series in which the former royal nanny, 'Crawfie', disclosed her 'secrets' about Margaret, entitled 'The Full Story of a Very Modern Young Woman'.[78] Readers were treated to Crawfie's revelation that the young princess liked to dress up and had once posed scarlet-mouthed as a glamorous spy in the palace: they were reassured, however, that she was never so racy in real life.[79] She used pale pink nail varnish, Crawfie insisted, *never* red.[80] As the 1950s progressed, and Margaret's own life became more scandalous, she slowly became more cutting-edge. Her hair was cut in a chrysanthemum, petal-cap style, and she was not averse to sporting eyeliner, and a darker lipstick. By the early 1960s she was a peripheral, but highly recognisable member of the fashion set.

Model schools in this period taught elocution, deportment, charm and manners: in effect they set out to transform girls into ladies. Even so, Lucie Clayton complained that too many girls aspired to become models out of a desire to improve their prospects socially, and in hope of marrying up.[81] Cherry Marshall, looking back on her experiences in modelling in the postwar years, remembered that the life had had its arduous side and was often boring: 'As for the glamour, that was still more of an illusion than reality. Behind the scenes were unromantic studios, stuffy dressing rooms full of cigarette ends and cold mugs of tea, laddered stockings and grubby make-up.'[82] There had been little around in the way of cosmetics, and she recalled much making do with liquid paraffin and boot polish. Hair was often washed in soft green soap.[83] Perspiration was a terrible hazard:

> *This was my biggest stumbling block, trying to find a reliable deodorant. I nearly gave up modelling on more than one occasion because I perspired under my arms when I was hot and nervous, and this was considered very unladylike and working class.*[84]

Woman and Beauty had recommended sponging armpits with diluted peroxide followed by a liberal application of boracic powder.[85] Marshall remembers sweat as a source of deep shame, until she discovered water-proof dress shields: even these were embarrassing, though, and they couldn't be worn with sleeveless ball gowns.

The world of modelling offered hazards as well as the lure of social success. In Susan Chitty's humorous novella *The Diary of a Fashion Model* (1958), the innocent Mavis Bone enters a crazy world of make-believe, in part seedy, in part highlife, and peopled by upper-middle-class daughters wearing real pearls and 'chatting over the phone about cubbing'. She discovers that the word 'mannequin' is safer than 'model', since the latter might include 'girls who stick snapshots outside tobacconists in South Kensington'.[86] Cherry Marshall was ruefully aware of both the dubious reputation of some forms of glamour modelling and goings-on in the less select model schools. Reputations could slither easily: 'Up we went with the Society girls and down we went with call-girls, night-club hostesses and the dollies in the pin-up magazines.'[87] It was a world in which glamour and class could appear to contradict each other rather sharply.

Plenty of veteran glamour girls resisted the feminising trends of the 1950s, though they risked doing so at the cost of their reputations. One woman recorded her memories of the decade for Mass Observation thirty years later:

> *My husband was nearly asked to resign from his golf-club over one dress I wore on Xmas Eve to the club's party. It was in fuchsia courtelle, with a plunging neckline, tight waist and full ruffled skirt. The sleeves were tight to the elbow, with a cascade of ruffles falling to the wrist. I was wearing a bra with it (although that was difficult to believe) and*

*one dear old gentleman of about 90 tottered over to me and said 'My
dear, you look delicious – just like a page out of Esquire'! I was quite
innocent of the uproar that had been created until my husband told me
a couple of weeks after.*[88]

Not that innocent – a little while later she wore a pale blue négligée to
the annual dinner of her husband's new company. This evidently stunned
the other wives into silence: she triumphantly recorded that they froze
her out of the conversation.

Glamorous celebrities were still visible, but might occupy uncertain
territory socially, and in relation to high fashion. Lady (Norah) Docker,
the openly gold-digging wife of the British industrialist Sir Bernard
Docker, became a working-class heroine of sorts. She usually faced her
public decked out in mink and diamonds, and designed and had custom-
built various Daimler cars covered in glitz: a gold model, spangled with
stars on the side panels, and one in dark blue, with an interior of croc-
odile leather and silver brocade. She justified her lifestyle as publicity
for Daimler, but was well aware that she herself had come to constitute
a form of public entertainment.[89] Lady Docker confessed to an early

Lady Docker,
wearing mink,
touches up
her make-up
in her custom
built 'Stardust'
Daimler, 1954.

*(© Fox Photos/
Hulton Archive/
Getty Images)*

determination to marry money, and boasted of her success. All three of her husbands had been millionaires.[90] 'For a girl from Birmingham, whose school life was an utter and miserable failure, and who became an artificial blonde among thousands of artificial blondes searching for stardom in London', she concluded (with palpable satisfaction), her life had been 'nothing short of a miracle'.[91] In the end her enjoyment of notoriety went too far. Sir Bernard lost his position in the Birmingham Small Arms Company not least because of mounting concern about his wife's expenses, which had included a wardrobe bill for £7,910 for attending the Paris Motor Show.[92] The couple eventually retired to Jersey as tax exiles.

Norah Docker's autobiography was a best-seller. It opened with a repudiation of passive, domestic forms of femininity. She declared unequivocally that she had never been able or bothered to cook and that, since she had been a failure at school, she thought her ambition was best served by attracting a rich male. The secret of her success, she suggested, lay in a determination 'to make myself expensive'.

> *When most girls were ready to accept a fur coat, I would demand a mink. When the other girls would be satisfied by a zircon, I would insist on a diamond ... In the same way, I always asked for champagne because I knew it was expensive, and it tasted expensive. It had to be pink champagne, because I loved the colour.*[93]

This was the kind of attitude later taken to extremes by Zsa Zsa Gabor, the ultimate gold-digger, who was born in 1917 and married her ninth husband in 1986. She remained famous only for being famous. Gabor memorably described herself as a wonderful housekeeper on the grounds that 'Every time I leave a man, I keep his house,' and boasted that she 'had never hated a man enough to give his diamonds back'.[94] In the 1930s, too, glamour had been used as a weapon to fight back in a patriarchal world; by the 1950s, it had become open warfare for some.

Lady Docker's glamour was flagrant and ostentatious. British 'sex-bombs' Sabrina and Diana Dors went still further in courting (and ignoring) accusations of vulgarity. Sabrina, born Norma Sykes, 'the Stockport glamour girl', was launched to fame playing the dumb blonde on Arthur Askey's TV show in the mid 1950s. Her celebrity really depended on her body measurements: forty-two inches of bosom

Week ending December 31 1955   EVERY THURSDAY

3½

Picturegoer

THE NATIONAL FILM AND
ENTERTAINMENT WEEKLY

ARE WE
LOSING
DAVID
WHITFIELD?
see page 5

I was
SHOCKED
by Hollywood
—says Nicole Maurey
see page 6

OUR NEW
YEAR GIFT
TO DIANA DORS

◀

on top of a waist of (allegedly) some 19 inches.[95] Diana Dors was born Diana Fluck, a surname that she considered, for a girl, little short of disastrous.[96] Dors was another 'sweater girl', described by *Picture Post* as 'having cornered the market in fast blondes'.[97] Dors herself had no illusions about her reputation, admitting that 'I am, by English standards, a fairly flamboyant character ... I am paid large sums of money not because I look and act like the girl next door, but because my name is linked immediately with mink, fast cars and pink champagne.'[98] A 'photographic essay' by Horace Roye, *Diana Dors in 3D*, sold complete with red-and-green viewing spectacles, featured the actress reclining around her home 'on tiger skins, satin bedspreads and the like ... to give the book a sensual and erotic flavour'.[99] It came close to being labelled obscene by magistrates in Halifax.[100] Dors's most enduring image comes not from that booklet, memorable though it was, but from her publicity shots for the 1955 film festival in Venice where she was photographed in a fur bikini (she claimed it was mink, but later confessed that it had been rabbit), with paste diamonds lacing the G-string below.[101] Film historian Sue Harper aptly described Dors as 'a sort of Lady Docker of the Screen'.[102]

A reading of glamour as unrespectable and even morally contaminated was reflected in newspaper accounts of Ruth Ellis's trial and conviction for the murder of her lover David Blakely in the mid 1950s. Ruth Ellis's appearance in court, her hair newly peroxided to a dazzling shade of platinum blonde, has been argued to have damaged public sympathy for her case. What for her was probably mainly an issue of self-respect was widely misinterpreted, an outrage in the eyes of moralists bent upon condemning her for tartiness and sexual promiscuity, if not for the social ambition she had showed in consorting with a young man well above her in social station. Glamour, so often linked with sex and ambition, could easily be made to look distastefully predatory.[103]

The notion that glamour slid too easily into seediness was reflected in women's magazines. The word 'glamour' itself – which had been used almost to death in the 1930s and 1940s – started to fall out of use. Elegance was more fashionable. An article in *Woman and Beauty* in May 1952, entitled 'School for Glamour', began: 'Glamour is a word we hesitate to use as a rule in this magazine because it is so often misused. It has come to suggest the false and the unreal – the purely artificial.' The copy bravely goes on to attempt to redefine and in part to reclaim the quality in terms of a gleam and polish on the outside that reflects and highlights a vitality within, but the tone is uncertain.[104] There followed the usual promptings about regular habits, manicured fingernails and clear skin. Real glamour was in danger of being swamped by apple-blossom soap, moral hygiene and domesticity.

Contradictory ideas about femininity, reflecting the opposition between glamour and class, were embedded in the material culture of the 1950s, and especially in clothing and advertisements for cosmetics. In fashion, for instance, a vogue for the 'housecoat' or 'hostess gown' reflected tension between the ideal of the leisured society hostess and the realities of the new servantless household, its mistress struggling to make a social impression on neighbours or her husband's work colleagues whilst struggling to cope with domestic chores.[105] The cost of failure to match up to expectations was poignantly illustrated in a film by J. Lee Thompson of 1957 entitled *Woman in a Dressing Gown*, in which Yvonne Mitchell's Amy slumps and blunders her way round the house in a grubby dressing gown while her husband lusts after a trim and efficient rival. Hostess gowns were a bit like sexy satin wraps crossed with the evening wear that distinguished the middle class who had routinely dressed for dinner before the Second World War. You were supposed to wear them by candlelight while serving guests at the table. Amy uses the sleeves of her wrap to soak up the gravy slopped around plates at her chaotic kitchen table.

'Mrs Exeter', *Vogue*'s archetypal older woman of the shires, made her entrance in the British version of the magazine in 1949.[106] She was portrayed as a comfortable figure, not too worried about her expanding waistline, respectably presentable in her sensible suits and cocktail dresses, good coat and brogues. Even her fur stoles looked 'serviceable'. Mrs Exeter embodied security and was at ease with her own status in the community. Not so the young of the decade, who were anything but comfortable. Mrs Exeter didn't really need help with dress codes, although hints on budget and sensible investment on the clothing front never came amiss. But the young women of the decade were much more troubled and their clothing could reflect this. Female singers and performers in the public eye sometimes dressed very oddly indeed. Glamour warred with class in the remarkable outfits worn by the singer

▶

Alma Cogan performs for the BBC Home Service in one of her trademark frou-frou crinolines, 1954.

(© Popperfoto/ Getty Images)

Alma Cogan, for instance, at this time. Cogan designed her own dresses and they were made up by a local dressmaker in north London.[107] The legendary bell-shaped skirts and sparkly crinolines, swagged and feathered (which she referred to as her 'tea cosies'), hint at a fine-lady-combined-with-showgirl look which is ill at ease with her vocal style and the emerging ambience of youth and rock and roll.

Advertisements for cosmetics similarly gave out mixed messages about glamour, class and femininity. Charles Revson, founder of Revlon, famously declared that he wanted his models to look like 'Park Avenue whores, elegant, but with the sexual thing underneath'.[108] Lipsticks in various shades, textures and packaging were now flooding the market: naming them was a challenge. Imaginative names and big promotions brought huge profits, as products themselves became glamorous and objects of desire. Revlon notched up a number of successes, with Pink Lightning (1944), and in the early 1950s, Love that Red, Fire and Ice, and Cherries in the Snow. The magic of Cherries in the Snow has lasted, and the company still produces a colour so-named. But the launch in 1952 of Fire and Ice, celebrated for its combination of 'dignity, class and glamour', has become the stuff of advertising legend.[109] The advertisement showed model Dorian Leigh, a graduate in mechanical engineering who had worked as a tool designer during the Second World War. According to Michael Gross, she had resented earning less than male co-workers and quit the job, only to find that under wartime regulations she was effectively unemployable. Gross suggests that for Leigh, becoming a model represented an act of 'pre-feminist' rebellion.[110] For the Fire and Ice advertisement she was photographed posing in an icy silver-sequinned dress, under a scarlet cape, alongside fifteen questions or challenges for the viewer. These ranged from the banal 'Have you ever danced with your shoes off?' or 'Do you blush when you find yourself flirting?' to the rather more interesting 'Do sables excite you, even on other women?' A reminder that too much spontaneity might threaten domestic harmony is hinted at in question thirteen, which asked 'Would you streak your hair platinum without asking your husband?'[111]

There were social messages, similarly, in scent. Flowery scents – as described earlier – were a hallmark of the 1950s. Dior's Diorissimo dates from 1956, and is by far the best known of a number of lily-of-the-valley fragrances launched at the time. The Duchess of Windsor – by now rather eccentric but safely holed up in France – was said to spray the real flowers in her table arrangements with it.[112] The names and packaging of many other successful new scents of the period hinted at fine ladies and high society: Balmain's Jolie Madame (1953), Rochas's Femme (1944) and Madame Rochas (1960), Revillon's Carnet de Bal (1960) and Desprez's Bal à Versailles (1962). In large numbers of advertisements for perfume at this time, fur and scent were linked to signify class and luxury. Goya No. 5 was marketed by Douglas Collins as 'the perfume for mink-coated evenings',[113] Raphael perfumes were described as 'deliciously clinging, wonderful on fur', and Jovan dubbed its new scent Mink and Pearls. Not to be outdone, Steiner added Pink Mink and Blue Mink to its White Mink range of toiletries. In John Braine's novel *Room at the Top* (1957), working-class and ageing women scent themselves with Phul-Nana, whilst the young and desirable middle-class girl aspires to Coty.[114] But the securely well-off bourgeois wife might well have settled for Patou's Joy, widely advertised as the most costly scent available. Joy had been made since 1930, and Patou boasted that the production of every ounce of the scent required twenty-eight dozen roses and over ten thousand jasmine blooms. Eve Merriam tartly commented in 1960 that Joy had become 'an ostentatious Christmas special' in the United States, but was also 'bought in steady, all-year quantities by men who want to make up to their wives for unexplained absences'.[115]

Many perfumes were still advertised as bounty showered by men upon their women, girlfriends or wives. An advertisement for Coty in 1960, for instance, showed a drawing of a woman coddled in a fur stole and muff being offered perfume bottles by male hands.[116] We are reminded that this was an era when the vast majority of women could only better themselves socially through marriage, and when respectability itself was conferred by marriage. Lisa Cohen has argued that there is a sense in which British *Vogue* and indeed the whole industry of fashion at this time depended upon marriage, through which women acquired financial and social capital as wives.[117] The Alison Settle archive in Brighton contains a Christmas card she received one year from Cecil Beaton, featuring one of his designs for the film *My Fair Lady*, a drawing of a woman in furs trailed by an elderly bourgeois male burdened with a vast number of ribbon-tied bandboxes and parcels.[118] The female shopper was represented as a kept woman. But this was beginning to change. Fashion writers and women working in the fashion industries such as Madge Garland and Alison Settle were themselves a new breed of professional women workers, with independent means of support. Settle herself contributed a piece to the *Observer* in 1956 entitled 'Mothers with a Pay Packet' in which she argued that women who were becoming used to their own spending power were increasingly reluctant to relinquish their autonomy on marriage, and could not be expected to take kindly to dependence on their husbands.[119]

Ptember, 1954

PICTURE
POST

JOAN COLLINS—
BRITISH FOR
GLAMOUR

4ᴰ

11 SEPTEMBER 1954

BRITAIN STAGES WORLD'S GREATEST AIR SHOW
A NEW PLAN FOR THE OVER SEVENTIES
ALEC GUINNESS SHOWS A GIRL ROUND PARIS

HULTON'S
NATIONAL
WEEKLY

VOL 64 · NO 11

As the 1950s gave way to the 1960s, film stars still inspired emulation – especially those stars who seemed to offer a new kind of fresh, youthful sexuality, less worldly than traditional glamour, but more intriguing than a femme-fleur. Marilyn Monroe, Brigitte Bardot and Audrey Hepburn were the icons of the time. Designer Barbara Hulanicki remembered being much influenced by Audrey Hepburn in the film *Sabrina Fair* (1954). '*Sabrina Fair* had made a huge impact on us all at college: everyone walked around in black sloppy sweaters, suede low-cut flatties and gold hoop earrings. Few of us, though, could imitate Audrey Hepburn's skinny elegance.'[120] This was a new kind of young look: halter-neck beach suit with little shorts, ballet pumps and huge dangling hoop earrings. Italian glamour made its impact in Britain during these years, not only through the stars of Italian cinema – Sophia Loren, Claudia Cardinale, Gina Lollobrigida and Silvana Mangano – but also in the fashionableness of Vespas and Lambrettas, 'Capri pants' and cappuccino. These influences were absorbed into youth culture particularly. Alongside the growing popularity in Britain of package holidays on the Italian Riviera their impact was widespread.[121] The 'Woltz Italiana Capri Carnival Collection' of nail enamels advertised in women's magazines, for example, featured four up-to-the-minute colours: Amalfi, Positano, Pompeii and Sorrento.

The most prominent screen glamour girl of the period, Marilyn Monroe, had a childlike, vulnerable quality, described by Diana Vreeland as 'fluffy zaniness'.[122] But Monroe herself embodied many of the contradictions of the era. In the early days of her career, photographed by Tom Keeley nude and stretched out on red satin, she came close to being labelled as 'cheesecake'. She appeared to lack the self-possession that had distinguished many of the screen goddesses of the 1930s, and she seemed more innocent than other pin-up girls. Monroe was never the girl next door however, and could be capable of a sharp realism. 'I guess I've always had too much fantasy to be only a housewife,' she confessed on one occasion, adding 'Well, also, I had to eat. I was never kept, to be blunt about it. I always kept myself. I have always had a pride in the fact that I was on my own.'[123] References to 'sex kittens' or 'sexpots' in the 1950s were essentially belittling, undermining women's autonomy and the power of their sexuality with elements of cuteness, passivity and dependency.[124] As early as 1939, George Cukor's film *The Women* had pitted the genteel, upper-middle-class lady against the glamorous, ambitious shopgirl. The film *Cover Girl*, starring Rita Hayworth, in 1944 pitted the false lure of glamour against true love. Love won, of course, even if not wholly convincingly. Glamour faded, damned or deluded. Poignant cinematic illustrations of this included *Sunset Boulevard* (1950), *The Bad and the Beautiful* (1952), *All About Eve* (1950) and *Whatever Happened to Baby Jane?*(1962). The sunny glamour girls of the 1930s and early 1940s gave way to the darker, moody, bad girl beauties of *film noir*. Gloria Grahame, Mamie van Doren, Ava Gardner. Gardner's glamour, in particular, had a threatening edge to it, more than a tinge of menace. The cinema itself was in decline by this time: as early as 1948, weekly attendance figures had plummeted to their lowest figure since 1933, largely due to the growing popularity of television.

Perhaps one of the last high moments in the classic Hollywood celebration of glamour was when Marilyn Monroe, in a memorable public performance, sang 'Happy Birthday' to John F. Kennedy in Madison Square Garden in May 1962. She wore a gown by Jean Louis in nude marquisette covered with rhinestones, described by Adlai Stevenson as all 'skin and beads'.[125] In 1999 the gown sold at auction by Christie's for $1.2 million.

Revolutions

The 1950s in Britain can be seen as a decade in which attempts to rehearse familiar ideas about class and gender were increasingly undercut by new conditions. Expectations about how young people would grow up had been enshrined in social systems such as sex-segregated education, the presentation of aristocratic and upper-middle-class girls at court as debutantes, and the requirement between 1947 and 1963 that young men do national service in the armed forces. Young men and women from upper-class backgrounds usually had little interaction with each other socially until they were expected to precipitate themselves into courtship. Girls would 'come out', 'do the season' and look for husbands who would support them in the manner to which they had been accustomed (or better). Lower down the social scale, systems of sex segregation (in schooling, for instance) were less watertight, and courting might begin at a much earlier age, but girls' hopes for respectability or social advancement would still primarily depend upon netting a husband with prospects. This was a society in which many still trusted that boys would look to fathers for lessons in how to grow up and that daughters might see their mothers as role models.

But however much British girls might have been expected to learn from the example of their mothers in the postwar years, autobiographical literature and written memories of the period show that daughters were increasingly uneasy about doing so. Emma Tennant provides vivid descriptions of the process of coming out, and the ways in which clothing embodied the social expectations of the time, in her novel *Girlitude* (2000), which draws to some extent on her own experience as an upper-middle-class girl growing up in the 1950s and 1960s. In the novel, preparing to launch her nineteen-year-old daughter into society, the heroine's mother orders a pale blue ball dress from Dior for herself, of 'understated elegance', whilst her daughter is provided with three ball gowns, the most memorable of which is 'a puff of white net in which wreaths of pink roses, like mice hidden in the folds, writhed in their lairs on my bosom and behind as I danced'.[1] On the eve of coming out, the debutante's uncle sends a 'muff of gardenias'.[2] Later, as the central character in the book prepares for marriage, the family dressmaker works on her trousseau. Tennant poignantly describes her heroine's uneasy anticipation of the event through the clothes themselves and the way in which they seem to constrain her identity:

> *a raspberry tweed overcoat, with 'raglan' shoulders so sloping that my chin seemed to slope into nothingness as well when I sat there for a fitting. I feel the panic of class, the trap of marriage: am I to be a housewife? an upper-class lady of leisure?[3]*

Charlotte the dressmaker warns the heroine to take particular care with the gold fabric ordered for her wedding gown: 'The gold dress will tarnish, so Charlotte says. I shall appear after the marriage ceremony green in the armpits like a coin made from a base alloy.' They both stare at the wedding dress, 'which lies in a white cardboard coffin on the floor'. And indeed, the gown does react to the bride's sweating armpits, turning into 'a kind of verdigris, at my nervous reaction to matrimonial ties'.[4] Photographs of debutantes from the 1950s show many of them looking rather matronly and old-fashioned, even by the standards of the time. Respectability, of course, was crucial, and there was something of a uniform: full-skirted calf-length dresses, petal hats, court shoes and set hair. Fiona MacCarthy, one of the last debutantes to be presented at Buckingham Palace, remembers queuing outside in 1958: 'The

▶

A mother takes her daughter shopping in the 1950s, before the teenage revolution.

(© Bert Hardy/ Hulton Archive/ Getty Images)

atmosphere, although excited, was peculiarly docile. You could hardly call us teenagers: we were altogether too formal and submissive, imitations of our mothers …'[5]

'We were all lamb dressed as mutton in those days,' remembered journalist Maureen Cleave.[6] Photographer Bert Hardy took a memorable photograph in 1956 showing a mother, suited and formal, considering the effect of a very matronly, unflattering ball gown on her gauche-looking daughter. The effect is claustrophobic and unsettling.[7] Barbara Hulanicki (later founder of Biba clothing) remembered that 'fashion in the late 1950s was definitely for thirty-year-olds and over. I was looking forward to the day when I would be that old and able to cope with all the elegance.'[8] After seeing Grace Kelly in the film *High Society* (1956), she had combed the clothes shops for a pale-pink twinset and fantasised about becoming a debutante, with a palace presentation and a coming-out dance.[9]

But curtseying was destined to become something of a lost art: presentations at court ceased after 1958. Although coming-out balls were still held in private, the accompanying ritual of royal pomp and aristocratic deference was gone. Why did it go? Fiona MacCarthy suggests that the system had been failing in its mission of upholding social exclusivity. A system designed to perpetuate the known hierarchies of inherited wealth and status was being besieged by newcomers, the *nouveaux riches* and socially aspirant. MacCarthy quotes a comment attributed to Princess Margaret at the time, 'We had to put a stop to it. Every tart in London was getting in.'[10] The remark nicely illustrates the snobbery of the 'establishment' in the 1950s, some women's complicity therein, and a particular harshness towards other women perceived as getting above themselves.

Middle-class ladies in Britain in the 1950s showed their class credentials by knowing how to dress correctly for the right occasion. As Elizabeth Wilson has emphasised in her autobiographical account, *Mirror Writing*, there were 'afternoon frocks', and one wore brown for the country: 'To find yourself wearing a pair of black "court" shoes in a country lane would be to let the Absolute leak away. To stick to these strict rules was a symbolic reassurance. A correct outward appearance meant that inwardly one was "all right".'[11]

These rules did not disappear overnight, and a more youthful style of dress for women evolved rather more gradually than is usually suggested. Schools – particularly girls' secondary schools – continued to insist on ladylike hats and gloves, indoor and outdoor shoes and respectable skirt lengths, for at least another couple of decades. But there were signs of change even in the early 1950s. *Picture Post* in December 1952 showed Brigitte Bardot and Annick Morice in woolly tights, ballet pumps and circular felt skirts.[12] Alison Settle noted the fashion for 'circle skirts': they could be purchased, appliquéd with poodles, from Marshall and Snelgrove.[13] Those at the cutting edge knew to wear them with petal-cut or 'baby pompadour' hairstyles; or, better still, with pony tails. This was the 'sex kitten' look, but there were more sophisticated variants. Hulanicki remembers walking around Brighton in the 1950s feeling like Cinderella in her 'brown formal crêpe dress, peach lisle stockings and a row of little pearls': 'to crown it all, I was made to wear one of those half-chewed hats that ladies wore then'.[14] Meanwhile she studied the outfits worn by fashionably dressed Jewish girls on the seafront flaunting dirndl skirts puffed out by swishy paper-nylon petticoats, ballerina pumps and button earrings.[15]

A little earlier, and just along the coast in Worthing, the young Alma Cogan had sat at her kidney-shaped dressing table (festooned with pictures of Rita Hayworth and Ava Gardner cut out from *Picturegoer*), practising hairstyles.[16] Cogan's ambitions as a singer had been nurtured in regular performances for tea-dances at Sherry's nightclub in Brighton, and at the Aquarium. Her parents had been in the dressmaking business, and were middle class. Now there were signs that innovation in fashion was coming from 'the street', that is, from the social classes beneath the middle class, with little deference to personal dressmakers, let alone couturiers. Hulanicki remembered the queues in the Strand, outside the Lyceum, for lunchtime dancing:

> *As time went by the clothes or the girls became more and more exaggerated. Their hair was now backcombed into a tall cone on top of their heads. They hobbled in their tight pencil skirts and on shoes with stiletto heels and the most vicious pointed toes.*[17]

Styles depended on where one lived as well as class and – increasingly – age group. The young Anita Roddick, later famous for establishing the Body Shop line of cosmetics, also grew up on the South Coast, where her mother presided over an 'Americanised' café in Littlehampton, with a Coca-Cola machine and images of Vargas girls on promotion cards.[18] Her mother's eccentric, exotic brand of glamour found later expression in the El Cubana nightclub, over the jukebox of which she presided in a lamé cocktail gown.[19] Anita went on to teacher training college near Bath, where she remembers that her fellow students dressed like members of the Women's Institute: meeting students from Bristol University dressed like beatniks introduced her to a different sartorial world.[20]

Youth became much more visible, not least because of new modes of dress and style. The fashion designer Mary Quant's beatniky, schoolgirl-type tunics and pinafore dresses were available from the late 1950s, and boutiques sprang up along the King's Road in Chelsea and in Carnaby Street.[21] Nancy Mitford, visiting London, found working-class girls and boys particularly smartly dressed; Oxford Street, she observed, was becoming much more exciting than Bond Street.[22] Colin MacInnes recorded the 'lavish, colourful eruption of gay stores selling "separates" to the girls, and sharp schmutter to the kids: shining enticing shops like candy-floss.'[23] These trends are usually seen as indicating the decline of haute couture and the rise of street style, alongside the new affluence of the working class in Britain. But neither the French, nor their designers, were wholly out of step. Alison Settle, on her way to a party hosted by Madame Carven in Paris in 1956, noted that she was driven across the city by a blonde woman cab-driver with horse-tail hairdo, wearing a duffle coat and jeans.[24] The following year, Settle's columns in the *Observer* drew attention to collections by Balenciaga, Balmain and Laroche, all of whom were showing short sheath-line or 'sack' dresses worn with black stockings.[25] An article in February 1958 on the Paris dress collections commented on St Laurent's new clothes as being specifically designed for youth, 'which is what American buyers want', but noted with some relief that 'he has not fallen into the error of turning women into dolls and babies, as have various other designers'. Settle was decidedly ambivalent about Givenchy's 'little girl coats' and especially about the 'pleated, "Baby Doll" chemises' shown by Jacques Griffe. Her article was headed, 'This Frightening Passion for Childhood's Look'.[26]

Nabokov's *Lolita* was published (in Paris) in 1955: the book caused great controversy and was banned in the USA and the UK until 1958.[27] *Baby Doll*, the equally contentious film with a screenplay by Tennessee Williams, starring Carroll Baker in the role of its lubriciously regressive, thumbsucking heroine, appeared in 1956. The sexualisation of young girls in the culture of the 1950s had complex roots, but was probably at least in part a male reaction to stereotypes of idealised, adult femininity. Little girls were less scary than adult women, especially when the latter looked like the elegant Barbara Goalen and wielded sharp-pointed parasols. Images of 'baby dolls' in short, flimsy nightdresses infantilised and grossly objectified women: they segued into the image of the 1960s 'dolly bird', undercutting any assertiveness associated with women's role in the 'youthquake' of the decade.

Explanations for the new assertiveness of young people in the late 1950s and 1960s have been well-rehearsed: the extension of opportunities to young people in education and the labour market; increasing affluence, and the rise of the teenage consumer documented by Mark Abrams.[28] Some aspects of these changes were deftly represented with a sharp eye for the detail of fashion and material culture in Colin MacInnes's novel about teenagers in London in the 1950s, *Absolute Beginners* (1959). There was a good deal of ambivalence around the status of young people at this time. The extension of secondary education, to be followed by two or three years at college or university, at least for many of the middle class, brought with it a kind of extended adolescence, raising difficult questions about personal sexual practice, autonomy and dependence. The age of marriage was falling dramatically in these years: with the official age of majority then set at twenty-one, young people from less privileged backgrounds were often married well before they were classed as adults. This had worrying implications: for instance, young fathers (let alone mothers) were legally prohibited from taking on mortgages or signing contracts or hire purchase agreements. These problems, together with difficult questions of wardship in relation to young people under twenty-one years of age marrying without the necessary parental consent, led to the government's decision to lower the age of majority: it was reduced from twenty-one to eighteen in 1969.[29]

In the meantime, the predicaments of the young – and the question of youth generally – occupied the forefront of media attention. Older generations might deplore the new assertiveness of the young: the lack of deference to established authority, trouser suits and miniskirts (making girls look unladylike), the long hair on boys (making them look like girls) and so forth, but the carnival of youth and the new permissiveness were seemingly unstoppable. Several of the older-established magazines for young women foundered and lost their grip: *Glamour*, in the 1950s, offered a weird mix of stories featuring the old stalwart romantic lovers (Arab sheikhs) alongside guitar-wielding boys from the hit parade.[30] Magazines catering for the new market mushroomed, especially those aimed at teenage girls. *Marilyn, Mirabelle, Romeo, Valentine, Roxy* and *Boyfriend* date from the mid to late 1950s, *Honey* and *Flair* from 1960, *Nova* from 1965, *Petticoat* from 1966. The first six of these clearly reflected the way pop culture and an interest in male singers (Frankie Vaughan, Perry Como, Elvis), coffee bars and rock groups had started to rival Hollywood and film culture in the dream world of young females. *Honey* and *Flair* catered for the increasingly well-off and fashion-conscious young woman, *Petticoat* her even younger sisters. (The short-lived *Poppet* targeted girls who were younger still.) The stylish and cutting-edge *Nova* tried a rather

Casual Counterpoint from Hogg of Hawick

MILLBANK HAWICK SCOTLAND

Her black and red sweater/cardigan duet completely captures the mood of the moment . . . slightly trad, gently soft, rather beat, casually chic. The cardigan is straight from the shoulder and low fastening; the sweater has long sleeves and a trim roll collar. It's the kind of casual partnership that could only have been inspired by clothes from Hogg of Hawick. See the Hogg of Hawick range at your nearest stockist. Write to us for his name.

different formula, with more intellectual and critical content. The more established magazines responded with new features or a younger look: *Vogue* introduced its 'Young Idea' section in 1961.

Above all, youth was fashionable. By the mid 1960s, fashionable women had stopped dressing like mature, sexually confident women, or even like perfectly groomed princesses. Instead, they started to dress like little girls. There were girly smocks in sugar pink, empire-line dresses in pastel colours, little coats with Peter Pan collars in tangerine, primrose, or daffodil yellow. These were often in new synthetic fabrics such as Crimplene and could be purchased cheaply from C&A, Richard Shops or even Marks and Spencer – they were not confined to the Chelsea set or those shopping in fashionable boutiques in London. There were floaty, synthetic fabrics decorated with swirling, psychedelic colours made into négligées and caftans, and many women found it easy to run these up at home from paper patterns. Childlike dressing reached extremes with short culottes like romper suits and baby bonnets decorated with white daisies or rabbit-fur pompons. Shrimpton, long-legged and Bambi-eyed, and the startlingly thin and pre-pubescent-looking Twiggy, became fashion's new icons.

Glamour was too grown up for the dolly birds of the sixties. In these years, even cosmetics lost sophistication and turned into something more like sweets or finger paint. Red lips were out: pale, opalescent shades and 'milkglass' colours were introduced by Revlon early in the decade, while cheap lines such as Miners' and Outdoor Girl produced opaque shades of ochre, cream and delicate pink for pale lips or what Eve Merriam unflatteringly termed 'the slug-white' look.[31] Eyes became darker: ringed with black, fringed with thick mascara or false lashes; sometimes over the top with silver-painted sun rays or doodled petals. If the aim was a kind of adorable wide-eyed innocence, the result was often a curiously vacant, disembodied stare. The childlike theme was extended into the names chosen for the Quant cosmetics line – Starkers foundation, Bonkers eye make-up, with even a Jelly Babies range in baby-bottle containers with teat-shaped tops.[32] Perfumes were marketed playfully, too: Max Factor's Primitif came packaged in a toy tiger, Hypnotique in a furry lion, and Electrique boasted a 'particularly cute' presentation in the shape of a pink elephant.[33]

▲

Adverts for Marchioness velvets (Martin & Savage Ltd) and Hoggs of Hawick, both from *Flair* magazine, early 1960s. In the Martin & Savage advert the model (Jean Shrimpton) exemplifies the kind of classy, regal femininity fashionable in the 1950s. In the Hogg of Hawick image she is starting to look like a 'Beat girl', heralding the 1960s.

The fur trade was in trouble. As Eve Merriam pointed out, sales of mink in the postwar United States never reached the value of the fur trade in the interwar years. Incomes were rising and supply was no problem, but market research conducted by the fur industry showed that fur was increasingly associated with older women, and *kept* women at that.[34] The fur coat had come to stand for a system of sexual exchange. Mandy Rice-Davies, who with Christine Keeler was implicated in the Profumo scandal in the early 1960s, recalled in her autobiography how her relationship with her 'protector', the notorious landlord Peter Rachman, had revolved around a fur coat: she had tried to walk out on Rachman, but was penniless:

> 'Look', he said, 'I'll buy the mink from you.'
>
> I had my mink coat over my arm, ready to leave. As he had given it to me in the first place he knew its worth. He went to the safe and counted out £500 in cash.
>
> That was the beginning of our arrangement. Whenever I wanted to leave he gave me £500 and took the coat. When I returned, the coat was mine again. It was a charade enacted frequently during our eighteen months together.[35]

The furrier J. G. Links recounted a story of how a man had come to him asking to be shown two mink coats of the same quality costing up to £250 each. He then brought his wife and asked her to select one of them, with his advice. After paying, they left. The husband then returned in a cab with a younger lady friend, telling her that he had chosen a mink coat for her and that he hoped that she would like it. Links applauded his customer's sense of delicacy, which he judged to pre-empt any moral distaste or need for censure. Nevertheless he was at pains to emphasise that by far the majority of his customers were married men buying furs for their wives, and not for mistresses.[36]

But public perceptions died hard. Merriam emphasised that the US research showed that married women were more interested in washing machines and cars than fur coats, and younger women continued to be put off by the way mink coats had come to indicate mistress status or hussies on the make. One young college woman commented, 'You can't imagine a bareheaded child of nature swinging down the street in a beaver coat, can you?' In Britain, Alma Cogan had celebrated her rise to television fame in the late 1950s by buying two silver-blue mink coats: the first for her mother, the second for herself. Her sister records that she too had been offered one, but had considered fur the wrong style: she had wanted to be seen as a serious actress and 'a sort of beatnik' and thought a duffle coat more appropriate to this image.[37] In her study, Merriam concluded that the image of fur in the USA needed 'de-snobbing', and that the industry would have to dim the glamour accent if it wasn't to collapse.[38] Older women might still see fur as the epitome of glamour and luxury: Victoria Glendinning records that an 85-year-old Rebecca West went shopping for a new mink coat, taking Madge Garland (formerly the Royal College of Art's first professor of fashion) with her to advise on the purchase.[39] But mink was losing its cachet. The later 1960s and 1970s saw a fashion for flea market fur or embroidered Afghan leather coats, with the fur worn inside; but it was probably even more stylish to keep the fur on legs: there was a vogue for Afghan hounds and Saluki dogs as up-market fashion accessories at this time.

Many remarked on the new independence of young girls: the writer and editor Alexandra Pringle described the 'Chelsea girl' of the sixties as having 'confidence, and, it seemed, no parents', and Hulanicki remembered the classic Biba girl as looking sweet but 'as hard as nails', adding, 'She did what she felt like at that moment and had no Mum to influence her judgement.'[40] It was a far cry from Bert Hardy's image of the gauche young woman photographed shopping and trying on clothes with her mother, as described earlier in this chapter. But this new independence sat uneasily with the little-girl image of the early 1960s. Elizabeth Wilson remembered her outfits at that time as reflecting sexual ambiguity, combining elements of 'trendy dolly' and 'pretty boy', but she also observed that 'in the sixties the aim was no longer to make a social statement, but to fuse, narcissistically, the glamour of the sexual object with the glamour of the sexual predator. But ambiguity and confusion hid behind this blank-eyed sexual pose.'[41] There is something about the animal startled by car headlights in the photographs of the young models who posed for the fashionable photographers of the period. They can appear paralysed: exposed by rather than composed for the camera.

But independence was not all illusion. Although the majority of girls were still leaving school at fifteen or sixteen years of age, and drifting into short-term jobs in the hope of an early marriage, the social and educational changes of the post-1945 period were beginning to have an effect.[42] Greater numbers of girls were continuing through sixth form, teacher training college or university.[43] Very few, whatever their class background, were spared some kind of exposure to the labour market, and it became fashionable to contemplate a period away from home, of flat sharing or city living, before settling down. These conditions, away from parental surveillance and control, allowed much more scope for sexual experimentation. Magazines such as *Boyfriend, Petticoat* and *Flair* began to introduce stories and features discussing these new conditions and predicaments, alongside advertisements for stomach-compressing 'roll-ons', Quant perfumes (Day Bird and Night Bird) and images of 'trendy chicks' in synthetic miniskirts ('Beat a modern rhythm in Courtelle').[44]

Helen Gurley Brown's book *Sex and the Single Girl*, published in America in 1962 and in Britain the following year, made being young, single and in the city sound fun.[45] The book was filled with advice on how to avoid being a 'mouseburger', urging its readers to glam up and flirt in order to get the best men available. The plural was intentional: there was no rush to find Mr Right; girls were exhorted to look around. 'Acquire men for your charm-bracelet,' suggested Gurley Brown.[46] Marriage should not be seen as the Holy Grail, to be sought desperately lest one was left on the shelf – a fate worse than death in the eyes of some – but as something rather banal that might even be experienced as boring. Derided though it was by feminists and intellectuals, *Sex and the Single Girl* was hugely popular. It is easy to condemn much of the book's message as trite. Readers were encouraged to prioritise needs ('you *need* iridescent gold eye-shadow, but what about that essence-of-pine purifier somebody was selling door to door?')[47] and urged to dress better than they could afford. This has led some historians, including Hilary Radner, to argue that the new independent girl of the 1960s temporarily escaped from patriarchy only to fall into the trap of consumerism.[48] However, Gurley Brown's book eloquently scorned older forms of femininity as self-denial; in doing so it legitimated a new form of agency for women, and at the same time it asserted unequivocally that 'career girls are sexy'.

Sex and the Single Girl appeared before the contraceptive pill became widely available in Britain. Women's sexual autonomy was still constrained by fears of illegitimacy or the spectre of illegal, backstreet abortion. Following the Abortion Law Reform Act of 1967, more liberal access to contraception, and the widespread use of the contraceptive pill in the early 1970s, the trend towards early marriage went into reverse, a dramatic change with important repercussions in the decades that followed.[49] In April 1970 *Honey* magazine celebrated its tenth birthday, looking back on the changes seen over the decade. Some girls were still marrying shortly after leaving school, as an advertisement for diamond engagement rings from de Beers, which appeared in this issue, made clear. The copy ran as follows:

> *At eighteen she'd wanted to travel the world; to see the ancient towns of Israel, the high white temples of Greece and the sun-warmed beaches of the Pacific. But at twenty she fell in love. When they got engaged he said, 'One day I'll give you the earth. But until then will you be content with a diamond ring and a gentle stroll in the park?'*[50]

The same issue contained an article on the pros and cons of living together before marriage, and a comment from the young singer and career woman Cilla Black on how the 1960s had altered her outlook on life. 'When I was at school I thought that if I was not married by the time I was 18 I'd kill myself', she mused, 'now I think I'd be mad to marry before I'm 35. Money changes a girl's attitude to romance, I can tell you.'[51]

The late 1960s and early 1970s were in many respects a turning point, as new freedoms and aspirations went hand in hand with the rise of second-wave feminism in the USA and Britain. Amid an efflorescence of feminist literature, three texts made a particular impact. A translation of Simone de Beauvoir's *Le Deuxième Sexe* was published in Britain in 1953 (although its impact was not fully felt until the 1960s); Betty Friedan's *The Feminine Mystique* appeared in 1963, and Germaine Greer's *The Female Eunuch* came out in 1970.[52] De Beauvoir's text, identifying the social construction of woman as 'other', contained a somewhat ambiguous section on adornment. She saw woman's obsession with appearance as narcissistic and conducive to passivity: making an object of oneself, rather than acting as agent. At the same time she recognised both the transformative possibilities and the celebratory qualities of dress. Even so, she defined elegance as bondage.[53] Betty Friedan's analysis of the predicament of bored and unhappy housewives focused on work and domesticity, showing little interest in dress and appearance. Greer, like de Beauvoir, was primarily concerned with the passivity of women. As part of a complex analysis of this she adopted a critical stance towards what she saw as the idealisation or commodification of women whose desires and identities were bound up with self-adornment, consumption and display. According to her own rich polemic the woman bedecked with furs, jewels and false eyelashes was little more than a showcase for her husband's wealth, herself a commodity.[54] Without dignity, and alienated from her own sexuality, she was reduced to the status of 'female eunuch'.

Second-wave feminism was initially more concerned with rights and opportunities than the politics of dress. That being said, it was attacks on beauty contests (judged particularly demeaning to women) that attracted large-scale media attention and established the idea of women's liberationists as bra burners, opposed to glamour in all its forms. A mythology has grown around the feminist attack on the Miss America competition in Atlantic City in 1968, during which bras were allegedly burned or dumped into a Freedom Trash Can, and a live sheep was crowned as Miss America. Two years later, feminists in London disrupted the Miss World contest at the Albert Hall, hurling smoke bombs, flour and leaflets at the hapless compère Bob Hope before being ejected by Mecca bouncers: four of those arrested were hauled off to Holloway Prison.[55] They comforted themselves with the belief that this was the first militant confrontation with the law by women since the suffragettes, but in retrospect, 'freaking out at phoney glamour' seemed a drop in the ocean compared with what was needed to fight the oppression of women.[56]

'We're not beautiful, we're not ugly, we're angry', announced an activist leaflet at the time.[57] A more sustained feminist consideration of the sexual politics of appearance was to emerge in the 1980s, but in the meantime, the high-heeled, cosmeticised, corseted and constricted forms of 1950s glamour were certainly beginning to look politically dubious as well as old hat.[58] Increasingly, for second-wave feminists, glamour's associations were no longer with female agency and power: instead, glamour was seen as demeaning, and women's investment in their appearance was a form of 'false consciousness' fostered by patriarchy and capitalism. Not all went along with this, and some feminists – Gloria Steinem, Erica Jong, Germaine Greer – were of course themselves highly glamorous figures and feted by the media as such. Greer staged her famous confrontation with Norman Mailer in New York Town Hall in 1971 wearing clinging black and fur, and looking for all the world like a 1930s film star.[59] There were indeed women who joyfully binned their cosmetics and took to the physical freedom and expansiveness associated with dungarees and desert boots, and others who were defensive about wanting to look sexy or dressing up. But most women probably enjoyed the liberty to choose from a new and ever-widening range of codes about how to dress. The feminist academic Lynne Segal remembered that in her politically active youth in the 1970s she was rarely without 'some subtle form of high heels, lipstick and eyeliner: the dress code was never as rigid as subsequent caricature would suggest'.[60] But the social and political messages embodied in clothing were increasingly discussed.

Whether politically incorrect or not, glamour was still out of fashion. Alongside the new freedoms of the early 1970s went a clear preference for a natural look, even though this look itself often depended on careful construction. The miniskirts of the 1960s gave way to longer, flowing dresses, and dolly birds or space-age trendies were replaced by pre-Raphaelite maidens and Guineveres. Adverts for cosmetics and shampoos showed women with long tresses floating through cornfields and soft-misted, flowery meadows. Youthful radiance was still much more important than sophisticated glamour, although this particular youthful look was slightly more grown up than that of the earlier baby dolls or flower children. Homespun stuffs were desirable, if impractical, but by way of substitute for hippie-ish maternal types there were Clothkits, obtainable by mail order from Lewes in Sussex. These were sewing kits for the making up of smocks, dungarees, quilted jackets and the like: instructions for assembly were printed on the back of the fabric. Laura Ashley smocks and frocks were particularly fashionable at this time. The pastel cottons were sprigged with small flowers. It was a look reminiscent of rural milkmaids, accessorised with shawls, sandals and rustic rush baskets.

Perfumes and cosmetics followed this 'natural' trend, with a vogue for patchouli, herbs, the scents of meadow grass and hay. In 1976 Anita

Roddick founded the Body Shop: its first outlet was a small store, fortuitously positioned between two funeral parlours in Brighton's North Laine. A new emphasis on aromatherapy and environmentalism was in the air: Clinique, introduced by Estee Lauder in 1968, was a range of cosmetics with an emphasis on fragrance-free, allergy-tested ingredients. Aveda – specialising in plant-based beauty products – was founded by Horst Rechelbacher two years after the Body Shop in 1978. Roddick once said that her original concern was merely to find a way of earning a living, and that the Body Shop's first gestures in the direction of environmental awareness – such as washing and refilling the small plastic bottles used for shampoos and lotions – were pragmatic rather than deliberate policy. But she insisted in 1991 that the growth of the venture was fuelled by her dislike of the beauty industry and its exploitation of women and the environment: 'I hate the beauty business ... It lies. It cheats. It exploits women. Its major product lines are packaging and garbage.'[61] And again: 'In my view the cosmetics industry should be promoting health and well-being; instead it hypes an outdated notion of glamour and sells false hopes and fantasy.'[62]

The Body Shop was a runaway success. By 1991, the year in which Roddick published her autobiography, *Body and Soul* (on recycled paper of course), it had established some 700 branches. Its products were far removed from the gilt and luxuriously packaged concoctions of the traditional cosmetics houses, catering for what Roddick contemptuously quoted Estee Lauder's son as having described as 'the kept woman mentality',[63] and they were not tested on animals. This helped to build consumer loyalties which were to be shaken somewhat in 2006, when the company was sold to global cosmetics giant L'Oréal.

But glamour did not disappear entirely from fashion in the 1960s and 1970s. Perhaps its most obvious manifestation was in Barbara Hulanicki's designs for the cult clothing company Biba. Biba's 'postal boutique' took off in 1964 with an advertisement in the *Daily Mirror* for a pink gingham dress with a keyhole opening in the back, and a matching headscarf. The design was said to have been inspired in part by a gingham wedding dress worn by Brigitte Bardot in 1959. The dress certainly embodied the current dolly or little-girl look, and it cost 25 shillings. It was an instant success: some 17,000 orders followed.[64]

Hulanicki herself has described in her autobiography how difficult it was to find young-looking clothes in the 1950s, and how her mission had been to get the price of fresh young designs down so that they could be bought by ordinary working girls: 'I didn't want to make clothes for kept women,' she insisted.[65] She aimed at a market somewhat wider than that of Mary Quant, whose Ginger Group designs tended to be bought by middle-class Londoners. Biba designs soon moved away from the little girl references – smocks, gingham and knitted jumpsuits – into a more sophisticated look, which owed a good deal to both Hollywood glamour and Art Nouveau. Hulanicki had been much influenced by her aunt, a wealthy widow who had lived a life of style and luxury in the grand manner in the Brighton Metropole Hotel during her niece's teenage years. Barbara grew up with a rich visual vocabulary and style lexicon in part derived from familiarity with her aunt's jewellery and the contents of her voluminous wardrobe. She frequently referred to Biba's signature colour palette – a wonderfully murky range of visceral reds, dusky pink, ochre and cream, shading into bruise colours, plum, sage and aubergine – as 'auntie colours', her aunt having impressed on her during childhood that clear bright colours verged upon vulgarity.[66] Biba's premises, first in Abingdon Road, then in Kensington Church and High Streets, were dark, seductive boudoirs, full of bentwood and potted palms. Satin cushions were heaped on velvet upholstery, feather boas were draped around mirrors.

Biba's look became even more vampish following the introduction of a cosmetic range in 1970. Hulanicki recalled that she had been keen to get away from scarlet lips and nails, or 'the usual corals and bright pinks': 'I had seen a film when I was thirteen that I never forgot, with Rita Gam as a slave girl. She hadn't looked made up but her lips had obviously been painted brown. I couldn't wait to have brown lipstick and other natural shades.'[67] As a girl she had experimented, mixing the then standard 'peach paste' foundation with blobs of white poster paint and ochre gouache.[68] Biba's new cosmetic range was introduced at a celebratory tea dance, the centrepiece of which was a cake modelled in the shape of Mae West, reclining on a bed of red marzipan roses.[69] Soon Biba was producing cosmetics in non-standard colours; lipsticks in sepia, violet and black. Hairpieces with wired curls were tinted similarly. The effect was theatrical rather than 'natural': Hulanicki reported with satisfaction that her models would look 'as if they had just left a Fellini set'.[70]

▶

Shirley Bassey in one of her many memorable glamorous performances, here at the London Palladium in 1965.

(© Harry Thompson/ Evening Standard/ Hulton Archive/ Getty Images)

Success seemed assured and the performance rolled on. The shop in Kensington High Street was attracting some 100,000 shoppers per week when on May Day 1971 a group calling themselves the Angry Brigade planted a bomb in the basement. Customers were evacuated and there was a violent explosion; the store's security officer reported that half the basement had been demolished. Why Biba? The Angry Brigade was a militant group of anarchists, some of them apparently connected with the more radical fringe of the women's liberation movement.[71] According to Hulanicki: 'Their decision to blow us up, which came out at their trial, was based on the following crazy reasoning: women are slaves to fashion, Biba leads fashion, therefore blowing up Biba will liberate women.'[72]

These events were unnerving, but in the same year Biba embarked on its final, breathtaking performance by expanding into the legendary Art Deco premises in Kensington High Street which had earlier been occupied by the department store Derry and Toms. 'Big Biba' opened in 1973, and was 'more like a Busby Berkeley film set than a department store'.[73] There were echoes of classic Hollywood throughout: *Vogue* described 'a palace of apricot marble, coloured counters and fake leopard-skin walls, six floors of 1930s fantasy'.[74] The studied glamour bubbled over into camp. There were pink flamingos in the roof garden, and a cinema was planned for the space next to the Rainbow Room restaurant. The cinema never materialised, but the space was used for book launches, including that of Norman Mailer's *Marilyn Monroe*. The Liberace fan club held a private banquet – attended by Liberace himself – in the restaurant. Biba historian Alwyn Turner points out that as the economic situation in Britain worsened in the mid 1970s, there was an increasing demand for fantasy and escapism, and that the store supplied this, just as Hollywood cinema had offered dreams of escape in the depression years of the 1930s.[75]

Biba crashed in 1975. The attraction that the store held for the pianist and camp showman Liberace, and glam rock performers such as David Bowie and his first wife, Angie, in the early 1970s was fitting. For glamour may have hovered around the edges of mainstream fashion in the 1960s and 1970s but it had remained a central part of the music scene. During these decades black women Motown performers such as Diana Ross, Gloria Jones, Dionne Warwick and Gladys Knight discarded the cutesy, girlish bobbed hair and tunics of the mid 1960s in favour of

Claudia Jones, feminist, political activist and founder of the Notting Hill carnival with black beauty queen Marlene Walker at the second Caribbean carnival in London, in 1960. Carmen England, on the right, was a West Indian businesswoman who ran a successful hair and beauty salon in south Kensington.

(© This image was reproduced by kind permission of Lambeth Archives department)

floor-sweeping dresses, furs and diamonds. There were other successful black women performers who had never abandoned the opulent and showy glamour of the Hollywood years. Performances by the highly glamorous (and now often forgotten) black singer Adelaide Hall, who had often been compared with Josephine Baker, had drawn large audiences in Britain through and after the Second World War.[76] Cardiff-born singer Shirley Bassey had radiated glamour since the late 1950s: her stage gowns glittered, clung and were festooned with feathers in the best Hollywood tradition. Bassey's famous 'diamond dress', one of the first gowns made for her by her favourite designer, Douglas Darnell, in 1955, gained many additional garnishings of Swarovski crystals and ostrich feathers in repeated alterations through the years, before selling at Christie's in 2003 for £35,000. Glamorous stage performances were also the stock-in-trade of white women country-and-western stars, such as Dolly Parton and Tammy Wynette, who contrasted their impoverished roots in the Deep South with stage outfits rich with sequins and rhinestones.

Despite these parallels, glamour sometimes carried different meanings for black and white women in these years. In 1968, as women's liberation groups disrupted the Miss America proceedings in Atlantic City, the National Association for the Advancement of Coloured People staged the first Miss Black America contest as an affirmation of black beauty and a protest against the fact that the previous forty-eight Miss Americas had all been white.[77] In Britain, early in the 1960s Claudia Jones, a leading black activist and founder of the *West Indian Gazette* (as well as 'Mother of the Notting Hill Carnival'), had been a staunch supporter of black women's beauty pageantry as a celebration of cultural identity.[78] She had been particularly enthusiastic in her promotion of beauty and hairdressing salons organised by and run for African-Caribbean women in London, seeing them as a way of validating black women's beauty and self-esteem. Glamour was being claimed as a right rather than regarded as a form of repression.

Claudia Jones congratulating Carol Joan Crawford (Miss Jamaica 1960, Miss World 1963).

(© Photograph reproduced by kind permission of Lambeth Archives)

Glamazons, grunge
and bling

Seen as lacking in class in the 1950s, lacking in youthfulness, trendiness and even political integrity in the 1960s and 1970s, glamour was to return to mainstream fashion in a big way in the 1980s. As a style it had always appealed to aspirant groups, to the upwardly socially mobile, and to those with experience of hardship or exclusion who wanted to stake a claim to a share in affluence or the world's respect.

British women's lives had changed dramatically since the 1950s: education, employment, and the control of fertility had brought new freedoms and purchasing power, particularly to younger women. These changes provided the setting not only for the rise of second-wave feminism, but also for what came to be known as 'Cosmo Girl'.

The UK version of the magazine *Cosmopolitan* was launched in 1972, the same year that saw the first appearance of the feminist *Spare Rib*. Both publications saw themselves as appealing to a new breed of independent-minded women with interests outside the domestic sphere, although they were very different in layout, appearance and political tone, and these differences were to become much sharper through the following decade. The appearance of *Spare Rib* owed more to the underground press of the 1960s than to the traditional women's magazine format. Several of the early issues featured articles critical of the fashion and

beauty industries and questioning women's investment in their appearance. Even so, these early issues reflected a pragmatic and open-minded
approach to the exploration of women's lives and feminist issues. This
openness of tone was much less evident in later issues, where a concern
with orthodoxy and a feminist political identity tended to pre-empt
engagement with women's traditional sources of pleasure in romance,
appearance and femininity.[1] *Spare Rib*'s circulation – in the early years
estimated at around 20,000 per month – fell markedly in the late 1980s,
and the magazine eventually folded in 1993.

The first issue of the UK version of *Cosmopolitan*, with Helen Gurley
Brown as editorial director, featured a cover illustration of a blonde-
haired model in a red, frilled and low-cut dress. 'Cosmopolitan Girl'
was defined as interested in men and her appearance, but not exclusively so; with a job and a mind of her own she was said to exhibit a
new form of sexual confidence and agency.[2] Consumption was for her
pleasure, something earned rather than to be deplored. The tone was
liberal-feminist, up-beat, self-improving and competitive. Cosmo Girl was
described as 'gorgeous', 'curvy' and 'fantastic': interestingly, the word
'glamour' was sparsely used in early issues. An article on 'The Cover
Girl Look' by Deirdre McSharry in April 1972 featured model Paulene
Stone, described as 'one of the last great glamour girls', photographed
wearing flesh-coloured satin and lace and reclining awkwardly and coyly
on a tiger skin.[3] Stone looks anything *but* self-aware and in control of
the situation, an impression confirmed by the published interview in
which she assured readers that she avoided wearing blood-red lipstick
because her husband Larry (Laurence Harvey) hated it.[4] There was a
hesitancy or tentativeness about some of the first generation of Cosmo
Girls, mirrored by a patently instructional tone in some of the articles on
consumption and sexuality that faded as the magazine came of age in
the 1980s. But the emphasis on self-improvement was soon stepped up,
as readers were exhorted to shape up and take control of their jobs, lives
and relationships: one thing that Cosmo Girl was to repudiate entirely
was any form of passive femininity.[5]

There were many ways in which women, or at least educated, middle-
class women were much more in control of their lives in the 1980s. As
described in Chapter 5, the impact of the Abortion Law Reform Act
(1967) and the widespread availability of the contraceptive pill had

done much to erase the terrible fear of illegitimate pregnancy that had haunted young unmarried women in the 1950s. The Equal Pay Act of 1970 and the Sexual Discrimination Act of 1975 had begun to alter attitudes to women in the workplace. Women began to enter new forms of professional employment and to challenge the acceptability of masculine institutions and 'old boy' networks. Many began to earn more and the gap between the wages of men and women in full-time employment narrowed. These trends continued in spite of the socially regressive agenda of Margaret Thatcher's government. The prime minister herself modelled a new form of feminine agency, even if she was described as the 'best man for the job' and widely regarded as an honorary male. Traditional expectations about gender were radically challenged: by the end of the decade girls were not only catching up with boys in terms of their educational successes, they were even beginning to outperform them.[6]

Cosmopolitan was derided by feminists who saw it as emphasising individual achievement at the expense of a more radical social critique, as well as by those who were unhappy about its thoroughgoing consumerism and focus on fashion and appearance. The magazine relied heavily on revenue from advertisements, and was a magnet for manufacturers of the kinds of products that were anathema to many feminists: there were large numbers of adverts for vaginal deodorants, for example – Femfresh, Bidex, Fleur de Lis, Cosmea – in issues of the early 1980s. But there were also adverts for new kinds of financial products reflecting women's greater economic independence, such as Women's Individual Savings Plans offered by Langham Life Assurance Company.[7] There were many ways in which *Cosmopolitan* marked an important break with the traditional women's magazine formula of the 1950s and 1960s. Employment rather than domesticity was recognised as central to women's lives, and sexual self-awareness challenged self-sacrifice and familial duty as a basic component of health and happiness. Readers were encouraged to put aside their guilt and to 'discover themselves'. An article by Irma Kurtz in July 1973 emphasised a need to experiment sexually: 'a certain amount of promiscuity counts as "research" into what will make you happy'.[8] It is impossible to imagine a suggestion like this being made in any women's magazine before the 1970s. In August 1973 an intelligent article by Sally Vincent on contraception explored the possibility of the pill posing a threat to ancient arts of role playing, sexual posing, and conventional notions of masculinity and femininity.[9] And it wasn't all lipsticks and orgasms: the magazine offered lively reviews of books, film and the theatre from its inception.

Cosmopolitan spoke to young women on the make, and the economic boom of the early 1980s encouraged this group to celebrate their new status with a confident and sometimes brash materialism. The stage was set for a wholesale revival of glamour in the 1980s. But there was uncertainty about style. What would women wear in the workplace? Secretaries in earlier decades had dressed as subordinates, demurely, in twin sets and pearls. In the USA in 1980, J.T. Molloy counselled on 'dressing for success'.[10] Girly skirts and baggy cardigans were out. Just as women had taken to tailored skirt suits, collars and ties as they entered public spaces in the universities and business world in the late Victorian period, the young women professionals and executives of the 1980s adopted a version of male dress.[11] This was the era of the tailored, pinstripe suit, albeit with a short skirt, set off with enormous, mannish shoulder pads. Designers such as Azzedine Alaïa set out to clothe the sexy and powerful career woman. Status mattered.

Leafing through issues of British *Vogue* of 1985 reveals some astonishing examples of 'power dressing', or corporate drag: models wearing masculine suits and overcoats, collars and ties; flat-chested, with handkerchiefs peeping from breast pockets. Cropped hair is gelled and slicked, even the body language is male as the models slouch against street furniture, newspapers and umbrellas in gloved hands.[12] An advert for a suit by Krizia in the March 1985 issue has a woman looking decidedly butch in a trouser suit with enormous, prizefighter shoulder pads, hands thrust in pockets, aggressive posture and face to match.[13] A note of startling incongruity is introduced by the fact that she is wearing diamanté drop earrings and a glittery bangle. If not aggressive, the expression on the faces of the models is sullen: they never smile. But side by side with this look of the surrogate male went another variety of power dressing in the form of the unashamedly predatory female. This was a look that owed a great deal to the bitch-heroines of US television soap operas such as *Dallas* and *Dynasty*, and particularly to the outfits worn by Joan Collins as Alexis Carrington, designed by Nolan Miller. It was showy stuff, encrusted with sequins and heavily embroidered appliqué. It was no coincidence that the word 'glitz' to indicate ostentation and tawdry

A shoulder-padded glamazon muscles up for the boardroom. Advert for Krizia, photograph by John Bishop for British *Vogue*, 1985.

Régine

43/44 NEW BOND STREET, W1

Krizia

glamour came into its own at this time.[14] Big jewels and gilt earrings and buttons approaching the size of door knobs set off the look, along with heavy gold chains. Hair was also big (this was a period when mousse, gel and heavy-duty hair spray were much in demand), shoulder pads were inserted into everything from jackets to fine wool sweaters, and lipstick was bold, uncompromising and carnivorously red.

▶

Another example of 1980s tailored androgyny. Advert for Georges Rech, British *Vogue*, 1985.

The word 'glamazon', coined at this time, associated glamour with the female warrior. This was a kind of glamour that could suggest aggression, as well as self-assertion. Women signalled that they knew what they were about, even if this signal was sometimes a bluff, masking a degree of uncertainty. While the Iron Lady governed Britain, shoulder pads announced presence in the boardroom, 'killer heels' indicated that one was not to be messed with, and had no need for flight. Power dressing took up space, and went hand in hand with an assertive materialism. Success led those with new money to invest in clothes, and it was no co-incidence that there was a revival of haute couture, as Versace, Valentino and other designers began catering for 'new money with a demand for old money habits'.[15] Paris fashion shows began to attract ever larger audiences in the 1980s; the numbers attending in 1986 had almost quadrupled over the previous ten years.[16] Designer labels signified social arrival and savoir-faire. Supermodels boasted enormous salaries and became celebrities. *Vogue* was stuffed full with advertisements for showy jewellery by Bulgari, Cartier, Chaumet, Asprey: greed was suddenly good.[17]

Blood-red lips and nails indicated a definite lack of squeamishness, and, in the context of eighties glamour, fur staged a comeback. In spite of the high-profile 'American Legend' Blackglama mink advertising campaign of the late 1960s,[18] fur had remained fairly marginal in the fashion of the 1970s. *Vogue* itself had sent out contradictory messages. An advert for the furrier Maxwell Croft in autumn 1973 announced: 'Call it glamorous, call it mood-dressing, call it super-style', showing a woman half-buried in fox, but the same issue had featured actress Mia Farrow and her then husband Andre Previn both dolled up in fake fur 'for the sake of wildlife'.[19] The environmental lobby got louder in the 1970s, and even the veteran fashion writer Alison Settle, who had drooled over quality fur for most of her working life, had heralded the importance of fake fur in the interests of conservation.[20] Younger women in the 1970s might still have worn hand-me-down or flea-market fur but were increasingly less likely to invest in a new fur coat.

With Anna Wintour editing British *Vogue* from 1986, the desirability of real fur was reasserted. October 1986 saw the magazine announcing a return to 'pure glamour' and featuring a Revillon sable coat from Harvey Nichols priced at £57,895. There was also a full-length 'smoky blue fisher fur' at £53,460. For those whose budget couldn't quite reach to these there was a yellow ermine wrap coat at just under £14,000.[21] Wintour's predecessor at *Vogue,* Beatrix Miller, had been described by the fashion designer Jean Muir as translating American glamour into a more English version of glossiness.[22] With Wintour, the distinction was eroded by an unapologetic celebration of glamour, materialism and privilege.

Tension over fur rose in the 1980s as animal rights organisations such as Peta (People for the Ethical Treatment of Animals) and Lynx attracted large-scale public support. One Lynx poster showed a photograph by David Bailey of a woman trailing a fur coat behind her with blood seeping out of it. 'It takes up to 40 dumb animals to make a fur coat but only one to wear it,' the slogan claimed. Another poster carried the slogan 'Rich bitch, poor bitch' showing a girl wearing furs, alongside a trapped female fox. Peta started to persuade female celebrities to pose in the nude alongside the slogan 'I'd rather go naked than wear fur': some, like Naomi Campbell and Cindy Crawford, signed up but later reneged. The fashion for leather coats and leather trousers in the 1980s generally escaped censure.[23] Anna Wintour, lampooned as 'Cruella de Vil', was repeatedly castigated by the anti-fur lobby. As attitudes hardened, protest became more violent. In November 1984, there were raids on a mink farm in Elland, Yorkshire, and 1,000 mink were let loose. Three years later, coinciding with the stock market crash of 1987, a series of small bombs created costly damage in three Debenhams' department stores: the Animal Liberation Front claimed responsibility for these. Attacks on stores selling furs continued into the 1990s and the twenty-first century. Wearing an expensive fur coat in the 1980s required a certain arrogance or intrepidity which may have served to restore an aura of exclusivity. But wearing it in public constituted something of a risk, inviting disapproving glances, overt challenge from passers-by, or even spray-paint attacks from animal liberationists.[24] But with the spotlight and so much controversy focused on fur, feathers were creeping back into fashion. A staple of Vegas showgirl costumes, they had never left the stage, but now their use was beginning to expand back into millinery. The more squeamish could fall back on leopard print, which suddenly sprang into fashion. Once the apogee of bad taste – Gundle observes that leopard print, 'the stock in trade of the experienced working-class woman', had earlier been associated with pub landladies – leopard-skin print became 'reinvested with new postmodern desirability by Dolce and Gabbana'.[25] It was brazen and somewhat kitsch, even if ironic: in the 1980s, that was the point.

The showy glamour of the 1980s called for scents with stridency. Revlon's successful mass-market fragrance Charlie, introduced in 1973, had set out to appeal to the young, liberated females of the 1970s. The perfume historian Susan Irvine suggests that in a way it was 'the first feminist perfume', in that advertisements showed young women wearing trousers and there were hints of androgyny as women began to enter a male world.[26] The scent was code-named 'Cosmo' while it was being developed, since the idea was to appeal to 'Cosmo Girl'. The 'face' of Charlie was Shelley Hack of the popular television series *Charlie's Angels*: the scent itself was 'pretty and wearable', a lightish floral. Perfumes of the 1980s had a much stronger presence. Yves St Laurent's Opium (1977) set the tone and was a huge success.[27] It was a rich and tenacious oriental perfume that traced its ancestry through Estee Lauder's potent Youth Dew (1953) and Guerlain's Shalimar. Outdoing even Opium's tenacity was Giorgio Beverly Hills (1981), described by Steve Ginsberg in his story of the history of the fragrance, *Reeking Havoc*, as 'the elevator-gagger of the 1980s'.[28] Giorgio was launched by boutique owners Fred and Gayle Hayman, Gayle having set out to design a 'high-powered, entrance-making fragrance' for assertive women. The company used scent strips in magazines to advertise Giorgio, and it was first stocked in Britain by Harvey Nichols. Described by Susan Irvine as 'olfactory shoulder pads', it was a remarkable success, although less in Britain than in the USA, where restaurants sometimes banned the scent on account of its very intrusiveness.[29] The third of the legendary power scents of the decade was Christian Dior's Poison (1985).[30] Irvine quotes perfume industry consultant Joachim Mensing's view of Poison as being 'about power in sexual politics': packaged to resemble 'a magic fruit filled with belladonna', it suggested witchcraft, and a 'female fantasy of sexual domination'.[31] The scent itself was certainly aggressive, if not actually asphyxiating. Deborah Hutton wrote an article for *Vogue* on the new scents of the 1980s: the heading was 'Fragrance: Coming on Strong ...'[32]

Strong scents, 'glamazons' and supermodels: women were taking up more space in the 1980s. But they had to be fit to survive, and the fashionable body shape was sleek and honed through exercise.[33] The 1980s saw a rise in gym membership and a fashion for working out. It was the decade of legwarmers and the spandex leotard. An advertisement for Sunsilk hair styling mousse featured in *Vogue* in July 1986 showed women sporting lycra bodysuits in the two fashionably bright colours of the day, electric blue and fuchsia, with matching dumb-bells.[34] *Jane Fonda's Workout Book* (1981) was a runaway success; her first exercise video, which appeared in the following year, is said to have sold some 17 million copies, and it spawned many imitations. Fonda herself released a series of more than twenty exercise videos between 1982 and 1995. In the UK, Rosemary Conley's *Hip and Thigh Diet* rose to the top of the best-seller charts in the late 1980s, and Conley went on to establish a network of diet and fitness clubs in the 1990s. Those who could afford it aspired to the cachet of having a personal trainer. Exercise videos proliferated, along with diet books. The cult of fitness could be taken to extremes, and some sought body shapes that went beyond sleek curves towards a toned and muscular androgyny. In August 1986, for instance, *Vogue*'s article on 'Attitudes to Fitness Now' was illustrated by a photograph of a flat-chested model with cropped and gelled hair, lifting weights with what can only be described as masculine grace.[35] But it is notable that many of the best-selling books and videos of the 1980s and early 1990s were made by older women such as Fonda, Conley and Joan Collins, demonstrating that women over forty, fifty and even sixty years of age could take delight in their bodies and look glamorous well into years in which they were historically considered as old and 'past it'. Joan Collins's career as a glamour icon spanned more than half a century. In the 1950s, she had been featured in the magazine *Glamour* elaborating on 'What Hollywood taught me' about femininity. She had confessed to a weakness for mink coats and a white convertible but had insisted that a main lesson had been not to wear too much make-up.[36]

Many women remained unconcerned about – or at least, accepting of – ageing, and claimed to find the idea of 'mutton dressed as lamb' pathetic. In the spring of 1988 the British organisation Mass Observation issued a 'Clothing Directive' in which its body of voluntary observers – weighted towards the female, the ageing and the middle class – offered inventories of their wardrobes and delivered their views on clothes.[37] There were few thoughtless consumers here. Many of the women retained the prudent, economical and make-do-and-mend habits of an earlier generation, wearing cast-offs and recycling jerseys as cushions for the cat. There was a marked leaning towards the roomy and comfortable, affection for anoraks, and distaste for anything 'flash'. 'I'll do anything for comfort, and blow the style,' commented one woman, who suffered from bunions.[38] 'Flash' was described by one respondent as 'tight jeans, high heels, gold ankle chain, a jumper with feathers or glitter of some sort and a fur coat'.[39] Another described 'flash, in a woman' as 'long red fingernails and wreeking [*sic*] of Estee Lauder's Youth Dew'.[40] 'Flash' was not unlike glamour, it would seem: many of these women had grown up in the 1950s when glamour spelt vulgarity and was something of a dirty word. There was more than one affectionate reference to *Vogue*'s Mrs Exeter. 'Flash', concluded yet another observer, meant 'Too tight, too bright, too tanned, too much glitter, too spikey heels, too much make-up, too strong perfume, too shiny, especially leather, too much all round.'[41]

The 1980s focus on body shape generated sharp criticism from those who claimed that an obsession with slimness generated body dysmorphia, particularly amongst younger women at risk of developing eating disorders such as anorexia and bulimia. But at the same time, obesity was becoming even more widespread, suggesting that these problems were linked, and ultimately connected with distortions of appetite in the context of an increasingly affluent society.[42] Many feminists argued that rapid social change had given rise to contradictory demands on young women, leading to confusion about identity and low self-esteem. Growing up, for girls, had got harder. Several studies explored the ways in which eating disorders connected with low self-esteem and a sense of powerlessness in women, the most well known being Susie Orbach's *Fat is a Feminist Issue* (1979), Kim Chernin's *The Hungry Self* (1985), and Orbach's second book on the subject, *Hunger Strike* (1986).[43]

Where some saw the possibility of glamour in old age as liberating, others demurred. The rising popularity of cosmetic surgery in the USA in the 1980s rang alarm bells for many. Facelifts had been sought by the rich and famous as early as the 1930s, but by the 1980s, these and a whole variety of 'procedures' – rhinoplasty, breast augmentation, liposuction, 'filler' injections and so on – were becoming ever more available.[44] Advertisements for cosmetic surgery in the back pages of women's magazines proliferated. What was seen by some feminists as a war waged on women's bodies and self-esteem by patriarchy, advertisers and big business generated a new wave of feminist texts in the 1980s, most notably Naomi Wolf's *The Beauty Myth* (1990) and Susan Faludi's *Backlash: The Undeclared War against Women* (1991).[45] For Wolf, the glamorised images that were the currency of women's magazines lay at the heart of women's oppression. The myth of domesticity current in the 1950s had deployed images of women transported by joy in the possibilities of owning vacuum cleaners, fridges and other new domestic appliances. More recently, Wolf contended, the imperatives of commerce had generated 'a raving, itching, parching product lust' for cosmetics, dieting and the 'makeover', fostering a sense of personal inadequacy and self-hatred in women, manifested in body dysmorphia, obsessive dieting, and eating disorders.[46] Wolf admitted that, in essence, glamour was born of a fundamentally human urge to adorn, and did not have to be destructive. 'We need it', she concluded somewhat lamely, 'but redefined.'[47] In the bestselling *Backlash*, the US feminist Susan Faludi elaborated a theory of patriarchal conspiracy further, claiming that in the 1980s the fashion and cosmetics industries had mounted wholesale attacks on the more liberated social attitudes that had followed from the feminism of the 1970s. Faludi saw the 1980s as urging a return to more traditional and constricting models of glamorised femininity, which could only be seen as retrogressive.[48]

But any notion of a backlash against feminism in the 1980s has to be balanced against the real gains that women were making in education and employment. And the issues around cultural ideals of beauty and body shape are complex. There are gains in health and social advantage in avoiding obesity. Moreover, some historians have interpreted the late twentieth-century fashion for slimness and fitness in terms of a breaking out from traditional models of femininity as coterminous with and limited by domesticity and reproduction.[49] Both Faludi and Wolf tend to represent women a little one-sidedly, as victims. 'To airbrush age off a woman's face is to erase women's identity, power and history,' announces Wolf.[50] Novelist Fay Weldon, quoted on the back cover of *The Beauty Myth*, tells us that the book constitutes 'essential reading for the New Woman; word-of-warning to the Glamorous'. Wolf sees cosmetic surgery as the epitome of male violence towards women, but Weldon's treatment of the subject, in *The Life and Loves of a She-Devil* (1983), is rather more complex. The novel is a revenge fantasy in which a clumsy and oppressed suburban housewife, Ruth, magically transforms herself through surgery, revenging herself on her husband's mistress and gaining wealth, power and sexual adulation in the process.[51]

In *Reshaping the Feminine Body* (1995), Kathy Davis explores the motives and experiences of a group of women in the Netherlands choosing to undergo cosmetic surgery, emphasising that this is a choice made by increasing numbers of educated professional women, often with feminist views, and that these women cannot simply be dismissed as 'cultural dupes' of patriarchy or capitalism.[52] One may deplore the gender inequity which rates appearance as more important in women than in men, the reductive notion of a body as 'cultural plastic', and ethnically loaded standards of beauty that value some physical characteristics highly and denigrate others. But women are not responsible for these conditions: they are agents insofar as they make decisions about their own lives, albeit within historically determined circumstances that are not of their own choosing. The marketing of cosmetic surgery – the number of procedures doubled in Britain during the 1980s and 1990s – understandably gave (and continues to give) serious grounds for concern, particularly because the majority of operations have been carried out upon women.[53] But in order to understand why women subject themselves to surgery we need to go beyond dismissing them all as victims of patriarchy or false consciousness.

Notwithstanding the strictures of Wolf and Faludi, the numbers of those seeking cosmetic surgery in Britain, the USA and elsewhere in the world continued to rise as the twentieth century came to its close. And slenderness became ever more desirable in Britain in the 1990s as younger models such as Kate Moss came to prominence in fashion photography: the look was undernourished, waif-like.

Deborah Silverman has argued that the unabashed displays of conspicuous consumption in the USA in the 1980s saw history plundered by haute couture and itself misrepresented and distorted in museum exhibitions that celebrated opulence and privilege rather than seeking to promote a better understanding of the past.[54] Meanwhile in Britain, the shiny, over-the-top glamour of the

1980s had begun to look out of date by the early 1990s and had generated its own antithesis: grunge. Although the popularity of luxury and designer brands continued into the 1990s, it was as if the fashion world itself, having gorged on luxury over the previous decade, was showing signs of surfeit.

This was in part generational. The term 'grunge' was associated with West Coast USA, where young musicians in Seattle were experimenting with combinations of punk and heavy metal, accompanied by lyrics suggestive of angst and social despair. The term quickly crossed into fashion to indicate a style of anti-fashion, an espousal of cheap, serviceable, often distressed clothing. Where Madonna's early stage performances had both celebrated and parodied femininity, singer Courtney Love became famous for a pastiche of glamour with ripped négligées, dirty blonde hair, smudged red lips and a diamanté tiara worn askew. These fashions, and what became widely known as the 'kinderwhore look', were widely copied by younger women. Torn lace was often worn in conjunction with the faded jeans and Doc Marten boots that had been something of a uniform for the young since the 1970s. In Britain, the rising fame of designer Vivienne Westwood narrowed the gap between punk and high fashion, helping to ensure that an element of postmodern irony often kept company with traditional displays of glamour. In the early 1990s, even august publications such as *Vogue* were featuring images of waif-like, often unhealthy-looking models in layered and hand-me-down-looking clothing.

The cosmetics industry caught on to this trend, with brands such as Hard Candy and Urban Decay offering Stray Dog Eye Pencil, Asphyxia Lip Gunk, and Dropout Nail Polish. Urban Decay's first slogan was 'Does pink make you puke?'[55] The countercultural appeal of these products was more about attitude than reality, and they were soon available in Harvey Nichols, Selfridges and Harrods. Perfumes introduced in the 1990s were very different from the complex intrusive scents of the 1980s. There was a fashion for watery smells, as well as scents based on food (melon, vanilla, chocolate) which were evocative of childhood. Calvin Klein's CK-1 was light and fruity, addressed to what Irvine calls the 'glamour-free kids' of the 1990s.[56] Thierry Mugler's rather more invasive Angel smelt of candyfloss, or caramel. Demeter fragrances (from 1993), described by the company as 'a unique range of naturally derived down to earth scents' that were light and faded quickly, were meant to be layered, like the clothing of the day. Demeter's first fragrance, Clear Water, was soon supplemented by such offerings as Dirt, Grass and Waffle-Cake. Some of the references (Bubble-Gum, Brownie) were to kiddy food, and the range deliberately targeted younger women.

The kind of adolescent angst associated with grunge as street style repudiated glamour, while influential designers such as Issey Miyake, Rei Kawakubo, Ann Demeulemester and others were 'deconstructing' it on the catwalk. As in the 1960s, glamour found itself in the gutter, or at least in the bargain bin. But in a society driven by consumerism, grunge could not last, and was soon overtaken by a new wave of conspicuous consumption flaunting the old signs: fast cars, champagne, diamonds and fur. In the late 1990s 'bling' (defined memorably as 'the sound light makes when it bounces off a diamond'[57]) was associated with American hip-hop and R&B, and black American male rappers as well as female stars such as Li'l Kim, Foxy Brown, Jennifer Lopez and Beyoncé. Diamonds and fur as quintessential symbols of glamour had always carried with them a certain disregard for hierarchy and restraint. But popular queasiness about the use of fur in some Western countries, coupled with concern about the source of 'conflict diamonds' and criminal activity in Africa, had amplified the charge of transgression by this time. Bling was 'in your face' and simply didn't care. But for those women who did feel uneasy about fur and diamonds, other forms of conspicuous consumption were available in the form of expensive designer handbags, kitted out with a whole variety of buckles, chains and hardware, the new signifiers of affluence and style.

The final decades of the twentieth century witnessed a mounting obsession with celebrity, as the state of being in the public eye changed with the impact of new media, celebrity magazines and the Internet. *Hello!* magazine first appeared in Britain in 1988, a spinoff of the Spanish *Hola!* It was a huge success, spawning many imitations. *OK!* followed in 1990, becoming weekly from 1996, *Now* arrived in 1997, *Heat* two years later. Longer-established magazines were also affected by the highly successful formula. The Internet, and the development of the World Wide Web, gave the illusion of delivering celebrity right into people's homes, effectively licensing voyeurism on an unprecedented scale. Celebrities – and details of their private lives and day-to-day goings-on – could be scrutinised and pored over by an ever-widening public, and demand for gossip and images of the famous rocketed, providing employment for armies of investigative journalists and photographers.

Two icons of glamour who achieved celebrity status in the late twentieth century were Britain's Diana, Princess of Wales and American pop singer Madonna, both of whom have attracted massive attention from students of popular culture and cultural historians. For both women, glamour was a performance, and a performance that was bound up with defiance in the face of traditional expectations of femininity.

At the time of her engagement to Prince Charles, the young Diana Spencer projected an air of awkward innocence: the official engagement photographs show her costumed discreetly in a bland blue two-piece not unlike the working uniform of an air hostess. She was twenty years old, worried about her weight, and unsure about style. A first official engagement with Charles at a charity event saw her dressed in a sexy black silk gown by Elizabeth and David Emanuel, off the shoulder and strapless with a deep décolletage. She looked gorgeous, but uncertain in front of photographers, an insecurity that can't have been helped by an insecure neckline, and the fact that Charles had already found fault with her choice of clothing (he had evidently objected on the grounds that black was for mourning). Beatrix Campbell made much of the occasion in her book *Diana, Princess of Wales: How Sexual Politics Shook the Monarchy* (1998), maintaining that Diana's sexiness and desirability in the eyes of the public unsettled Charles, who was more comfortable with the idea of marrying an innocent and dependent subordinate.[58] His fiancée's 'glamorous reinvention in a great frock unsettled the problem of power that circulated between both the virgin and the prince and the virgin and the public': a sad augury of what was to follow.[59]

Diana's choice of a fairy-tale wedding dress, the ivory silk meringue-like confection designed by the Emanuels, betrayed her romanticism, probably in part derived from an avid reading of her step-grandmother, Barbara Cartland's romantic novels. Her clothes and demeanour went through a series of transformations as the years went by, as she struggled with persistent insecurities, an eating disorder, and an increasingly unhappy marriage.[60] Her sense of style grew more confident as her popularity with the public grew and she both reflected and initiated fashion trends of the 1980s with a combination of high street and haute couture.

The pie-crust frills, county tweeds and bashful fringe were abandoned in favour of taffeta, glitz and big hair. Blonde streaks, a tanned and toned body, fashion advisers from *Vogue* and close relations with leading designers including Bruce Oldfield, Catherine Walker, Victor Edelstein and Gianni Versace assured her reputation as the most (if not the only) glamorous member of the British royal family at that time, with what was effectively supermodel status in the world at large.[61]

In spite of her despair in the context of her husband's continuing love affair with Camilla Parker-Bowles and a failing marriage, Diana had sufficient *amour-propre* not to submit to the double standards of sexual morality still subscribed to by her husband and other royals. A determination to tell her side of the story led to her co-operation with Andrew Morton, whose biography of the princess was originally published in 1992, and to her agreement to be interviewed by Martin Bashir on *Panorama* three years later.[62] She put up a fight, and would not go quietly. Diana's determination to be a survivor rather than a victim was never more apparent than on the night Charles gave his side of the story, confessing his adultery in a television interview with Jonathan Dimbleby. The dress she wore to the event she attended at the Serpentine Gallery that night in March 1994 has become legendary: widely referred to as the 'revenge dress', this was a dramatic, off-the-shoulder, short black cocktail dress by Christina Stambolian. With it she wore towering heels and blood-red nail polish. Diana's photograph graced the cover of nearly every newspaper the following morning: she looked extraordinarily glamorous and self-possessed.[63] The Stambolian dress was not altogether unlike the low-cut, black Emanuel dress she had worn to her first official engagement all those years before: there was both defiance and closure in the wearing of it.

Diana got rid of many of her most elaborate dresses in a sale for charity in 1997, but lost nothing of her glamour in the process.[64] She reinvented herself as both private individual and public persona, looking for happiness in new relationships (which did little to heal conflict with the royal family), striving against all odds to make an impact on the world through charity work, her support for those infected with HIV, and her campaigns against land-mines. It was her many reinventions, and the ways in which these both colluded with and contested popular understandings about femininity that have fascinated both cultural theorists and feminists.

Glamour, a complex and ambivalent performance of femininity, reinventions, defiance: these are themes that resonate similarly in any consideration of the career of Madonna. From the ironic construction of herself as 'boy-toy' in the 1980s, in which she smudged the division between virgin and whore in glittery crucifix, fishnets and black lace, fingerless gloves, Madonna's influence on the way young women represented and perceived themselves was immense. In spite of the sexual revolution of the 1960s and 1970s, many girls still complained of a double standard of morality. They were stigmatised as 'slags' if they enjoyed sexual encounters with boys, 'drags' if they didn't.[65] This made it hard to own sexual desire, but Madonna demonstrated new possibilities and a complete lack of shame as a desiring subject. The posing was essentially a challenge: to received notions about gender and to any illusion of feminine sexual desire as quiescent and biddable, safely contained in the service of patriarchy.[66] Many critics have explored the elements of camp in Madonna's female impersonations, drawing comparisons with Mae West and gay drag.[67] In the 'Material Girl' video, she projected a confident, luminous glamour, rehearsing a debt to a parade of female Hollywood stars from the 1930s through to Marilyn Monroe – but crucially, as has often been pointed out, without any of Monroe's vulnerability. Madonna combined Hollywood glamour with the aggressive edge of US street style. By the time of the Blond Ambition tour of 1990, her constant changes of image were being interpreted as representing a postmodern playfulness unsettling of any fixed identity. Her glamour got tougher, with strong elements of androgyny and the striking Gaultier-designed corset with its shiny, bullet-shaped breasts. The charge of transgression was amplified with the appearance of the album *Erotica* in 1992 and the notorious coffee-table book *Sex*, published by Warner Books in the same year.[68] The highest-earning female pop singer of all time, Madonna showed ambition and shrewdness in forwarding her own business interests. Motherhood did not interrupt her career, and nor did reaching the age of fifty (once considered elderly for women) diminish her success as one of the most glamorous performers of the modern age.

Perspectives and reflections: glamour for all?

At least two magazines with the title *Glamour* have been launched in Britain. The first, published by C. Arthur Pearson, appeared in March 1938, declaring itself boldly 'The World's Greatest Love Story Weekly'. It lasted until 1956, when it retitled itself *The New Glamour*; two years later this amalgamated with *Mirabelle*. Condé Nast's *Glamour* magazine is of much more recent origin: following the success of the US title of the same name (which dates from 1937), a UK version first appeared in April 2001. The success of this 'handbag-sized' publication was meteoric: by 2005–6 it had established itself as the best-selling monthly magazine in the UK, with sales topping 600,000.[1]

To compare 2007's *Glamour* magazine to the British publication of the same name from 1938 is to see the shift that has taken place in the meaning of the word. There are interesting continuities as well as contrasts. Like so many other women's magazines, both *Glamour*s attempted to woo readers with free gifts: in December 2005 the Condé Nast publication offered a cheap synthetic clutch bag in place of its predecessor's 'Parisian mirror love rings', which were said to be 'miraculously lucky in ATTRACTING MEN TO THEIR OWNERS'.[2] The 'editress' of the earlier magazine frequently resorted to bellowing at her readers in capital letters with messages of this kind. But the 1938 *Glamour* was cheaply produced: costing twopence a week until the 1950s, when the price went up to threepence, it was printed on low-grade, absorbent newspaper, mainly in black and white. The content was mainly torrid romantic fiction. A serial romance featured in the first few issues gripped its audience with a tale of an English rose (Rosalie) seduced by a polygamous Indian rajah. A subtext indicates that, confronted by the sexy 'Prince of Darkness', Rosalie was uncertain whether 'this was love, or just mad glamour', interestingly preserving the older usage of the word 'glamour' to suggest delusion. Rosalie narrowly escapes a horrible fate, including death by being poisoned by the rajah's venomous, jealous mother, being rescued in the nick of time by a decent English bloke. 'White Girl, Dark Prince' was followed by several serials of similar ilk with titles such as 'Never a Bride', 'The Scarlet Nun' and 'The House of Hidden Secrets'. The 'editress' herself described these as 'throbbing' romances 'pulsating with the rhythm of love'.[3] There were regular problem pages. In early editions, contemporary film hero Ramon Navarro offered to solve the problems of readers' love affairs on the basis of his trumpeted experience in knowing 'WHAT MAKES A GIRL ALLURING TO MEN', but he seems to have tired of offering succour to the heartsick rather early on and in his place an avuncular-looking Nigel Mansfield proffered ideas and tips on 'how to get a boy of your own'.[4] A column entitled 'Confessions of a Hollywood Beauty Expert' lasted for some years, as did an even longer-running feature on cosmetics, beauty and glamour by Diana Carr. In the 1950s there were added features written by Evadne Price ('My Friends the Stars'), advice columns by 'Nurse Janet' on health and hygiene and on relationships by Marion Dark, but the basic structure of the magazine stayed remarkably constant throughout its history.

Most of the advice dispensed by the beauty experts in these early magazines was pretty homespun, and of the cold cream, nailbrush, olive oil and lemon juice variety, often making use of simple culinary ingredients, although one can trace a growing emphasis on commercially produced skin products and cosmetics. Advertisements for such products were there from the start, although the space occupied by advertising was nowhere as extensive as in modern magazines. Many of the advertisements have an irresistible period flavour: Tetlow's Swan Down Petal Lotion, which could 'defeat facial perspiration', Snowfire Vanishing Cream, pink, green or blue milk baths 'to make you feel like a millionairess'.[5] Other products sound less alluring: Kozy Kaps for 'seaside hair protection … glisten most attractively and are absolutely waterproof'; a scary-looking apparatus manufactured by 'Mr Trilety' to be strapped to the face by those seeking 'nose correction'.[6] Many of the advertisements remind us of the poverty, hard work and ill-health which were clearly features of so many of the readers' everyday lives: images of knackered-looking women faced by piles of ironing who are advised to drink Bourn-vita to deal with exhaustion; promotion of pink pills to 'take the lead out of your legs' and 'female pills' for anaemia, listlessness and 'female disorders'. The tone of reassuring intimacy fostered by personal messages from 'Your Editress' was often undercut by strident admonitions from advertisers and beauty editors about hygiene, posture, grooming and bad teeth. An advertisement for 'Dor cream deodorant' in 1938 warned that 'under-arm odour destroys all charm', asserting that 'lots of girls lose their jobs and miss romance simply because they think that a bath is enough … it isn't!'[7] The novelty value of cosmetics is very apparent in the 1930s: a new 'Tokalon BLACK LIPSTICK' was introduced as 'the rage of Paris': 'This amazing lipstick, though black, turns from light, to medium, to dark red according to how much you moisten your lips …'[8] At the same time girls were bombarded with dire warnings against turning themselves into 'painted horrors'; the copyline for Guitare lipstick, for instance, asserted that 'men are repulsed, even disgusted by the heavy painted look that comes from old-fashioned cosmetics'.[9]

Magazines like this received short shrift from middle-class social observers of the time. For A. J. Jenkinson and Pearl Jephcott, analysing the reading habits of working-class girls during the Second World War, *Glamour* was typical of a group of magazines they categorised as 'erotic bloods', a genre that included *Oracle, Miracle, Lucky Star, Silver Star* and *Red Star Weekly*.[10] These magazines were universally known amongst young people from working-class homes, they discovered. Jephcott was scathing about the content of such publications, which she saw as capitalising on the emotional and intellectual underdevelopment of girls whose formal education ended with the elementary school. She somewhat grudg-ingly acknowledged the use girls made of advice columns: 'how to get a boyfriend even when you have pimples on your face'. But whilst she conceded the importance of dream-world longings for glamour, expen-sive clothes and exotic settings to girls living humdrum lives in humble circumstances, she considered the serial fiction, even where exciting, ultimately sordid and sickly in nature, 'second-rate' or 'low-grade' food which could only debase 'the mental and spiritual quality of the consumer'.[11]

This is a little harsh. The short story and serial fiction that appeared in magazines such as *Glamour* in the 1940s may have been sensational, far-fetched and lacking in conventional literary merit, but in spite of the lure of exoticism and the *frissons* of scandal and suspense the basic messages or values exemplified in the genre were markedly conventional and respectable to the point of rigidity. Heroines hungered after riches and luxury but they learned, through bruising experience, the value of the familiar and the everyday. Even Richard Hoggart, who somewhat surprisingly devoted several pages of *The Uses of Literacy* (1957) to a discussion of this kind of magazine, confessed to finding a kind of authenticity and what he defined as 'decency' in these stories.[12] Erring heroines longed for glamour but came to appreciate modesty and sincerity. They strayed and misbehaved but they invariably learned their lesson in the end, came to their senses and married Mr Right. Mr Right was always white, of course: the sexy sheikhs, maharajahs and oriental princes who featured so commonly in the narratives inevitably turned out rotten, requiring the heroine to be rescued by an upstanding English chap. If these stories are to be judged debased from a present-day perspective, then this must surely be on account of their thoroughgoing racism. For all their exoticism, they are ultimately cautionary tales of a parochial, conservative cast. The glamour of the foreign is a dangerous illusion: girls should be thankful to return to the *terra firma* of the familiar, the virtues and decencies of everyday life. Readers were offered adventure and escape, then, at the imaginative level, but a constant series of subtexts – the narrative structures of the fiction, advertisements and editorial interventions – served to anchor them to the everyday, to the distinctly *unglamorous* circumstances of contemporary women's working lives.

Comparisons with Condé Nast's *Glamour* magazine, published in the USA from the 1930s, and the much more recent UK edition of this same publication are interesting. The US version of *Glamour* magazine had grown out of the *Hollywood Pattern Book*, Nast's attempt to exploit the potential of selling paper patterns for home dressmaking to women who wanted to copy the fashions worn by movie stars.[13] This venture into mass

marketing in the early 1930s had proved so successful that a new magazine, *Glamour of Hollywood*, was launched in 1939. As Nast's biographer,
Caroline Seebohm, points out, this new publication was very different
from his earlier publishing enterprises in that he set out deliberately to
appeal to the average woman, to emphasise 'mass' instead of 'class', and
to woo young women in particular, exploiting the magic of movie stars.[14]
The magazine (which soon dropped the 'of Hollywood' from its title)
was hugely successful: the March/April edition of 1941, for example,
sold approximately a quarter of a million copies. In terms of appearance
and content the US publication was strikingly different from C. Arthur
Pearson's *Glamour*. Instead of lurid illustrations of illicit passion and love-
tortured heroines the covers of the US magazine sported photographs
of snappily dressed young girls about town, offering fashion advice to
girls at college and career girls at affordable prices, whilst radiating an
affluence and fashionable self-possession utterly foreign, at that time, to
their counterparts in austerity-ridden Britain.

How does Condé Nast's twenty-first-century UK edition of *Glamour*
magazine compare with its domestically produced predecessor? There
are some continuities, as indicated above, but the contrasts are also
striking. One might be forgiven for putting on sunglasses to contemplate the cover of the modern magazine: the title appears in fluorescent, flame-coloured letters, some of the subtext in fluorescent fuchsia.
Inside, there are no line drawings depicting lovelorn heroines in despair,
no images of exhausted women needing tonics or pep pills, no serials
or even short stories – just glossy, digitally perfected glamour. Page
after page of it. Images of flawless complexions, slinky torsos, pouting
lips, perfect breasts; clothes, food and almost equally luscious-looking
cosmetics. Readers are lured into the magazine like wasps to a honeypot,
invited to gorge on glamour. It is tempting to consider the possibility
that where once the world of glamour offered an imaginary escape from
dullness and routine, the modern imagery constructs reality itself as
glamorous, representing the pursuit of glamour as an imperative, the
new feminine routine.

Should we infer from this that glamour, once an escape, has now
become a prison? This would imply an overly passive view of the female
reader, who probably turns to women's magazines in much the same
spirit as her predecessors, in search of pleasure and light relief. But

along with increasing affluence, there can be little doubt that glamour has become democratised and more available in the West. As women have become richer and more independent, they have chosen to spend more, not less on their appearance. Rosie Boycott, one of the founders of the feminist magazine *Spare Rib* in the 1970s, recalls that one of the hopes she had cherished at the time 'was that women would become less obsessed about their looks, but the reverse has happened'.[15] Are we to consider this one of the failures of feminism in the face of global capitalism?

Excoriating women for vanity and an obsession with personal appearance is as old as literature. As we saw in Chapter 1, the idea of glamour as seductive and artificial, luring away from truth and real worth, was implicit in the meaning of the word from the outset. Towards the end of the twentieth century, theory on the connection between glamour, false values and consumerism was given impetus by the influential writing of John Berger in his *Ways of Seeing* (1972), based upon the television series of the same name.[16] Berger's famous dicta that 'men act and women appear' and that 'men look at women; women watch themselves being looked at' were a starting point for subsequent work on the 'male gaze', whilst his assertion that 'glamour cannot exist without personal social envy being a common and widespread emotion' influenced thinking about consumption.[17] In Berger's opinion, the industrial society, 'which has moved towards democracy and then stopped halfway', was a fertile breeding ground for envy because workers had to live out the contradiction between who and what they were, and what they would ideally like to be. They had the choice between political action or a retreat into daydreams. Since capitalism by its very nature enshrined acquisitiveness as the wellspring of social action, all their hopes would centre on consumption.[18]

Colin Campbell's study *The Romantic Ethic and the Spirit of Modern Consumerism* (1987) started from the premise that consumerism needed investigation and explanation rather than criticism and condemnation.[19] Paying homage to the work of Thorstein Veblen on the ways in which social status might be maintained through 'conspicuous consumption', Campbell argued that more work was necessary to understand the importance of 'imaginative hedonism': daydreaming, fantasy and longing in sustaining desire – and patterns of consumption – in the modern world.[20]

The spirit of modern consumerism, according to Campbell, was imaginative rather than materialistic, the relentless desire for goods depending upon a continuing dynamic relationship between illusion and reality.[21] In the 1990s, academic interest in consumption blossomed, developing ideas generated earlier by Bourdieu, especially the concept of taste as 'cultural capital' and the symbolic meanings of goods and lifestyle.[22] There was growing interest in the status of the body in consumer culture: in particular, in the ways in which technology and advances in cosmetic surgery had given rise to new ideas about the plasticity of the body, and of the performing – and perfectible – self. [23]

Many writers have explored the ways in which appearances have come to count for a great deal in the modern world: an individual's appearance is increasingly seen as an expression of his or her self, and as a key, in part, to personal impact in a society characterised by an abundance of visual imagery and fleeting impressions. In *Modernity and Self-Identity*, Anthony Giddens has argued that 'the body has become a core part of the reflexive project of self-identity'.[24] But there is no shortage of critics ready to deplore this. In *The Fashioned Self* (1991), Joanne Finkelstein declared:

> It is the argument of this book that as long as we continue to value personal appearances, and sustain the enormous industries which trade on this value, namely, the consumer-oriented cosmetic, fashion and therapeutic industries, we authenticate a narrative of human character which is spurious ...[25]

Leaving aside the question of whether society *only* judges on the basis of appearances, there is something of Canute in raillery of this kind. Finkelstein slightly undercuts the force of her own argument by using as her preface the mischievous quotation from Oscar Wilde 'It is only shallow people who do not judge by appearances. The true mystery of the world is the visible, not the invisible.'[26]

Second-wave feminist concern with the sexual politics of appearance from the 1980s fed into discussions about glamour and consumerism, given women's mounting expenditure on beauty products, dieting, fitness, clothing and cosmetics. In *Female Desire* (1984), Rosalind Coward argued that the scrutiny of women's appearance amounted to social and sexual control in a patriarchal society and that insecurity about looks generated widespread anxiety and a sense of inadequacy in women.[27] She observed that the images of women on the covers of magazines in the 1980s no longer smiled ingratiatingly at observers, suggesting that the challenging gaze of the new glamour models connoted sexual arousal and was essentially derived from pornography.[28] Wendy Chapkis's *Beauty Secrets* (1988) dealt in detail with women's insecurities about appearance. Improving one's appearance 'offered a first class journey through life to the second sex'.[29] She concluded that 'the only way enhanced appearance can be a source of pleasure rather than anxiety, is if it is firmly rooted in a sense of our own value independent of it'.[30] Similarly, in *Beauty Bound* (1988), Rita Freedman set out to explore 'how beauty increases women's status by maintaining woman's subordination'. Freedman also asserted the need for women to base their self-image on something other than their appearance.[31] *Face Value: The Politics of Beauty* (1984), by Lakoff and Scherr, is more sophisticated, taking on board the confusion and ambivalence many feminists feel about these issues, and providing some insightful historical analysis.[32] The authors' conclusion, however, that women need to base their self-esteem on something more solid and enduring than physical beauty, is much the same as those of the others.[33] It is hard to imagine anyone disagreeing with this particular line of argument.

As discussed in the previous chapter, feminist writing about the beauty industries developed a harder edge with the publication in 1990 of Naomi Wolf's *The Beauty Myth* and Susan Faludi's *Backlash*.[34] Both envisaged patriarchy as fighting back against the gains in freedom women had made in the 1970s. Wolf emphasised the violence against and resentment of women that she saw as inherent in cosmetic surgery and argued that the ideal of slenderness was alienating women from the realisation of their sexuality. Women's magazines might publish interesting articles with sensible arguments about work, fashion and the body, she argued, but the imagery and photographs used in advertisements undermined these:

> Young women now are being bombarded with a kind of radiation sickness brought on by overexposure to images of beauty pornography, the only source offered them of ways to imagine female sexuality. They go out into the world sexually unprotected: stripped of the repressive assurance of their sexual value conferred by virginity or a diamond ring

> *– one's sexuality was worth something all too concrete in the days when*
> *a man contracted to work for a lifetime to maintain access to it – and*
> *not yet armed with a sense of innate sexual pride.*[35]

The vulnerability of young women, and the ways in which they come to develop self-esteem, are highly important concerns, as of course is the rising incidence of eating disorders, but it is unlikely that these can all be laid squarely at the door of imagery in magazines. The (almost certainly related) problem of obesity is much more widespread than anorexia or bulimia, and its rising incidence prompts important questions about the ways in which appetite and autonomy can become distorted in wealthy consumer societies, and affluence can sometimes fail to deliver satisfaction and well-being.[36] Peter Stearns's wide-ranging study, *Fat History* (1997), shows how a culture of dieting has become bound up with the moral fabric of contemporary US life, and how a broad chronological, comparative historical approach can enlighten our understanding of these issues.[37] Banning photographs of 'size zero' models is unlikely to solve deep-rooted problems of consumer societies in the West: in any case, glamour has historically required rather more ample curves.

The feminist philosopher Sandra Lee Bartky has argued that 'the fashion–beauty complex' parallels 'the military–industrial complex' in the maintenance of capitalist patriarchy.[38] Like many of the theorists discussed so far, she sees the fashion and beauty industries as responsible for creating anxieties about the body, estranging women from their true interests and being conducive to a state of narcissism and alienation. She concedes that there is a problem here, in that many women appear actively to *embrace* this state of alienation. She admits ruefully that 'most teenage girls would rather be Miss America than Madame Curie'.[39] In *Femininity and Domination,* Bartky speculates on the ways in which accusations of narcissism and alienation may have undermined the appeal of feminism to younger women:

> *Feminists are widely regarded as enemies of the family; we are also seen*
> *as enemies of the stiletto heel and the beauty parlor – in a word, as*
> *enemies of glamour. Hostility on the part of some women to feminism*
> *may have its origin here. The women's movement is seen not only to*
> *threaten profound sources of gratification and self-esteem, but also to*
> *attack those rituals, procedures and institutions upon which many*
> *women depend to lessen their sense of bodily deficiency.*[40]

She nevertheless sticks to her philosophical guns, insisting that however much women may enjoy cosmetics and the rituals of adornment, these represent a form of oppression, and concludes that:

> *Repressive narcissistic satisfactions stand in the way of an emergence of an authentic delight in the body ... the woman unable to leave home in the morning without 'putting on her face' will never discover the beauty, character and expressiveness her own face already possesses.*[41]

But is this really the case? What if we were to draw an analogy with gardening, for instance? The beauty of formal gardens doesn't necessarily obscure the beauty of 'natural' growth. An appreciation of 'art' doesn't preclude love of nature. There is more than a streak of Puritanism here.

A search for theoretical or political rigour may have tempted some feminists to underestimate or dismiss the pleasures – and profit – many women derive from bodily adornment. Many of the pleasures – the social and therapeutic benefits of taking time out to visit the hairdresser, beauty parlour, or masseuse – can be real enough. The sociologist Paula Black's work on the use of beauty parlours has highlighted the importance, for many women, of a space in which they can find time for themselves, away from the pressures of work and domesticity.[42] Most of the women she questioned wanted to look acceptable rather than beautiful, to make the best of themselves rather than to measure up to some illusory ideal. Much of the criticism of women's exploitation by the beauty industries has centred on struggles over body shape, but these criticisms need to be balanced against the advantages in terms of nutrition, exercise and fitness that have benefited many women. The unrealistic claims of manufacturers of anti-ageing creams are also regularly targeted as a form of exploitation. There is nothing new in this, of course, but nor is there in many women's scepticism about the efficacy of such claims, which often tempers any real belief in the existence of 'miracle creams'. Eve Merriam, the American poet, feminist and sometime fashion editor of *Glamour* magazine, included a drily witty chapter 'Never too old to be young' in her insightful 1960 study of the fashion industry, *Figleaf*:

> *Tint your hair, slather on the hormone creams, the honey bee jellies, the secret ingredient of the latest youth inducing formula. Try water lily*

lotion – men respond to the dewy fresh look. Try oil of pure sesame seed,
try oil of pure hogwash …[43]

Cosmetics may well represent 'hope in a jar', but this is not say that women *en masse* are duped by manufacturers and advertisers into brainless acceptance of their promises.[44]

Nor can opting for cosmetic surgery necessarily be dismissed as proof of social oppression or 'false consciousness'. In Kathy Davis's study of a group of women in the Netherlands who elected to have cosmetic surgery, *Reshaping the Female Body* (1995), some certainly described themselves as feminists: their motives were complex and their decisions often carefully judged.[45] Decidedly uneasy about the many ways in which surgery may be sought to transcend differences of age, ethnicity and gender as well as simply to look 'normal', Davis powerfully resists any explanation that would deny the subjectivity or agency of those seeking surgery by presenting them as simple victims of ideological manipulation. In a later essay exploring the life and work of Suzanne Noël, a French feminist and pioneer cosmetic surgeon who operated in France between the two world wars, Davis argues that Noël carried out cosmetic surgery in 'a different voice'.[46] She compares Mme Noël's practice and approach with those of the predominantly male cosmetic surgeons of today, and emphasises that most of Noël's female patients sought surgery because they were desperate to earn a living and found their ageing faces a barrier to this. If they were married, it was generally their husbands who were uneasy about their motives for undergoing surgery. Noël saw her intervention – and her craft – as a feminist practice. Decisions about surgery are partly shaped by context, and Davis reiterates her conclusion that women make choices, although not necessarily in circumstances of their own choosing.[47]

Beauty practices, cosmetic interventions, choices about fashion and adornment are all made in a social – and historical – context. Postmodern understandings of identity as fluid rather than fixed, as constructed at least in part through performance rather than set in stone, encourage us to see style not simply in terms of the reflection of the self, but as part of the construction of identity, a continuing and creative process. Elizabeth Wilson has argued eloquently that to see fashion or style simply in terms of women's oppression is to ignore the richness of its cultural and political meanings.[48] More recently, Linda Scott has urged historians to rethink the often complex relationships between fashion and feminism.[49] Glamour – like twentieth-century fashion – has a history inseparable from patriarchy, but the relationships between men and women have changed radically in Britain and the USA over the past century and the task of the historian is to try to make sense of the ways in which dreams, aspirations and style have related to social change, to find a pattern in the richness of fashion's cultural and political meanings.

'Glamour' is a slithery concept. Reka Buckley and Stephen Gundle have described it as a 'fashion buzzword', conveying an idea rather than any precise meaning.[50] They point out that in 1947 the lexicographer Eric Partridge referred to the word 'glamour' somewhat disapprovingly as a 'vogue word' having a momentum of its own, and as having invaded stage gossip, journalism and even the vocabulary of respectable novelists.[51] But words do indeed have a life of their own, which can supply historians with insights into the nature of cultural change. If the word 'glamour' originally connoted magic and enchantment, it had come to mean much more by the time Partridge subjected it to scrutiny. The word's associations with the Hollywood dream factory in the 1930s were to prove enduring, certainly: even into the twenty-first century there would be common reference to 'classic, Hollywood glamour'. But the word was still running away with itself, acquiring connotations of seediness and even soft pornography in the years after the Second World War, a patina of middle age and suggestions of 'the kept woman' in the 1950s and 1960s. Glamour was back with a vengeance, materialistic and brash, in the 1980s. But whereas at the beginning of the twentieth century, glamour implied modernity, its 1980s reincarnation involved a degree of looking back: Hollywood still furnished a reference point, a visual lexicography, a constant source of images and ideas.[52] There was an element of nostalgia, an echo from the past, not always audible, as designers such as Versace or Dolce and Gabbana turned the volume up. Glamour got louder as it became more widely available and became democratised.

Glamour is and probably always has been about fantasy, desire and longing. In the 1920s and 1930s it was linked with modernity and especially the possibilities opened by new technologies such as cinema and fast travel. There was a widening of horizons as people were confronted with different possibilities of living their lives as men and women. A fashion for exoticism reflected the romance, the dreams of escaping from the everyday. The horrors and deprivations of two world wars, with the harshness of social conditions during the Depression, intensified the need for imaginative escape. In spite of the anxieties and strictures of the social critics of cinema and other forms of popular culture of the day, most people were all too aware of the distinction between fantasy and reality. They had little glamour in their lives apart from the cinema, dressing up, and the dance floor.

But there was a sense in which the critics were right, in that aspirations were indeed changing. A central characteristic of modernity in social history is the transition from societies dominated by ascribed status – status based on birth, inheritance and social class – to a more fluid system where an individual (in theory at least) has more scope to shape his or her destiny through personal achievement. Horizons are less circumscribed; there is more movement, geographically and socially. People invest more in education, move to cities, and take their chances. They are judged more on appearances, and by impressions, than would ever have been possible in a less mobile society. This is the case for both men and women, but women's appearances were especially important given the gendered inequities of the time. Women's investment in how they looked became even more important as they entered the workforce in greater numbers during the twentieth century.

Glamour has always been about aspiration. In the 1930s, glamorous women were often seen as gold-diggers, as women on the make. But there was an ambivalence here, reflected in many of the films of the decade. Shrinking violets and submissive women could be boring, on screen as in life, and gutsy, good-looking and glamorous women couldn't always be dismissed as bloodsuckers. Pre-Code Hollywood films such as the Warner Brothers' *Gold Diggers of 1933* played around with some of these contradictions: the women in the film plot to ensnare rich men to revenge themselves on these particular exemplars of capitalism and patriarchy, but somehow romance triumphs and it all turns out just fine. Before the strictures of the Hays Code took effect, actresses such as Barbara Stanwyck, Jean Harlow and Marlene Dietrich had the opportunity to play some wonderfully assertive (and transgressive) roles as resourceful, sexy women. Research on cinema audiences of the day suggests that these powerful and confident performances – when they were not censored, and when they had the opportunity to see them – were particularly enjoyed by women.

The old hierarchies of birth and wealth were symbolically reasserted in Britain with the coronation of Elizabeth II in 1953. Hollywood still influenced British popular fashion to some degree, but reinventions of idealised femininity in the form of the New Look were eclipsing 1930s glamour; debutantes and deference pervaded the popular press. Middle-class respectability reasserted itself, no doubt partly because it was increasingly insecure, but in the meantime glamour was made to look tacky. The bosom-flaunting antics of Diana Dors, Jayne Mansfield and Sabrina, the 'look at me' extravagances of Lady Docker, had a certain popular appeal but little to do with fashion or style; glamour faded into the shadowy world of calendar girls, pin-up models and soft pornography. In the meantime, new challenges to the worlds of both the English lady and the glamour model were brewing, with the efflorescence of youth, pop culture and the sexual revolution.

The 1960s emphasis on the revolutionary and transformative power of youth has probably obscured some of the continuities between the interwar period and that decade, not least the ways in which rising aspirations were acting as a catalyst in the transition from a society based on ascription and deference to one in which social mobility through education and personal achievement was seen as increasingly possible. Women's aspirations, particularly, began to change after the First World War.

War had allowed many to gain experience of work formerly reserved for men. The loss of so many male lives during the war destroyed many women's chances of marriage and as single women they often had no choice but to remain in the labour market.[53] At the same time, widening – though still limited – opportunities for education led many young women to seek work in urban areas, in shops and offices, in local administration, in communications and in journalism. Young, independent women constituted a new market for clothes, cosmetics and new magazines such as *Miss Modern*. These young women patronised the cinemas and dance halls, worked out new living arrangements away from the family home, and the more professionally successful amongst them – secondary school teachers and doctors, for instance – might aspire to holidays abroad and to drive their own cars.

Some of the most important social changes of the twentieth century have been around gender. It is a common complaint that twentieth-century sociologists consistently ignored women in large-scale studies of social mobility, and it can be argued that this has held back our full understanding of the impact of modernity on women.[54] A rising proportion of single women sought to better their own lives in the 1920s and 1930s, and would continue to do so through the Second World War. But rising marriage rates, together with an idealisation of the family and of domesticity in the postwar years, complicated women's ambitions. They received ambiguous messages from an education system which suggested that work and family were difficult to combine, and sometimes it seemed a lot easier to opt for early marriage than to wrestle with limited career options and a patriarchal workplace.[55] At the beginning of the 1960s, some three quarters of all girls left school at the age of fifteen.[56] The majority of women were well aware that it was easier to improve their social status by marrying a successful man than through their own efforts in the labour market. To aspire to becoming a 'kept woman' was still a shrewd career move. A fur coat from a male protector – ideally one's husband – might be seen as proof of having made it.

This situation changed slowly, although it has probably never changed completely. Women still stand to gain more than do men from investing in their appearance: this may be deplored, but can scarcely be denied. At the same time, young educated women of the last quarter of the twentieth century enjoyed a new autonomy, were not unlikely to have feminist views, and had enough self-respect to feel uneasy about resigning their economic independence. They enjoyed having money to spend upon themselves and the idea of being accountable for every penny to a husband seemed unacceptably demeaning. It seemed imprudent, too. With divorce rates rising, who could ensure that the husband would not later go off with a younger – and more glamorous – alternative? If he did this, the wife would probably be censured for not having taken sufficient pains to make herself attractive, and for 'letting herself go'. Aside from the sexual politics of this, a majority of young women now combine paid work with family responsibilities because they have no alternative: soaring property values from the 1990s into the early twenty-first century, and the cost of maintaining a home, have required them to continue earning.

As women have become wealthier and more autonomous through education and employment, they have spent more rather than less on their appearance. In part, the rituals of hairdressing, grooming and body care might be read as supplying some respite from the exhausting

demands of the double shift, of combining domestic and family responsibilities with employment. Against a background of rising prosperity,
there were also issues of self-respect, optimism and pleasure. Those who
studied patterns of expenditure and consumption in working-class life
in the 1900s in Britain recorded that women rarely bought new clothes:
they constantly sacrificed their own needs, whether for clothing or food,
for the sake of husbands and children. The French celebrity hairdresser
Antoine, visiting London in 1905, found shop-window displays full of
clothes for men, and observed that almost everywhere women were
much worse dressed than their menfolk.[57] It was a common observation
that many working-class women in Britain looked middle-aged when
they were still young. Margery Spring-Rice noted in the 1930s that erst-
while pretty girls looked drab after a few years of marriage and appeared
worn out by the age of thirty.[58] The contrast between the appearance
of married and unmarried women remained for a long while – Mass
Observers had commented on this in the 1940s. But by Antoine's own
account, things had changed remarkably between 1905 and the time
of the Second World War: there were many more clothes for women in
the shops and the gulf between the standards of male and female dress
was less apparent.[59] Film footage from the 1930s and 1940s of women
queuing for the sales in big department stores is nevertheless revealing:
to modern eyes the majority of women look old, tired and down-at-heel.[60]
Poverty still makes women look old before their time, but it would be
hard to argue against the contention that the majority of women look
much better today, and well into what used to be regarded as old age,
than did their predecessors. Affluence, aspirations, better nutrition,
dietary awareness, exercise, clothing, 'beauty culture' and cosmetics
have all contributed to this.

It is difficult to reconcile these changes with any all-embracing theory
of women as victims, imprisoned by false consciousness or deluded by
the snares of patriarchy. There are aspects of the glamour industries that
we may deplore, particularly the ways in which advertisers and manufacturers exploit the insecurities of consumers. This is a criticism that can
be levelled at most consumer industries. There are clearly problems with
the extent to which we invest in appearances, and younger women are
prone to particular anxieties about their appearance, as older women
are prone to lament their wrinkles and the loss of their youth. But we

do have choices, and most women are probably capable of enjoying glamour without deluding themselves into a denial of other values or wholly distorting their understanding of life.

Has what we might call the democratisation of glamour led to a bland conformity in standards and ideals of feminine attractiveness? This is an important question if we adopt a wider focus and consider skin whitening, hair straightening, and the ways, for instance, in which women with Asiatic features may aspire to a more 'Westernised' appearance. Standards of beauty are undeniably linked with ethnicity and carry cultural weighting: this argument is propounded strongly by black models and the organisers (since 2006) of beauty contests to select a Miss Black Britain.[61] As noted earlier, these issues were raised in Britain by Claudia Jones in the early 1960s. Issues around ethnicity, skin colour and ideals of feminine beauty are regularly debated in the pages of *Pride*, a British magazine founded in 1990, which is addressed to 'the aspirational modern woman of colour'. But glamour, bound up with artifice, style, performance and attitude is less subject to ethnic hijacking than 'essentialist' conceptions of beauty. And if a certain vision of glamour framed the bland, busty blonde and sun-kissed look fashionable in late twentieth-century California, this must be set against glamour's long association with the oriental and the exotic. In part this has represented the eroticism displaced onto non-white women (and men too), which has allowed for a degree of cultural diversification and heterogeneity in standards of appearance worldwide. But there has undoubtedly been two-way traffic: the glamour that India had for the British in the 1920s, for instance, was reflected in the cosmetics and perfumes popular in Britain at that time, and the glitter and gorgeousness of Bollywood cinema feeds into contemporary notions of glamour in the UK.

Exploring the role of glamour in history shows that it has often served to express a sense of aspiration and entitlement for women as well as a dream of escape from hardship and the everyday. Glamorous women have often expressed an attitude of self-possession and assertiveness in conflict with traditional models of femininity rather than in conformity with them. Glamour has often been perceived as transgressive. There was no shortage of observers in the 1930s prepared to dismiss it as artificial and self-regarding, in the 1950s as vulgar and lacking in class, in the 1960s and 1970s as lacking in youth and innocence, in the 1980s as associated with ambition and an unfeminine materialism.

The word 'glamour' is so widely and loosely used today that we may well argue that it has lost edge and meaning. But it maintains its power of suggestion, a connection with the dreams of the past, a whole history of associations and longing. One writer who understood this well was the British novelist Angela Carter, whose work reflects both a fascination with Hollywood glamour and continual engagement with themes of femininity, performance and illusion.[62] Her last novel, *Wise Children*, explored the lives of twin female chorus girls, Dora and Nora Chance ('the Lucky Chances'), seen through the eyes of the 75-year-old Dora. The writing is exuberant and subversive in the spirit of the carnivalesque. Dora and her sister live out their lives in glorious defiance of patriarchy, poverty and ageing. Deprived (or relieved) of paternal protection by their illegitimacy, raised in highly unconventional circumstances by their grandmother, and embarking on careers that go steadily downhill, they triumph through wit, wisdom, generosity and sheer *joie de vivre*. The end of the story has them putting on their gladrags and glamming up for their distant father's birthday celebrations.[63] They strut their stuff, shouldering off their silver fox fur trench-coats as they ascend the grand staircase, flash bulbs popping, flaunting their still shapely ('not quite catastrophic') legs in starry tights, mutton dressed as lamb, out of sheer delight in the sense of still being alive and kicking. A pair of elderly *grandes dames*, they are a poignant contrast with Gloria Swanson's famous representation of the ageing star Norma Desmond in the film *Sunset Boulevard* precisely because they are so self-aware, with no illusions: their fading glamour no disguise but rather, in the face of all that has to be endured, a celebration of the human condition.

Notes

Introduction

1   Information from *Oxford English Dictionary Online.* There is a very full discussion of the etymology and meaning of the word 'glamour' in Gundle, S., and Castelli, C., *The Glamour System,* Basingstoke: Palgrave Macmillan, 2006, pp. 2–6.

2   See, *inter alia,* Wolf, N., *The Beauty Myth: How Images of Beauty Are Used against Women,* London: Vintage, 1990; Faludi, S., *Backlash: The Undeclared War against Women,* London: Chatto and Windus, 1991. The most extreme representation of this argument is probably Jeffreys, S., *Beauty and Misogyny: Harmful Cultural Practices in the West,* London: Routledge, 2005.

3   See, for instance, Offer, A., *The Challenge of Affluence: Self-Control and Well-Being in the US and Britain since 1850,* Oxford: Oxford University Press, 2006; Barber, B., *Consumed: How Markets Corrupt Children, Infantilize Adults, and Swallow Citizens Whole,* New York and London: Norton, 2007; Bauman, Z., *Consuming Life,* London: Polity, 2007.

4   Grieve, M., *Millions Made My Story,* London: Gollancz, 1964, p. 136. Some introduction to recent work on women and consumption can be found in Andrews, M., and Talbot, M. (eds.), *All the World and*

Her Husband: Women in Twentieth Century Consumer Culture, London: Cassell, 2000, and de Grazia, V., with Furlough, E., *The Sex of Things: Gender and Consumption in Historical Perspective*, Berkeley: University of California Press, 1996.

5   Bowlby, R., *Just Looking: Consumer Culture in Dreiser, Gissing and Zola*, London: Methuen, 1985; see esp. p. 152.

6   See, for instance, Pember Reeves, M., *Round about a Pound a Week*, London: G. Bell and Sons, 1913.

7   Berger, J., *Ways of Seeing*, London: BBC, 1972, p. 148.

8   An argument suggested in a sociological study of working-class girls by Beverley Skeggs; see her *Formations of Class and Gender*, London: Sage, 1997, p. 109. See also Jacobowitz, F., and Lippe, R., 'Empowering Glamour', *Cineaction*, vol. 26/27, 1992, pp. 2–11.

9   This reference cited in the *OED* is from the *Illustrated London News*, 1940, CXCVI, 464/2.

10   Professor Laura Marcus.

11   Glamour is defined as 'a visual language of the enticing that seduces through the deployment of images of theatricality, luxury, sexuality and notoriety' by two recent scholars of the phenomenon. See Buckley, R., and Gundle, S., 'Flash Trash: Gianni Versace and the Theory and Practice of Glamour' in Bruzzi, S., and Gibson, P. Church (eds.), *Fashion Cultures: Theories, Explanations and Analyses*, London: Routledge, 2000, pp. 346–7. See also Stephen Gundle's recent book, *Glamour: A History*, Oxford: Oxford University Press, 2008. The connections between perfume, magic and dreams were memorably explored by the anthropologist Alfred Gell in 'Magic, Perfume, Dream …', in Lewis, I. (ed.), *Symbols and Sentiments: Cross Cultural Studies in Symbolism*, London: Academic Press, 1977.

12   See, for instance, Edwards, M., *Perfume Legends: French Feminine Fragrances*, Paris: H. M. Éditions, 1996. The exhibition in Newcastle was organised by Christine Clennell, and was described in the private subscription magazine *Common Scents*, 2001, issues 10, 11, 12.

13   For an eloquent defence of the claims of dress history see Taylor, L., *The Study of Dress History*, Manchester: Manchester University Press, 2002.

1   The origins of glamour

1   See Gundle, S., and Castelli, C., *The Glamour System*, Basingstoke: Palgrave Macmillan, 2006, pp. 2–6.

2   Berry, W., *A Victim to Glamour, and Other Poems*, Leeds: J. Barmley, 1874.

3   My approach in this book is to examine what contemporaries actually described as 'glamour'. Stephen Gundle's recent *Glamour: A History*, Oxford: Oxford University Press, 2008, adopts a very different approach, arguing that the history of glamour dates back to the eighteenth century.

4   According to the *OED*, 'glamour boy' became slang for members of the RAF, especially flying crews.

5   Beaton, C., *The Glass of Fashion*, London: Weidenfeld and Nicolson, 1954, pp. 36, 38, 40.

6   Hartnell, N., *Silver and Gold*, London: Evans Bros, 1955, p. 17.

7   Beaton, *Glass of Fashion*, p. 38.

8   Hartnell, *Silver and Gold*, pp. 58–9.

9   Glyn, E., *Three Weeks*, London: Duckworth, 1907.

10   Glyn, A., *Elinor Glyn: A Biography*, London: Hutchinson, 1955, pp. 94, 320.

11   Fowler, M., *The Way She Looks Tonight: Five Women of Style*, New York: St Martin's Press, 1996, p. 116.

12   Glyn, E., *Romantic Adventure*, London: Ivor Nicholson and Watson, 1936.

13   See, *inter alia*, Etherington-Smith, M., and Pilcher, J., *The 'It' Girls: Lucy, Lady Duff Gordon, the Couturière 'Lucile', and Elinor Glyn, Romantic Novelist*, London: Hamish Hamilton, 1986.

14   Glyn, E., *The Career of Katherine Bush*, London: Duckworth, 1917. Anthony Glyn comments that the story illustrates Elinor's (highly unromantic) aphorism that 'It is wiser to marry the life that you like, because after a little while, the man doesn't matter', Glyn, A., *Elinor Glyn*, p. 235. He also points out that the novel was extremely popular, especially in Britain.

15   Glyn, A., *Elinor Glyn*, pp. 301–2; Glyn. E., *'It' and Other Stories*, London: Duckworth, 1927.

16   Glyn, A., *Elinor Glyn*, p. 279.

17 For discussion of some of these images see, *inter alia*, Melman, B., *Women and the Popular Imagination in the Twenties: Flappers and Nymphs*, Basingstoke: Macmillan, 1988.

18 See Bingham, A., *Gender, Modernity and the Popular Press in Inter-War Britain*, Oxford: Clarendon Press, 2004, pp. 47–50.

19 Barlow, T., Yue Dong, M., Poiger, U., Ramamurthy, P., Thomas, L., and Weinbaum, A. (The Modern Girl around the World Research Group), 'The Modern Girl around the World: A Research Agenda and Preliminary Findings', *Gender and History*, 2005, vol. 17, no. 2, pp. 245–94.

20 Hammerton, J., *For Ladies Only? Eve's Film Review, Pathé Cinemagazine, 1921–1933*, Hastings: The Projection Box, 2001, pp. 102, 92–106.

21 Hutchinson, A. S. M., *This Freedom*, London: Hodder and Stoughton, 1922. A film based on the novel was made in the following year.

22 Information from IMDb, www.imdb.com/title/tt0021273/.

23 Arlen, M., *The Green Hat: A Romance for a Few People*, London: Collins, 1924.

24 Display advertisement for Harrods, 'Exhibition of Japanese Kimonos', *The Times*, 20 November 1922, p. 9.

25 See Horwood, C., '"Girls Who Arouse Dangerous Passions": Women and Bathing, 1900–1939', *Women's History Review*, 2000, vol. 9, no. 4, pp. 653–73.

26 See, for instance, www.screenonline.org.uk/history/id/1195318/index; also www.britishpathe.com. There is a useful list of *Eve's Film Review* items in Hammerton, *For Ladies Only?*, Appendix 2, pp. 119–24.

27 Lee, J., *This Great Journey*, New York and Toronto: Farrar and Rinehart, 1942, p. 59.

28 Arlen, *The Green Hat*, pp. 30, 42, 47, 305, 309.

29 Beaton, C., *The Book of Beauty*, London: Duckworth, 1930, p. 41.

30 Bankhead, T., *Tallulah*, London: Gollancz, 1952, p. 157.

31 Graves, R., and Hodge, A., *The Long Weekend*, London: Faber, 1940, p. 39.

32 See Woodhead, L., *War Paint: Elizabeth Arden and Helena Rubinstein, Their Lives, Their Times, Their Rivalry*, London: Virago, 2004.

33 *Ibid.*, p. 6; see also Peiss, K., *Hope in a Jar: The Making of America's Beauty Culture*, New York: Henry Holt, 1998.

34 Woodhead, *War Paint*, p. 52.

35   *Ibid.*, p.101.

36   Rubinstein, H., *The Art of Feminine Beauty*, London: Gollancz, 1930, pp. 55–6.

37   Angeloglou, M., *A History of Make-up*, London: Studio Vista, 1970, p. 115.

38   *Common Scents*, 2001, issue 11.

39   'Hasu-no-Hana' (Japanese Lotus), 'Shem-el-Nessim' (Scent of Araby), 'Wana-Ranee' (Scent of Ceylon), 'Phul-Nana' (Indian Flowers), 'Tsang-Ihang' (Perfume of Tibet). For reference to 'servant girls' perfume' see Angeloglou, p. 115, who suggests that 'only the poorest girls or a fast woman used Phul-Nana'. See also the reference in Angela Carter, *Wise Children*, London: Vintage, 1991, p. 61.

40   Edwards, M., *Perfume Legends: French Feminine Fragrances*, Paris: H. M. Éditions, 1996, pp. 32–7; Irvine, S., *The Perfume Guide*, London: Haldane Mason, 2000, p. 111.

41   Edwards, *Perfume Legends*, pp. 54–9; Irvine, *Perfume Guide*, p. 139.

42   'Dubarry Toilet Luxuries are World Famous', *Brighton Standard*, 29 August 1951, p. 3.

43   For connections between modern girls, smoking, eroticism and exoticism see Tinkler, P., *Smoke Signals: Women, Smoking and Visual Culture*, Oxford: Berg, 2006, esp. chapters 4 and 5; Kalmar, I., 'The Houkah in the Harem: On Smoking and Orientalist Art', in Gilman, S. L. and Xun, Z. (eds.), *Smoke: A Global History of Smoking*, London: Reaktion, 2004.

44   Edwards, *Perfume Legends*, pp. 38–47.

45   Quoted by Kennedy, W., *Birds and Their Protection* (Society for the Protection of Birds), Hertford: Stephen Austin, 1895, pp. 15–16.

46   Hudson, W. H., *Osprey; or Egrets and Aigrettes*, London: Royal Society for Protection of Birds, 1894. See also Cocker, M., and Mabey, R., *Birds Britannica*, London: Chatto and Windus, 2005, p. 50.

47   Rushton, P., *Mrs Tinne's Wardrobe: A Liverpool Lady's Clothes, 1900–1940*, Liverpool: Bluecoat Press, 2006, pp. 114, 139–40.

48   'Violet Hopson's Fashion Fancies', *Girls' Cinema*, no. 1, 16 October 1920.

49   Ewing, E., *Fur in Dress*, London: Batsford, 1981.

50   Laut, A., *The Fur Trade of America*, New York: Macmillan, 1921, pp. 25, 50.

51   Editorial article, 'Our Policy and Other Matters', *British Fur Trade*, September 1923, no. 1, p. 25.

52   Rushton, *Mrs Tinne's Wardrobe*, pp. 64–70.

53   Sally Alexander notes that Arthur Harding in *East End Underworld* dated the passion for fur coats amongst women in Bethnal Green from the beginning of the First World War (Samuel, R. [ed.], *East End Underworld: Chapters in the Life of Arthur Harding*, London: Routledge and Kegan Paul, 1981, p. 237, cited in Alexander, S., *Becoming a Woman and Other Essays in 19th and 20th Century Feminist History*, London: Virago, 1994, pp. 222–3). Harding comments that 'Fur coats became the ambition of all the young girls', and his tone is infused with resentment: 'There were people buying fur coats who never had a bed to lay on. One man, Mr Easton, he was getting his bloody legs blown off in Flanders and his kids were sleeping on the floor, but his wife had a fur coat which cost about seventy guineas.'

54   *Our Animal Brothers*, vol. 1, London: Wells Gardner, 1906, and vol. 2, London: Simpkin, Marshall, Hamilton and Kent, 1907; Carrington, E., *The Dog: His Rights and Wrongs*, London: Bell and Sons, 1896; *Peeps into Birdland*, London: Nelson, 1989; and *Grandmother Pussy*, London: Cassell, 1904.

55   Our Animal Brothers' Guild, *Fashionable Furs: How They Are Obtained*, Bristol: 1911.

56   Ewing, *Fur in Dress*, pp. 106–10.

57   Advertisement for J. Woolf, 'Dressers and Cleaners' (in East End of London), *British Fur Trade*, 23 October 1923, p. 135.

58   *British Fur Trade Yearbook, 1933*, London: Hutchinson, 1933, Appendix: Hudson's Bay Company sales, pp. 419–45.

59   Advertisement for Revillon Frères in *Vogue*, 31 October 1928, p. 3.

60   On the romance of fur-getting see Mallet, Captain Thierry, *Glimpses of the Barren Lands*, New York: Revillon Frères, 1930; Sexé, M., *Two Centuries of Fur Trading, 1723–1923: The Romance of the Revillon Family*, Paris: Draeger Frères, 1923. Pudovkin's film *Storm over Asia* (1928) explores and dramatises the social class, political and gender dimensions of fur-getting.

2 Hollywood glamour

1   Nicholson, V., *Singled Out: How Two Million Women Survived without Men after the First World War*, London: Viking, 2007.

2   Cited in Castelbajac, K. de, *The Face of the Century: 100 Years of Make-up and Style*, New York: Rizzoli, 1987, p. 76.

3   Hollander, A., *Seeing through Clothes*, New York: Viking, 1978, pp. 342–3.

4   Bordwell, D., *Hollywood Glamour, 1924–1956: Selected Portraits from the Wisconsin Center for Film and Theater Research*, Introduction to Exhibition Catalogue, Elvehjem Museum of Art, University of Wisconsin: Madison, 1987.

5   Vieira, M., *Hurrell's Hollywood Portraits: The Chapman Collection*, New York: Harry N. Abrams, 1997, p. 51.

6   For discussion of the colour red as indicative of transgression in Hollywood cinema see, *inter alia*, Gundle, S., and Castelli, C., *The Glamour System*, Basingstoke: Palgrave Macmillan, 2006, pp. 116–22.

7   McConathy, D., and Vreeland, D., *Hollywood Costume: Glamour! Glitter! Romance!*, New York: Harry N. Abrams, 1976, p. 23.

8   *Ibid.*, p. 28.

9   Fowler, M., *The Way She Looks Tonight: Five Women of Style*, New York: St Martin's Press, 1996, p. 155.

10 Harlow, G., 'Diamonds in the Twentieth Century,' in Harlow, G. (ed.), *The Nature of Diamonds*, Cambridge: Cambridge University Press in association with the American Museum of Natural History, 1998, esp. pp. 211–13; Epstein, E., 'Have You Ever Tried to Sell a Diamond?', www.edwardjayepstein.com/diamond/chap20.

11 Spiegel, M., 'Hollywood Loves Diamonds', in Harlow (ed.), *Nature of Diamonds*, pp. 199–206.

12 *Ibid.* Epstein, chapter 13, 'The Diamond Mind'.

13 Epstein, chapter 13, 'The Diamond Mind'.

14 Loos, A., *Gentlemen Prefer Blondes*, London: Hamish Hamilton, 1926.

15 Chierichetti, D., *Hollywood Costume Design*, London: Studio Vista, 1976, p. 218.

16 Sontag, S., *Against Interpretation*, New York: Dell Publishing, 1966, p. 283.

17 McConathy and Vreeland, *Hollywood Costume*, pp. 61–2.

18 Society for the Protection of Birds, 'Feathered Women', pamphlet no. 10, originally published anonymously as a letter to *The Times*, 17 October 1893.

19 *Ibid.*

20 McDowell, C., *Hats: Status, Style and Glamour*, London: Thames and Hudson, 1992, p. 114.

21 McConathy and Vreeland, *Hollywood Costume,* p. 22.

22 Fowler, *The Way She Looks Tonight*, p. 130; Naudet, J., and Riva, M., *Marlene Dietrich: Photographs and Memories*, New York: Alfred A. Knopf, 2001, p. xxvi.

23 Fowler, *The Way She Looks Tonight*, p. 167.

24 In the film *Ziegfeld Girl* (1941), 'Red' (Lana Turner) boasts to a boyfriend from back home that she is now wealthy enough to throw frocks away when they are dirty, and in her Park Avenue apartment she shows him a cupboard stuffed with fur coats. She recalls that her first fur coat smelt of dog when it got wet, emphasising that she is now successful enough to be able to walk on fur coats if she wants to.

25 Tapert, A., *The Power of Glamour: The Women Who Defined the Magic of Stardom*, London: Aurum Press, 1999, p. 23.

26 McDowell, C., *Dressed to Kill: Sex, Power and Clothes*, London: Hutchinson, 1992, p. 30.

27 LaVine, W. Robert, *In a Glamorous Fashion: The Fabulous Years of Hollywood Costume Design*, London: Allen and Unwin, 1981, p. 64.

28 Chierichetti, *Hollywood Costume Design*, p. 25.

29 Bill Nichols, quoted in DelGaudio, S., *Dressing the Part: Sternberg, Dietrich and Costume*, New York: Associated University Presses, 1993, p. 54.

30 *Ibid.*, p. 140.

31 Forbes, J., 'Furs – and Whence They Come', *The Morning Post* (Fur Supplement), 1 October 1934.

32 *Furriers' Journal*, 30 May 1936, p. 5.

33 Rogers, P., *What Becomes a Legend Most? The Blackglama Story*, New York: Simon and Schuster, 1979. See also Fowler, *The Way She Looks Tonight*, pp. 121–4, for Dietrich's participation in the Blackglama advertising campaign.

34 Fowler, *The Way She Looks Tonight*, pp. 162, 167.

35   Quoted by Castelbajac, *The Face of the Century*, p. 80.

36   Advertisements for Espanol in *Miss Modern*, November 1930, p. 8; for Marmola in *Woman and Beauty*, 30 April, p. 11.

37   Young, J., *The Medical Messiahs: A Social History of Health Quackery in Twentieth-Century America*, Chapter 6, 'Truth in Advertising', at www. quackwatch.com/

38   Horwood, C., '"Girls Who Arouse Dangerous Passions": Women and Bathing, 1900–1939', *Women's History Review*, 2000, vol. 9, no. 4, pp. 653–73.

39   *Ibid.*, p. 662.

40   Matthews, J., 'They Had Such a Lot of Fun: The Women's League of Health and Beauty', *History Workshop Journal*, 1990, vol. 30, pp. 22–54.

41   Tapert, *Power of Glamour*, p. 21.

42   Carr, L., *Four Fabulous Faces: The Evolution and Metamorphosis of Garbo, Swanson, Crawford and Dietrich*, New Rochelle, NY: Arlington House, 1970, pp. 124–30, 272–3.

43   Tapert, *Power of Glamour*, p. 242; Fowler, *The Way She Looks Tonight*, p. 170.

44   Carr, *Four Fabulous Faces*, pp. 123–30.

45   *Ibid.*, pp. 275–97.

46   Tapert, *Power of Glamour*, p. 242.

47   Castelbajac, *The Face of the Century*, p. 71.

48   Rubinstein, H., *The Art of Feminine Beauty*, London: Gollancz, 1930, p. 264.

49   Castelbajac, *The Face of the Century*, p. 68.

50   *Ibid.*, p. 80.

51   Antonia White in *Picture Post*, 8 October 1938, p. 57.

52   Corson, R., *Fashions in Make-up*, London: Peter Owen, 1972, p. 540.

53   'Charlady into Glamour Girl', *Picture Post*, 17 June 1939, pp. 52–5.

54   *Ibid.*

55   Pickford, M., *Sunshine and Shadow*, London: Heinemann, 1956, quoted in McConathy and Vreeland, *Hollywood Costume*, p. 39.

56   Banner, L., *American Beauty*, New York: Knopf, 1983, p. 136.

57   Tapert, *Power of Glamour*, p. 97.

58   Beaton, C., *The Book of Beauty*, London: Duckworth, 1930, pp. 46–7.

59   Antoine, *Antoine by Antoine*, London: W. H. Allen, 1946, p. 128.

60   Newquist, R., *Conversations with Joan Crawford*, New Jersey: Citadel Press, 1980, frontispiece.

61   Trent, P., *The Image Makers: Sixty Years of Hollywood Glamour*, London: Octopus, 1973, p. 54.

62   McConathy and Vreeland, *Hollywood Costume*, p. 55.

63   Hartnell, N., *Silver and Gold*, London: Evans Bros, 1955, p. 56.

64   Advertisements for Chanel's Glamour by Fenwicks, *Newcastle Daily Journal*, 22 November 1934. I owe the reference to Christine Clennell, *Common Scents*, issue 17, 2003.

65   Massey, A., *Hollywood Beyond the Screen: Design and Material Culture*, Oxford: Berg, 2000, pp. 133–5.

66   Thorp, M., *America at the Movies*, London: Faber and Faber, 1945, p. 52.

67   *Ibid.*, chapter 3.

68   *Ibid.*, p. 50.

69   See useful collections of photographs in Bordwell, *Hollywood Glamour*; also Vieira, *Hurrell's Hollywood Portraits*.

70   McConathy and Vreeland, *Hollywood Costume*, p. 137.

71   Quoted in Tapert, *Power of Glamour*, p. 232.

72   *Ibid.*, p. 63.

73   Chierichetti, *Hollywood Costume Design*, p. 50.

74   Vieira, *Hurrell's Hollywood Portraits*, pp. 175–6.

75   Quoted by Cadwalladr, C., in review of Chandler, C., *The Girl Who Walked Home Alone*, London: Simon and Schuster, 2006, published in the *Observer*, 18 June 2006.

76   Thorp, *America at the Movies*, p. 55.

77   Kuhn, A., *An Everyday Magic: Cinema and Cultural Memory*, London: I. B. Tauris, 2002, p. 110.

3 Dreams, desires and spending

1   Richards, J., *The Age of the Dream Palace: Cinema and Society in Britain, 1930–1939*, London: Routledge and Kegan Paul, 1984, pp. 12–15.

2   Stacey, J., *Star Gazing: Hollywood Cinema and Female Spectatorship*, London: Routledge, 1994, pp. 95–111.

3   A classic early analysis of this can be found in Powdermaker, H., *Hollywood the Dream Factory: An Anthropologist Looks at the Moviemakers*, Boston: Little Brown, 1950. See also Thorp, M., *America at the Movies*, London: Faber and Faber, 1945.

4   Spencer, D. A., and Waley, H. D., *The Cinema Today*, Oxford: Oxford University Press, 1956, p. 153.

5   *Ibid.*

6   Mayer, J. P., *British Cinemas and Their Audiences*, London: Dobson, 1948, p. 36.

7   *Ibid.*, p. 52.

8   *Ibid.*, p. 57.

9   *Ibid.*, p. 66.

10   For the USA, see Berry, S., *Screen Style: Fashion and Femininity in 1930s Hollywood*, Minneapolis: University of Minnesota Press, 2000; for Britain, Massey, A., *Hollywood beyond the Screen: Design and Material Culture*, Oxford: Berg, 2000.

11   *Girls' Cinema*, 9 July 1932, p. 23.

12   Alexander, S., *Becoming a Woman and Other Essays in 19th and 20th Century Feminist History*, London: Virago, 1994, p. 223.

13   Walsh, J., *Not Like This*, London: Lawrence and Wishart, 1953, p. 31.

14   Brittain, V. (ed. Bishop, A.), *Chronicle of Friendship: Diary of the Thirties*, London: Gollancz, 1986, p. 58.

15   *Film Fashionland*, May 1934.

16   *Woman's Filmfair*, 1934, vol. 1 no. 4, p. 54.

17   Kuhn, A., *An Everyday Magic: Cinema and Cultural Memory*, London: I. B. Tauris, 2002, chapter 5.

18   *Ibid.*, p. 114.

19   Mayer, *British Cinemas and Their Audiences*, p. 57.

20   Kuhn, *An Everyday Magic*, pp. 112–14.

21   Mayer, *British Cinemas and Their Audiences*, p. 83.

22   Tapert, A., *The Power of Glamour: The Women Who Defined the Magic of Stardom*, London: Aurum Press, 1999, p. 215.

23   *British Fur Trade Yearbook*, London: Hutchinson, 1933.

24   'Fur Farming an Industry for Women?', *British Fur Trade*, February 1936, p. 41.

25   *Hutchinson's Woman's Who's Who*, London: Hutchinson, 1934, pp. 629–30.

26   'Furs on the Move', 8 January 1931, www.britishpathe.com, ref. 930.04. See also Hammerton, J., *For Ladies Only? Eve's Film Review, Pathé Cinemagazine, 1921–1933*, Hastings: The Projection Box, 2001, pp. 78–9.

27   Waugh, E., *A Handful of Dust*, London: Chapman and Hall, 1934.

28   Listed in *British Fur Trade Yearbook*.

29   *Furriers' Journal*, 25 July 1936, p. 5.

30   Advertisements for Imperial Fur Traders in the *British Fur Trade*: 'Three Selected Quick Sellers', January 1937, p. 45; 'Four Forceful Selling Lines', March 1937, p. 33.

31   Advertisement for Swears and Wells, 'The World's Biggest Fur Sale – by the World's Biggest Furriers', *Daily Herald*, 1 October 1938, p. 4.

32   Mass Observation Topic Collection 18 (Personal Appearance and Clothes), Box 2; Notes on closing-down sale at Revillon, Regent St, January 1940. In MO Archive, University of Sussex.

33   'Women Rush for Fur Bargains', press cutting from *Evening Standard*, 1 January 1940, in MO Topic 18, Box 5.

34   Notes of interview with Elizabeth Wray, 15 December 1939, MO Topic 18, Box 2.

35   Notes of interview with manageress of Samuel Soden (Regent Street furrier), 27 February 1942, MO Topic 18, Box 4.

36   *Ibid.*

37   'Utility Furs', 23 April 1944, www.britishpathe.com, ref. 1215.09.

38   Angeloglou, M., *A History of Make-up*, London: Studio Vista, 1970, p. 122.

39   Reference from example shown in *Common Scents*, issue 17, Summer 2003.

40   Rodaway, A., *A London Childhood*, London: Virago, 1985, p. 149.

41   *Ibid.*, p. 124.

42   *Ibid.*

43   Wyndham, J., *Love Lessons*, London: Virago, 2001, p. 30.

44   MO Topic 18, Box 2, Observer notes dated 8 August 1940.

45   Glyn, E., 'It', *Miss Modern*, October 1930, p. 31.

46   'Is the Modern Girl a Gold-Digger?', *Woman's Film Fair*, December 1934, pp. 21–2.

47   Banning, M., 'The Lipstick Mood', *Woman and Beauty*, January 1931, pp. 12–15.

48   *Ibid.*

49   Carter, A., 'The Wound in the Face', in *Nothing Sacred: Selected Writings*, London: Virago, 1982, p. 94.

50   Photograph in Imperial War Museum of ambulance worker, Kennington; see also Ragas, M. C., and Kozlowski, K., *Read My Lips: A Cultural History of Lipstick*, San Francisco: Chronicle, 1998.

51   *Picture Post*, 26 April 1947, p. 29.

52   Windsor, HRH Edward, Duke of, *A King's Story*, London: Prion, 1951, pp. 187–8.

53   MO Report, July 1939, Personal appearance: Hands, Face and Hair (A 21).

54   Advertisements for Chanel and Schiaparelli by Fenwick's, *Newcastle Daily Journal*, 22 November 1934, cited by Christine Clennell, *Common Scents*, 2003, issue 17.

55   Advertisement for Californian Poppy, *Picturegoer*, 13 December 1941, p. 15.

56   Settle, A., *Clothes Line*, London: Methuen, 1937, p. 97.

57   Advertisement for Yardley's Orchis, *Vogue*, 30 October 1935, p. 14.

58   *Woman's Fair*, October 1939, p. 103.

59   *Woman's Fair*, December 1939, p. 54.

60   Collins, D., *A Nose for Money: How to Make a Million*, London: Michael Joseph, 1963, pp. 93–4.

61   *Ibid.*, Chapter 19.

62   *Ibid.*, p. 106.

63   Advert for Coty Chypre, *Woman's Journal*, November 1938, p. 135.

64   *Film Fashionland*, February 1935, pp. 24–5, and March 1935, pp. 24–5.

65   Stacey, J., *Star Gazing: Hollywood Cinema and Female Spectatorship*, London: Routledge, 1994.

66   Priestley, J. B., *English Journey*, London: Heinemann, 1934, p. 401;
      Orwell, G., *The Road to Wigan Pier*, Harmondsworth: Penguin, 1972
      (1937), p. 79.

67   Burke, T., *London in My Time*, London: Rich and Cowan, 1934, pp.
      65–6, quoted in Robson, J. M., 'The Role of Clothing and Fashion in
      the Household Budget and Popular Culture; Britain, 1919–1949',
      unpublished University of Oxford D.Phil thesis, 1997–8, p. 172.

68   Mayer, *British Cinemas and Their Audiences*, pp. 83, 90; see also Kuhn,
      An Everyday Magic, pp. 114–16 and *passim*.

69   See Kuhn, A., 'Cinema Culture and Femininity in the 1930s', in
      Gledhill, C., and Swanson, G. (eds.), *Nationalising Femininity: Culture,
      Nationality and British Cinema in the Second World War*, Manchester:
      Manchester University Press, 1996.

70   Kuhn, *An Everyday Magic*, pp. 173–4.

71   From a letter in *Picturegoer*, 17 March 1945, quoted in Stacey, *Star
      Gazing*, p. 58.

72   Stacey, *Star Gazing*, p. 113.

73   *Ibid.*, pp. 154–62.

74   Basinger, J., *A Woman's View: How Hollywood Spoke to Women, 1930–
      1960*, London: Chatto and Windus, 1994, pp. 6–7 and *passim*.

75   'It's a Tough Life Being Glamorous', *Picture Post*, 19 October 1946,
      pp. 12–13.

76   The full advertisement in *Glamour* (4 May 1948) went as follows:
      'Holly-Pax from Hollywood: A Promise of Freedom from the City
      of Stars, Modern insertion-type Sanitary Protection'. There was an
      accompanying verse:

> *These modern days need modern ways*
> *That's why so many girls approve*
> *The name of Holly-Pax today –*
> *So up-to-date in every way*
> *No can't-wear-that or can't-do-this*
> *Here's freedom for the Modern Miss*
> *The old restrictions go for good*
> *With Holly-Pax from Hollywood.*

77   Sforzia, T., 'Glamourizing the English Girl', *Women's Filmfair*, July
      1934, pp. 12–13.

78   Advert for Bile Beans, *Picturegoer and Film Weekly*, 18 January 1941.

79   Horwood, C., *Keeping Up Appearances: Fashion and Class Between the Wars*, Stroud: Sutton Publishing, 2005.

80   Rushton, P., *Mrs Tinne's Wardrobe: A Liverpool Lady's Clothes, 1900–1940*, Liverpool: Bluecoat Press, 2006, pp. 60–1.

81   Settle, *Clothes Line*, p. 60.

82   Godfrey Winn in *Miss Modern*, January 1932, p. 9, quoted in Horwood, *Keeping Up Appearances*, p. 67.

83   Winship, J., 'Culture of Restraint: The British Chain Store, 1920–1939', in Jackson, P., Lowe, M., Miller, D., and Mort, F. (eds.), *Commercial Cultures: Economies, Practices, Spaces*, Oxford: Berg, 2000.

84   Lehmann, R., *Invitation to the Waltz*, London: Virago, 2001 (1932).

85   Brittain, *Chronicle of Friendship*, p. 339.

86   Quoted in Lee, H., *Virginia Woolf*, London: Vintage, 1997, p. 390.

87   Collins, *A Nose for Money*, p. 130.

88   MO Topic 18, Box 2, File 1/F, Observation dated 8 August 1940.

89   *Ibid.*

90   *Ibid.*

91   Langhamer, C., *Women's Leisure in England, 1920–1960*, Manchester: Manchester University Press, 2000, pp. 95–6.

92   MO Topic 18, Box 2, File 1/F.

93   *Ibid.*, Files 1/B, 1/F. In some of the tabulated results, the word 'Jewess' is typed in red; see Box 5, File E.

94   *Ibid.*, Box 2, 1/E.

95   *Ibid.*, Box 2, 1/C.

96   Harrisson, T., 'MO on Fashions', Press release dated April 1939, MO Topic 18, Box 2.

97   *Ibid.*

98   *Ibid.* See also 2/C, 2/F and notes on 'Mad Hattery', Box 5 (5/A and 5/B).

99   Garland, A., *Lion's Share*, London: Michael Joseph, 1970, p. 47.

100   Notes on interviews dated 15 December 1939, MO Topic 18, Box 2, File A.

101   Harrisson, T., 'Mad Hattery', in MO Topic 18, Box 5.

102   From MO, *Preliminary Report on Fashion Covering the Period September 1939 to February 1940*, A 28, p. 15.

103   Press cutting from *Daily Telegraph*, 15 April 1940 in MO Topic 18, Box 5, File C.

104 Press cutting of article 'Hats', by 'Mr K. P.', from *Daily Mirror*, 18 March 1940, in MO Topic 18, 5/A.

105 Ironside, J., *Janey*, London: Michael Joseph, 1973, p. 45.

106 From *Miss Modern*, November 1940, p. 18, quoted in Tinkler, P., *Constructing Girlhood: Popular Magazines for Girls Growing Up in England, 1920–1950*, London: Taylor and Francis, 1995.

107 'Trying on a Lipstick', *Picture Post*, 7 October 1939, pp. 40–1.

108 MO Topic 18, Box 2, File 1/G.

109 Wilson, E., and Taylor, L., *Through the Looking Glass: A History of Dress from 1860 to the Present Day*, London: BBC Books, 1989, p. 111.

110 Castle, C., *The Duchess Who Dared: Margaret, Duchess of Argyll*, London: Pan, 1994, p. 32.

111 Summerfield, P., *Reconstructing Women's Wartime Lives*, Manchester: Manchester University Press, 1998, p. 91.

4 Princesses, tarts and cheesecake

1 See Myrdal, A., and Klein, V., *Women's Two Roles*, London: Routledge and Kegan Paul, 1956.

2 Webster, W., *Imagining Home: Gender, 'Race' and National Identity, 1945–64*, London: UCL Press, 1998.

3 Advert for Kestos, *Woman's Own*, 25 September 1957, p. 6.

4 MO, *Preliminary Report on Fashion Covering the Period September 1939 to February 1940*, A 28, p. 3.

5 Settle, A., 'AS Notes on Fashion in the War Years 1939–45/6', B 405.31, Alison Settle Archive, University of Brighton.

6 Quoted in Lakoff, R., and Scherr, R., *Face Value: The Politics of Beauty*, London: Routledge and Kegan Paul, 1984, p. 87.

7 Steele, V., *Fifty Years of Fashion: New Look to Now*, New Haven and London: Yale University Press, 1997, p. 11.

8 Garland, A., *Lion's Share*, London: Michael Joseph, 1970, p. 40.

9 Marshall, C., *The Cat-Walk*, London: Hutchinson, 1978, p. 29.

10 Settle, A., 'Viewpoint', *Observer*, 11 March 1956. From a collection of cuttings in Alison Settle Archive, University of Brighton Library.

11 *Ibid.*

12 Settle, A., 'Viewpoint', 12 May 1957.

13   Merriam, E., *Figleaf: The Business of Being in Fashion*, Philadelphia and New York: Lippincott, 1960, pp. 212–13.

14   The Elizabeth Arden 'giant roller' was pictured in *Harper's Bazaar*, January 1950, p. 52.

15   Merriam, *Figleaf*, p. 20.

16   Turim, M., 'Designing Women: The Emergence of the New Sweetheart Line', in Gaines, J., and Herzog, C., *Fabrications: Costume and the Female Body*, London: Routledge, 1990, p. 225.

17   MO *Report on the New Look*, 3095, March 1949, p. 11.

18   *Woman's Own*, 24 January 1952.

19   Steedman, C., *Landscape for a Good Woman: A Story of Two Lives*, London: Virago, 1986, p. 32.

20   Settle, A., 'AS Notes on Fashion in the War Years 1939–45/6', B 405.38, Alison Settle Archive, University of Brighton.

21   Hartnell, N., *Silver and Gold*, London: Evans Brothers, 1955, p. 76.

22   Settle, A., 'Viewpoint', 12 May 1957.

23   Mulvagh, J., *Costume Jewellery in Vogue*, London: Thames and Hudson, 1998, p. 84.

24   Settle, A., 'Viewpoint', 27 February 1955.

25   Mulvagh, *Costume Jewellery in Vogue*, pp. 84 ff.

26   Settle, A., 'Viewpoint', 16 December 1956.

27   *Costume Jewellery and Fashion Accessories*, no. 1, 1956, p. 19.

28   Boston, J., 'All That Glitters', *Film and Fashion*, September 1948, p. 10.

29   Settle, A., 'Viewpoint', 17 July 1955.

30   Mulvagh, *Costume Jewellery in Vogue*, p. 111.

31   Links, J., *The Book of Fur*, London: James Barrie, 1956, p. 139.

32   Settle, A., *Clothes Line*, London: Methuen, 1937, pp. 220–1.

33   Settle, A., 'Viewpoint', 14 August 1955.

34   Settle, A., 'Viewpoint', 4 March 1956.

35   Settle, A., 'AS Notes on Fashion in the War Years 1939–45/6', B 405.5, 7.

36   *Glamour and Peg's Paper*, January 1948, p. 10.

37   Settle, A., 'Viewpoint', 17 October 1954.

38   Links, *Book of Fur*, p. 184.

39   Durbar, Leslie, *British Fur Trade*, January 1957, p. 4.

40   *Vogue*, July 1952, p. 16, and August 1952, p. 16.

41   Settle, A., 'Viewpoint', 9 December 1956.

42   Settle, A., 'Viewpoint', 25 November 1956.

43   Haugland, H. Kristina, *Grace Kelly: Icon of Style to Royal Bride*, New Haven: Yale University Press, 2006, p. 15.

44   Day, Diana, *Woman's Own*, 14 August 1952, p. 17.

45   *Oxford English Dictionary Online.*

46   *Ibid.*

47   *Ibid.*

48   Hoggart, R., *The Uses of Literacy: Aspects of Working Class Life, with Special Reference to Publications and Entertainments*, London: Chatto and Windus, 1957, p. 177.

49   Buszek, M. E. 'War Goddess, the Varga Girls, WWII and Feminism', *N. Paradoxa*, issue 6, 1998. web.ukonline.co.uk/n.paradoxa/buszek.

50   *Ibid.*

51   *Ibid.* For 'nose art' see Wood, J., *Aircraft Nose Art: 80 Years of Aviation Artwork*, London: Salamander, 1992.

52   'An Experiment in Taste – What Is a Pin-Up Girl?', *Picture Post*, 23 September 1944, pp. 14–15, 25.

53   'Horace Roye' was a pseudonym for Horace Narbeth. Roye's publications included *Perfect Womanhood: 48 Photographic Studies*, London: George Routledge, 1938; *The English Maid*, London: George Routledge, 1939; and, with Vala, *Stereo-Glamour Series: Transatlantic Authors for the Camera Studies Club*, London, 1958.

54   Jane first appeared in the *Daily Mirror* in 1932: see Bingham, A., *Gender, Modernity and the Popular Press in Inter-War Britain*, Oxford: Clarendon Press, 2004, pp. 79–80; see also Saunders, A., *Jane: A Pin-Up at War*, Barnsley: Pen & Sword, 2005.

55   Gabor, M., *The Pin-Up: A Modest History*, London: André Deutsch, 1972, pp. 39–40.

56   *Ibid.*, pp. 30ff, 76ff.

57   The Jean Straker photograph collection found a home in Cymiarth Bwlchllan, Lampeter, Wales, in 1999.

58   Gabor, *The Pin-Up*, p. 78.

59   Hoggart, *Uses of Literacy*, p. 177.

60   *Ibid.*, p. 181.

61   *Ibid.*

62   Moseley, R., *Growing Up with Audrey Hepburn*, Manchester: Manchester University Press, 2002, pp. 33ff, 111–12.

63   Advertisement for 'English Rose nylons', *Vanity Fair*, September/October 1956, p. 111.

64   Woodhead, L., *War Paint: Elizabeth Arden and Helena Rubinstein, Their Lives, Their Times, Their Rivalry*, London: Virago, 2004, pp. 229–30, 272–3.

65   *Ibid.*, pp. 280–2.

66   *Woman's Own*, articles on Rita Hayworth, 11 and 18 September 1952.

67   *Ibid.*

68   Dawnay, J., *How I Became a Fashion Model*, London: Thomas Nelson, 1958, p. 2.

69   Reproduced in Castle, C., *Model Girl*, Newton Abbot: David and Charles, 1977, p. 34.

70   Clayton, L., *The World of Modelling; and How To Get the London Model Girl Look*, London: Harrap, 1968, p. 7. Cherry Marshall pointed out that Goalen was in fact a war widow with two young children to support; see Marshall, C., *The Cat-Walk*, London: Hutchinson, 1978, p. 30.

71   Wilson, E., and Taylor, L., *Through the Looking Glass: A History of Dress from 1860 to the Present Day*, London: BBC Books, 1989, p. 159.

72   Cannadine, D., *Class in Britain*, London: Yale University Press, 1998.

73   Hartnell, N., *Silver and Gold*, London: Evans Bros, 1955, p. 71.

74   *Ibid.*, p. 94.

75   'Hartnell and the Coronation', *Picture Post*, 24 January 1953.

76   *Picture Post*, 14 March 1953, pp. 11–12.

77   Dior, C., *Dior by Dior: The Autobiography of Christian Dior*, translated by Antonia Fraser, London: V&A Publications, Weidenfeld and Nicolson, 2007, p. 161.

78   'Crawfie', 'Princess Margaret: The Story of a Very Modern Young Woman', *Woman's Own*, from September 1952.

79   *Ibid.*, 2 October 1952, p. 14.

80   *Ibid.*, p. 17. See also Crawford, M., *The Little Princesses*, London: Transworld Publications, 1953.

81   Clayton, *The World of Modelling*, p. 12.

82   Marshall, *The Cat-Walk*, p. 77.

83   *Ibid.*, pp. 27–8.

84   *Ibid.*, pp. 35–6.

85   *Woman and Beauty*, June 1931, p. 53.

86   Chitty, S., *Diary of a Fashion Model*, London: Methuen, 1958, pp. 21, 10.

87   Marshall, *The Cat-Walk*, p. 65.

88   MO Directive, Spring 1988, Clothing, B 1898, p. 16.

89   Docker, N., *Norah: The Autobiography of Lady Docker*, London: W. H. Allen, 1969, esp. chapter 9.

90   *Ibid.*, pp. 9–10.

91   *Ibid.*, p. 11.

92   Lady Docker's own account is given in Docker, *Norah*, chapter 17.

93   *Ibid.*, p. 12.

94   See, *inter alia*, Gabor, Z. (with Wendy Leigh), *One Lifetime is Not Enough*, London: Headline, 1992; Gerald Frank, *Zsa Zsa Gabor: My Story*, London: Pan, 1962.

95   http://nylon.net/sabrina/

96   Dors, D., *Behind Closed Doors*, London: W. H. Allen, 1979, p. 139.

97   'The Frenchman's Guide to Our Girls', *Picture Post*, 28 March 1953.

98   Diana Dors, quoted in *Picturegoer*, 24 March 1956, from Harper, S., *Women in British Cinema: Mad, Bad and Dangerous to Know*, London: Continuum, 2000, p. 98.

99   Dors, D., *For Adults Only*, London: W. H. Allen, 1978, p. 172.

100 *Ibid.*

101 Photo reproduced in Dors, *For Adults Only*, and widely elsewhere.

102 Harper, *Women in British Cinema*, p. 98.

103 See, for instance, Marks, L., and Van Den Bergh, T., *Ruth Ellis: A Case of Diminished Responsibility?* Harmondsworth: Penguin, 1990, p. 134.

104 'School for Glamour', *Woman and Beauty*, May 1952, pp. 16–17.

105 *Woman's Own* offered patterns for elegant housecoats to home dressmakers on 24 January. 1952, p. 26. Most fashion magazines of this time included features on housecoats as 'leisure' wear and for entertaining at dinner.

106 'Mrs Exeter' was modelled by Margot Smyly, who died in 2005. See

obituaries in *Guardian Unlimited*, www.guardian.co.uk, 6 October 2005, and *Daily Telegraph*, www.telegraph.co.uk, June 2005.

107 Caron, S., 'Flashback' (recalling a night out with her sister, Alma Cogan, and mother, Fay, in 1959), *Telegraph* Magazine, 11 August 2007, p. 82.

108 Castelbajac, K. de, *The Face of the Century: 100 Years of Make-up and Style*, New York: Rizzoli, 1987, p. 115.

109 Quotation from *Business Week* cited in Corson, R., *Fashions in Makeup*, London: Peter Owen, 1972, p. 536. There are many accounts of the launch of Fire and Ice, the most complete being in Tobias, A., *Fire and Ice: The Story of Charles Revson, The Man Who Built the Revlon Empire*, New York: William Morrow and Co., 1976.

110 Gross, M., *Model*, London: Bantam Press, 1995, p. 74.

111 The advertisement has been widely reproduced. See for instance, Ragas, M. Cohen, and Kozlowski, K., *Read My Lips; A Cultural History of Lipstick*, San Francisco: Chronicle, 1998, pp. 56–7.

112 Fowler, M., *The Way She Looks Tonight: Five Women of Style*, New York: St Martin's Press, 1996, p. 242.

113 Advert for Goya No. 5, *Woman's Own*, September 1952, p. 36.

114 Braine, J., *Room at the Top*, London: Eyre and Spottiswoode, 1957; Penguin edition, 1960, pp. 104, 132. Alice, when still desired by Joe, is described as smelling of lavender, with 'her own personal smell as musky as furs and as fresh as apples', p. 79.

115 Merriam, *Figleaf*, p. 68.

116 Advert for Coty, 'Les parfums', *Vogue*, May 1960, p. 25.

117 Cohen, L., '"Velvet is Very Important": Madge Garland and the Work of Fashion', *Journal of Lesbian and Gay Studies*, 2005, vol. 11, no. 3, pp. 371–90.

118 Alison Settle Archive, University of Brighton, in Beaton File, BN 5.

119 Settle, A., 'Viewpoint: Mothers with a Pay Packet', *Observer*, 14 April 1957, in Alison Settle Archive.

120 Hulanicki, B., *From A to Biba*, London: Hutchinson, 1983, p. 54.

121 For the influence of Italian culture on 1950s youth in Britain, see, *inter alia*, MacInnes, C., *Absolute Beginners*, first published in 1959 (new edition London: Allison and Busby, 1980). On Italian glamour see Gundle, S., 'Hollywood Glamour and Mass Consumption in Postwar Italy', in Koshar, R. (ed.), *Histories of Leisure*, Oxford: Berg, 2002.

122 McConathy, D., and Vreeland, D., *Hollywood Costume: Glamour! Glitter! Romance!* New York: Harry N. Abrams, 1976.

123 'Marilyn Monroe: The Last Interview', *Life*, August 1992, pp. 73–8, quoted on p. 265 of Cohen, L., 'The Horizontal Walk: Marilyn Monroe, Cinemascope and Sexuality', *Yale Journal of Criticism*, 1998, vol. 11, no. 1, pp. 265–88.

124 Lakoff, R., and Scherr, R., *Face Value: The Politics of Beauty*, London: Routledge and Kegan Paul, 1984, p. 91.

125 www.screenlegends.com/History.htm

5 Revolutions

1 Tennant, E., *Girlitude*, London: Vintage, 2000, pp. 14–17.

2 *Ibid.*, p. 7.

3 *Ibid.*, pp. 35–6, 37.

4 *Ibid.*, p. 38.

5 MacCarthy, F., *Last Curtsey: The End of the Debutantes*, London: Faber and Faber, 2006, p. 6.

6 Cleave, M., *Punch*, 21 September 1983, quoted in Turner, A., *Biba: The Biba Experience*, Suffolk: Antique Collectors' Club, n.d., p. 9.

7 Bert Hardy, 'Junior Miss', Hulton Getty Archive, image no. 2666614 (www.gettyimages.com). Reproduced (but wrongly attributed to Roger Mayne) in Handley, S., *Nylon: The Manmade Fashion Revolution*, London: Bloomsbury, 1999, p. 100.

8 Hulanicki, B., *From A to Biba*, London: Hutchinson, 1983, p. 60.

9 *Ibid.*, p. 56.

10 MacCarthy, *Last Curtsey*, p. 14.

11 Wilson, E., *Mirror Writing: An Autobiography*, London: Virago, 1982, p. 19.

12 *Picture Post*, 20 December 1952.

13 Settle, A., 'Viewpoint', *Observer*, 25 November 1956, cuttings in Alison Settle Archive, University of Brighton.

14 Hulanicki, *From A to Biba*, pp. 37, 43.

15 *Ibid.*, p. 37

16 Caron, S., *Alma Cogan: A Memoir*, London: Bloomsbury, 1991, p. 20.

17 *Ibid.*, p. 57.

18 Roddick, A., *Body and Soul*, London: Ebury Press, 1991, p. 35.

19 *Ibid.*, pp. 46–7.

20 *Ibid.*, pp. 33–5.

21 Breward, C., *Fashioning London: Clothing and the Modern Metropolis*, Oxford: Berg, 2004, esp. Chapter 6.

22 *Ibid.*, pp. 152–3. Breward takes Nancy Mitford's comments from Colin MacInnes, *England, Half English: A Polyphoto of the Fifties*, Harmondsworth: Penguin, 1966, pp. 153–4.

23 MacInnes, *England, Half English*, p. 153.

24 Settle, A., 'Viewpoint', *Observer*, 12 February 1956, Alison Settle Archive, University of Brighton.

25 Settle, A., 'Viewpoint', 1 September 1957.

26 Settle, A., 'Viewpoint', 2 February 1958.

27 Nabokov, V., *Lolita*, New York: G. P. Putnam, 1958.

28 Abrams, M., *The Teenage Consumer*, London: London Press Exchange, 1961.

29 *Report of the Committee on the Age of Majority* (Latey Report), July 1967, Cmnd 3342, London: HMSO.

30 See, for instance, *Glamour*, January 1958.

31 Merriam, E., *Figleaf: The Business of Being in Fashion*, Philadelphia and New York: Lippincott, 1960, p. 28; advert for Revlon 'Milkglass' nailcremes, *Fashion*, July 1969.

32 Advert for Mary Quant 'Jelly Babies', *Honey*, July 1970, p. 84.

33 Advert for Max Factor perfumes, *Honey*, December 1960, p. 33.

34 Merriam, *Figleaf*, pp. 181–3.

35 Rice-Davies, M., with Shirley Flack, *Mandy*, London: Sphere, 1980, p. 97.

36 Links, J., *The Book of Fur*, London: James Barrie, 1956, pp. 43–4.

37 Caron, *Alma Cogan*, p. 69.

38 Merriam, *Figleaf*, pp. 191–4.

39 Glendinning, V., *Rebecca West: A Life*, London: Weidenfeld and Nicolson, 1987, p. 246.

40 Pringle, Alexandra, 'Chelsea Girl', in Maitland, S. (ed.), *Very Heaven: Looking Back at the 1960s*, London: Virago, 1988, p. 38; Hulanicki, *From A to Biba*, p. 98.

41 Wilson, *Mirror Writing*, p. 15.

42 Dyhouse, C., *Students: A Gendered History*, London: Routledge, 2006, pp. 92–4, chapters 4 and 5, *passim*.

43 *Ibid.*, chapter 5.

44 Advertisements for Quant perfume, *Honey*, December 1966, p. 47; for Courtelle, *Flair*, October 1963, p. 61.

45 Brown, Helen Gurley, *Sex and the Single Girl*, London: Frederick Mueller, 1963.

46 *Ibid.*, p. 113 and *passim*.

47 *Ibid.*, p. 107.

48 Radner, H., 'On the Move: Fashion Photography and the Single Girl in the 1960s', in Bruzzi, S., and Gibson, P. Church (eds.), *Fashion Cultures: Theories, Explanations and Analyses*, London: Routledge, 2000.

49 Cook, Hera, *The Long Sexual Revolution: English Women, Sex, and Contraception 1800–1975*, Oxford: Oxford University Press, 2004.

50 Advert for de Beers, *Honey*, April 1970.

51 Cilla Black, quoted in *Honey*, April 1970, p. 9.

52 De Beauvoir, S., *The Second Sex*, London: Cape, 1953; Friedan, B., *The Feminine Mystique*, Harmondsworth: Penguin, 1965; Greer, G., *The Female Eunuch*, London: Paladin, 1971.

53 De Beauvoir, *Second Sex*, p. 510.

54 Greer, *Female Eunuch*, pp. 55–6 and *passim*.

55 See 'Miss World' in Wandor, M. (ed.), *The Body Politic: Writings from the Women's Liberation Movement in Britain, 1962–1972*, London: Stage 1, 1972.

56 *Ibid.*, pp. 249–60.

57 Segal, L., *Making Trouble: Life and Politics*, London: Serpent's Tail, 2007, p. 67.

58 See, *inter alia*, Neustatter, A., *Hyenas in Petticoats: A Look at Twenty Years of Feminism*, Harmondsworth: Penguin, 1990, esp. chapter 5, 'Woman à la Mode: The Politics of Appearance'.

59 There is an account of Greer's New York Town Hall debate with Mailer in Wallace, C., *Germaine Greer: Untamed Shrew*, London: Richard Cohen, 2000, pp.188–200.

60 Segal, *Making Trouble*, p. 80.

61 Roddick, *Body and Soul*, p. 9.

62 *Ibid.*

63 *Ibid.*, p. 12.

64 Hulanicki, *From A to Biba*, pp. 70–3.

65 Turner, *Biba*, p. 13.

66 *Ibid.*, p. 25.

67 Hulanicki, *From A to Biba*, p. 113.

68 *Ibid.*, p. 62.

69 Turner, *Biba*, p. 41.

70 Hulanicki, *From A to Biba*, p. 118.

71 *Ibid.*, pp. 116–18; Turner, *Biba*, pp. 47–9; see also Segal, *Making Trouble*, pp. 59–60.

72 Hulanicki, *From A to Biba*, p. 117.

73 *Observer*, 20 July 1975, quoted by Turner, *Biba*, p. 79.

74 *Vogue*, 15 September 1973, quoted by Turner, *Biba*, p. 69.

75 Turner, *Biba*, pp. 76–8.

76 Williams, I. C., *Underneath a Harlem Moon: The Harlem to Paris Years of Adelaide Hall*, London: Continuum, 2002.

77 Craig, M., *Ain't I a Beauty Queen?: Black Women, Beauty and the Politics of Race*, Oxford: Oxford University Press, 2002, pp. 4, 46ff.

78 See Lambeth Landmark website for images of Claudia Jones congratulating Miss Jamaica, 1960 (Joan Crawford), and the winner of the Notting Hill Carnival Beauty competition in the same year (Marlene Walker): http://landmark.lambeth.gov.uk/display_page.asp?section=landmark&id=6169. For Claudia Jones generally see Sherwood, M., *Claudia Jones: A Life in Exile*, London: Lawrence and Wishart, 1999; Schwarz, B., 'Claudia Jones and the *West Indian Gazette*: Reflections on the Emergence of Post-colonial Britain', *Twentieth-Century British History*, 2003, vol. 14, no. 3, pp. 264–85.

6 Glamazons, grunge and bling

1   Todd, S., 'Models and Menstruation: *Spare Rib* Magazine, Feminism, Femininity and Pleasure', 1999, www.sussex.ac.uk/Units/SPT/journal/archive/pdf/issue1-5.pdf.

2   See editorial, 'Our Cosmo World' by Joyce Hopkirk, in the first UK edition of *Cosmopolitan*, March 1972, p. 10.

3   McSharry, D., 'The Cover Girl Look', *Cosmopolitan*, April 1972, pp. 82–3.

4   *Ibid.*

5   See Ouellette, L., 'Inventing the Cosmo Girl: Class Identity and Girl-style American Dreams', *Media, Culture and Society*, 1999, vol. 21, no. 3, pp. 359–83; Berebitsky, J., 'The Joy of Work: Helen Gurley Brown, Gender and Sexuality in the White Collar Office', *Journal of the History of Sexuality*, 2006, vol. 15, no. 1, pp. 89–127.

6   Arnot, M., David, M., and Weiner, G., *Closing the Gender Gap: Postwar Education and Social Change*, Cambridge: Polity Press, 1999; Dyhouse, C., *Students: A Gendered History*, London: Routledge, 2006, pp. 92–4, chapter 5.

7   *Cosmopolitan*, December 1977, pp. 41–2.

8   Kurtz, I., 'The Simple Secret of Successful Sex', *Cosmopolitan*, July 1973, pp. 68–70, 111.

9   Vincent, S., 'You and the Pill', *Cosmopolitan*, August 1973, pp. 100–1, 176.

10 Molloy, J. T., *Women: Dress for Success*, New York: Peter H. Wyden, 1980.

11 See Entwistle, J., 'Fashioning the Career Woman: Power Dressing as a Category of Consumption', in Andrews, M., and Talbot, M. (eds.), *All the World and Her Husband: Women in Twentieth Century Consumer Culture*, London: Cassell, 2000.

12 See for instance *Vogue*, February 1985, p. 9, and April 1985, p. xvi.

13 Advert for Krizia, *Vogue*, March 1985, p. 44.

14 See *OED Online*, which dates 'glitzy' from the 1960s, 'glitz' from 1977, with increased use in the 1980s.

15 McDowell, C., *Dressed to Kill: Sex, Power and Clothes*, London: Hutchinson, 1992, pp. 151ff, 173; Quick, H., *Catwalking: A History of the Fashion Model*, London: Hamlyn/Reed International, 1997, p. 145.

16 Quick, *Catwalking*, pp. 142–5.

17 Adams, Tim, 'Forever Eighties', *Observer* Review, 23 April 2006.

18 Rogers, P., *What Becomes a Legend Most? The Blackglama Story*, New York: Simon and Schuster, 1979.

19 *Vogue,* November 1973, inside cover; Mia Farrow and André Previn, p. 17.

20 Settle, A., 'Leather Leads the Way', *The Lady*, 22 June 1972, from collection of cuttings in Alison Settle Archive, University of Brighton.

21 'Winter's Great Day Looks', *Vogue*, October 1986, pp. 325–31.

22 *Vogue,* August 1986, tributes to Beatrix Miller, p. 154.

23 Guest, K., 'Why Do We Still Wear Fur?', *Independent on Sunday*, 12 December 2004.

24 See, *inter alia*, Toolis, K., 'In for the Kill: Is Human Life of Greater Importance and Worth than Animal Life?', *Guardian Unlimited*, 5 December 1998.

25 Gundle, S., and Castelli, C., *The Glamour System*, Basingstoke: Palgrave Macmillan, 2006, p. 98.

26 Irvine, S., *The Perfume Guide*, London: Haldane Mason, 2000, p. 108; Craik, J., *The Face of Fashion: Cultural Studies in Fashion*, London: Routledge, 1994, p. 168.

27 Edwards, M., *Perfume Legends: French Feminine Fragrances*, Paris: H. M. Éditions, 1996, pp. 170ff; Irvine, *Perfume Guide*, p. 130.

28 Ginsberg, S., *Reeking Havoc: The Unauthorised and Outrageous Story of Giorgio the Bestseller Fragrance*, London: Hutchinson Business Books, 1989, pp. 7–9.

29 Irvine, *Perfume Guide*, p. 58.

30 Edwards, *Perfume Legends*, pp. 224ff.

31 Irvine, *Perfume Guide*, p. 124.

32 Hutton, D., 'Fragrance: Coming on Strong', *Vogue*, November 1986, pp. 248–51, 281ff.

33 Zweiniger-Bargielowska, I., 'The Body and Consumer Culture', in Zweiniger-Bargielowska, I. (ed.), *Women in Twentieth-Century Britain*, Harlow: Pearson Education, 2001, esp. pp. 189–195.

34 Advert for Sunsilk Styling Mousse, *Vogue,* July 1986.

35 Image of Claire Ringrose illustrating article 'Attitudes to Fitness Now', *Vogue*, August 1986, p. 170.

36   'Joan Collins Confesses', *Glamour*, 29 August 1956.

37   Mass Observation Directive on Clothing, Spring 1988, in Mass Observation Archive, University of Sussex.

38   *Ibid.*, B 56.

39   *Ibid.*, B 42.

40   *Ibid.*, L 1002.

41   *Ibid.*, R 1897; see also G 1655.

42   Offer, A., *The Challenge of Affluence: Self-Control and Well-Being in the US and Britain since 1850*, Oxford: Oxford University Press, 2006, pp. 144, 156 and *passim*.

43   Orbach, S., *Fat is a Feminist Issue*, London: Hamlyn, 1979; Orbach, S., *Hunger Strike: The Anorectic's Struggle as a Metaphor for Our Age*, London: Faber and Faber, 1986; Chernin, K., *The Hungry Self: Women, Eating and Identity*, New York: Times Books, 1985. See also Bordo, S., *Unbearable Weight: Feminism, Western Culture and the Body*, Berkeley: University of California Press, 1993.

44   For a history of cosmetic surgery see Gilman, S., *Creating Beauty to Cure the Soul: Race and Psychology in the Shaping of Aesthetic Surgery*, Durham, NC : Duke University Press, 1998, and Gilman, S., *Making the Body Beautiful: A Cultural History of Aesthetic Surgery*, Princeton, NJ: Princeton University Press, 1999.

45   Wolf, N., *The Beauty Myth: How Images of Beauty Are Used against Women*, London: Vintage, 1990; Faludi, S., *Backlash: The Undeclared War against Women*, London: Chatto and Windus, 1991.

46   Wolf, *The Beauty Myth*, pp. 70, 179–218 and *passim*.

47   *Ibid.*, p. 274.

48   Faludi, *Backlash*, esp. chapter 8.

49   Zweiniger-Bargielowska, *Women in Twentieth-Century Britain*, chapter 12.

50   Wolf, *The Beauty Myth*, p. 83.

51   Weldon, F., *The Life and Loves of a She-Devil*, London: Coronet, 1983.

52   Davis, K., *Reshaping the Female Body: The Dilemma of Cosmetic Surgery*, New York and London: Routledge, 1995.

53   Davis, *Reshaping the Female Body*, p. 20. For recent figures see annual reports of the British Association of Aesthetic Plastic Surgeons (BAAPS). 2005/6 saw an increase of nearly 35 per cent in the number of 'procedures' recorded. www.baaps.org.uk

54   Silverman, D., *Selling Culture: Bloomingdale's, Diana Vreeland and the New Aristocracy of Taste in Reagan's America*, New York: Pantheon, 1986.

55   www.urbandecay.com/about.cfm

56   Irvine, *Perfume Guide*, p. 96.

57   This definition is not mentioned in the *Oxford English Dictionary Online*, but is commonly attributed to New Orleans rapper B. G. See Wikipedia, http://en.wikipedia.org/wiki/Bling

58   Campbell, B., *Diana, Princess of Wales: How Sexual Politics Shook the Monarchy*, London: Virago, 1998, pp. 120–1.

59   *Ibid.*, p. 121.

60   See, *inter alia*, Bradford, S., *Diana*, London: Viking, 2006; Davies, J., *Diana, a Cultural History: Gender, Race, Nation and the People's Princess*, Basingstoke: Palgrave, 2001, chapter 3 and *passim*.

61   *Ibid.*, esp. chapter 4.

62   Morton, A., *Diana: Her True Story*, London: Michael O'Mara, 1993.

63   Sherwood, D., 'Secrets of Di's Revenge Dress', *Sunday Mirror*, 3 May 1998.

64   Davies, *Diana*, pp. 168ff.

65   Cowie, C., and Lees, S., 'Slags or Drags?', *Feminist Review*, October 1981, no. 9, pp. 17–31.

66   See, *inter alia*, Turner, K., *I Dream of Madonna: Women's Dreams of the Goddess of Pop*, London: Thames and Hudson, 1993; Skeggs, B., 'A Good Time for Women Only', in Lloyd, F. (ed.), *Deconstructing Madonna*, London: Batsford, 1993.

67   Robertson, P., *Guilty Pleasures: Feminist Camp from Mae West to Madonna*, London: Tauris, 1996.

68   *Madonna/Sex: Photographed by Steven Meisel*, London: Secker and Warburg, 1992.

7 Perspectives and reflections

1   Carr, D., 'Condé Nast's London Man Makes *Glamour* a Hit', *International Herald Tribune* (Business), 25 January 2005. Recent figures (2006/7) suggest a slight fall in circulation: www.magforum.com/glossies/womens_glossies.htm

2   *Glamour*, no. 1, March 1938, p. 23. The copy in the British Library no longer has this free gift.

3   Boxed observation from 'Your Editress', *Glamour*, no. 1, March 1938.

4   Navarro, R., 'Solved: The Problems of Your Love Affairs', *Glamour*, 12 March 1939, p. 23. Nigel Mansfield had taken over by September 1939.

5   Tetlow's Swan Down Petal Lotion, advertised in *Glamour*, 18 June 1938, p. 21.

6   Mr Trilety adverts appeared regularly; Kozy Kaps featured in *Glamour*, 29 July 1939.

7   Advert for Dor cream deodorant in *Glamour*, 13 August 1938, p. 29.

8   Tokalon lipstick described in 'Glamour Glimpses', *Glamour*, 14 January 1939, p. 28.

9   Advert for Guitare lipstick, headed 'Darling: Look at the Painted Horror!', *Glamour*, 13 August 1938, p. 29.

10   Jenkinson, A. J., *What Do Boys and Girls Read?*, London: Methuen, 1940, cited in Jephcott, P., *Girls Growing Up*, London: Faber and Faber, 1942, p. 100.

11   Jephcott, *Girls Growing Up*, pp. 98–111.

12   Hoggart, R., *The Uses of Literacy: Aspects of Working Class Life, with Special Reference to Publications and Entertainments*, London: Chatto and Windus, 1957, pp. 100–7.

13   Seebohm, C., *The Man Who Was Vogue: The Life and Times of Condé Nast*, London: Weidenfeld and Nicolson, 1982, p. 331.

14   *Ibid.*, pp. 332–9.

15   Boycott, R., 'What I See in the Mirror', *Guardian Weekend*, 14 April 2007, p. 95.

16   Berger, J., *Ways of Seeing*, London: BBC, 1972.

17   *Ibid.*, pp. 37, 148.

18   *Ibid.*, and p. 153.

19   Campbell, C., *The Romantic Ethic and the Spirit of Modern Consumerism*, Oxford: Blackwell, 1987, Introduction and chapter 3.

20   *Ibid.*, and Veblen, T., *The Theory of the Leisure Class*, New York: Macmillan, 1912, or see the selection published as Veblen, T., *Conspicuous Consumption*, London: Penguin, 2005.

21   Campbell, *The Romantic Ethic*, pp. 72–90.

22   Robbins, D., *Bourdieu and Culture*, London: Sage, 2000; Featherstone, M., *Consumer Culture and Postmodernism*, London: Sage, 1991.

23   Featherstone, M., Hepworth, M., and Turner, B., *The Body: Social Process and Cultural Theory*, London, Sage, 1991.

24   Giddens, A., *Modernity and Self-Identity: Self and Society in the Late Modern Age*, Cambridge: Polity, 1991, p. 178.

25   Finkelstein, J., *The Fashioned Self*, Cambridge: Polity, 1991, p. 12.

26   *Ibid.*, p. 1.

27   Coward, R., *Female Desire: Women's Sexuality Today*, London: Paladin, 1984.

28   *Ibid.*, 'Pouts and Scowls', pp. 55ff.

29   Chapkis, W., *Beauty Secrets: Women and the Politics of Appearance*, London: Woman's Press, 1988, p. 95.

30   *Ibid.*, p. 171.

31   Freedman, R., *Beauty Bound: Why Women Strive for Physical Perfection*, London: Columbus, 1988.

32   Lakoff, R., and Scherr, R., *Face Value: The Politics of Beauty*, London: Routledge and Kegan Paul, 1984.

33   *Ibid.*, p. 284.

34   Faludi, S., *Backlash: The Undeclared War against Women*, London: Chatto and Windus, 1991; Wolf, N., *The Beauty Myth: How Images of Beauty Are Used against Women*, London: Vintage, 1990.

35   Wolf, *The Beauty Myth*, p. 163.

36   See, *inter alia*, Offer, A., *The Challenge of Affluence: Self-Control and Well-Being in the US and Britain since 1850*, Oxford: Oxford University Press, 2006.

37   Stearns, P., *Fat History: Bodies and Beauty in the Modern West*, New York: New York University Press, 2002.

38   Bartky, S., *Femininity and Domination: Studies in the Phenomenology of Oppression*, New York and London: Routledge, 1990.

39   *Ibid.*, p. 36.

40   *Ibid.*, p. 41.

41   *Ibid.*, p. 42.

42   Black, P., *The Beauty Industry: Gender, Culture, Pleasure*, London: Routledge, 2004.

43   Merriam, E., *Figleaf: The Business of Being in Fashion*, Philadelphia and New York: Lippincott, 1960, p. 166.

44   'Hope in a Jar' is the title of Kathy Peiss's useful history of American beauty culture: Peiss, K., *Hope in a Jar: The Making of America's Beauty Culture*, New York: Henry Holt, 1998.

45   Davis, K., *Reshaping the Female Body: The Dilemma of Cosmetic Surgery*, New York and London: Routledge, 1995.

46   Davis, K., 'Cosmetic Surgery in a Different Voice: The Case of Madame Noël', www.let.uu.nl/~Kathy.Davis/personal/cosmetic_surgery.html

47   *Ibid.*

48   Wilson, E., *Adorned in Dreams: Fashion and Modernity*, London: Virago, 1985, esp. chapter 11, 'Feminism and Fashion'.

49   Scott, L., *Fresh Lipstick: Redressing Fashion and Feminism*, Basingstoke: Palgrave Macmillan, 2005.

50   Buckley, R., and Gundle, S., 'Flash Trash: Gianni Versace and the Theory and Practice of Glamour,' in Bruzzi, S., and Gibson, P. Church (eds.), *Fashion Cultures: Theories, Explanations and Analyses*, London: Routledge, 2000, p. 331.

51   Partridge, E., *Usage and Abusage: A Guide to Good English*, London: Hamish Hamilton, 1947, p. 361, cited in Buckley and Gundle, 'Flash Trash'.

52   See, for instance, Claxton, E., Dolce, D., and Gabbana, G., *Hollywood: Dolce & Gabbana*, New York; Assouline, 2003.

53   For a recent exploration of the predicament of single women between the wars see Nicholson, V., *Singled Out: How Two Million Women Survived without Men after the First World War*, London: Viking, 2007.

54   Payne, G., and Abbott, P. (eds.), *The Social Mobility of Women: Beyond Male Mobility Models*, London: Falmer Press, 1990.

55   Spencer, S., *Gender, Work and Education in Britain in the 1950s*, Basingstoke: Palgrave Macmillan, 2005; Dyhouse, C., *Students: A Gendered History*, London: Routledge, 2006, esp. chapters 4 and 5.

56   Ollerenshaw, K., *Education for Girls*, London: Faber and Faber, 1961, p. 107.

57 Antoine, *Antoine by Antoine*, London: W. H. Allen, 1946, p. 38.

58 Spring-Rice, M., *Working Class Wives: Their Health and Conditions*, Harmondsworth: Penguin, 1939.

59 Antoine, *Antoine*, pp. 38–9.

60 The Pathé News archive contains many film clips of women shoppers queuing for January sales, etc. See, for example, 'Sales, Storm and Sunshine: Winter Sales', 1431.09, 'January Sales', 3342.02, 'The Nation: January Sales', 1418.10. www.britishpathe.com.

61 www.missblackbritain.co.uk.

62 See, for instance, Carter, A., *Nights at the Circus*, London: Chatto and Windus, 1984, and *Wise Children*, London: Vintage, 1991.

63 Carter, *Wise Children*, p. 197.

Sources and select bibliography

Archives and collections

Alison Settle Archive, University of Brighton
Brighton Museum and Art Gallery, Clothing Collection
Fashion Museum, Bath
Mass Observation Archive, University of Sussex
National Museums, Liverpool, Tinne Collection
Victoria and Albert Museum
Worthing Museum and Art Gallery, Clothing Collection
International Movie Database (IMDb): www.imdb.com

Magazines and periodicals

The British Fur Trade
Common Scents
Cosmopolitan
Costume Jewellery and Fashion Accessories
Daily Mirror Beauty Book, 1910
Eve: The Ladies' Pictorial

Fanfare: Adventures of a Glamour Girl
Fashion Forecast
Film and Fashion
Film Fashionland
Flair
Funfare
Fur Farming
Fur Leader
Fur Record
Fur Times
Fur Weekly News
Fur World and Skin Trades Gazette
Furriers' Journal
Girls' Cinema
Glamour (published by C. Arthur Pearson), later *Glamour and Peg's Paper*
Glamour (published by Condé Nast)
Harper's Bazaar
Honey
Lucky Star
Marilyn
Miss Modern
Nova
Perfumery and Essential Oil Record
Perfumery and Toiletry: A Monthly Trade Record
Picture Post
Picturegoer
Poppet
The Queen
Vanity Fair
Vogue
Vogue Beauty Book
Woman
Woman and Beauty
Woman's Fair
Woman's Filmfair
Woman's Journal
Woman's Own

Books and articles

Abel, R. (ed.), *Silent Film*, London: Athlone, 1996.

Abrams, M., *The Teenage Consumer*, London: London Press Exchange, 1961.

Alexander, S., *Becoming a Woman and Other Essays in 19th and 20th Century Feminist History*, London: Virago, 1994.

Allen, M., *Selling Dreams: Inside the Beauty Business*, London: Dent, 1981.

Andrews, M. and Talbot, M. (eds.), *All the World and Her Husband: Women in Twentieth Century Consumer Culture*, London: Cassell, 2000.

Angeloglou, M., *A History of Make-up*, London: Studio Vista, 1970.

Antoine, *Antoine by Antoine*, London: W. H. Allen, 1946.

Arlen, M., *The Green Hat: A Romance for a Few People*, London: Collins, 1924.

Arnot, M., David, M. and Weiner, G., *Closing the Gender Gap: Postwar Education and Social Change*, Cambridge: Polity Press, 1999.

Ash, J. and Wilson, J. (eds.), *Chic Thrills: A Fashion Reader*, London: Pandora, 1992.

Bailey, M., *Those Glorious Glamour Years: Classic Hollywood Costume Design of the 1930s*, London: Columbus, 1982.

Ballard, B., *In My Fashion*, London: Secker and Warburg, 1960.

Banet-Weiser, S., *The Most Beautiful Girl in the World: Beauty Pageants and National Identity*, Berkeley: UCLA Press, 1999.

Bankhead, T., *Tallulah*, London: Gollancz, 1952.

Banner, L., *American Beauty*, New York: Knopf, 1983.

Barber, B., *Consumed: How Markets Corrupt Children, Infantilize Adults, and Swallow Citizens Whole*, New York and London: Norton, 2007.

Barlow, T., Yue Dong, M., Poiger, U., Ramamurthy, P., Thomas, L. and Weinbaum, A., 'The Modern Girl around the World: A Research Agenda and Preliminary Findings', *Gender and History*, 2005, vol. 17, no. 2, pp. 245–94.

Barron, L., '"Elizabeth Hurley is More than a Model": Stars and Career Diversification in Contemporary Media', *Journal of Popular Culture*, 2006, vol. 39, no. 4, pp. 523–44.

Bartky, S., *Femininity and Domination: Studies in the Phenomenology of Oppression*, New York and London: Routledge, 1990.

Basinger, J., *A Woman's View: How Hollywood Spoke to Women, 1930–1960*, London: Chatto and Windus, 1994.

Bassett, P., *List of the Historical Records of the Royal Society for the Protection of Birds*, Birmingham: Centre for Urban and Regional Studies, 1980.

Bauman, Z., *Consuming Life*, London: Polity, 2007.

Beaton, C., *The Book of Beauty*, London: Duckworth, 1930.

Beaton, C., *The Glass of Fashion*, London: Weidenfeld and Nicolson, 1954.

Beaton, C., *The Face of the World: An International Scrapbook of People and Places*, London: Weidenfeld and Nicolson, 1957.

Beaton, C., *The Wandering Years: Diaries 1922–39*, London: Weidenfeld and Nicolson, 1961.

Berebitsky, J., 'The Joy of Work: Helen Gurley Brown, Gender and Sexuality in the White Collar Office', *Journal of the History of Sexuality*, 2006, vol. 15, no. 1, pp. 89–127.

Berger, J., *Ways of Seeing*, London: BBC, 1972.

Berry, S., *Screen Style: Fashion and Femininity in 1930s Hollywood*, Minneapolis: University of Minnesota Press, 2000.

Berry, W., *A Victim to Glamour, and Other Poems*, Leeds: J. Barmley, 1874.

Bingham, A., *Gender, Modernity and the Popular Press in Inter-War Britain*, Oxford: Clarendon Press, 2004.

Black, P., *The Beauty Industry: Gender, Culture, Pleasure*, London: Routledge, 2004.

Black, P. and Sharma, U., 'Men are Real, Women are "Made Up": Beauty Therapy and the Construction of Femininity', *Sociological Review*, 2001, vol. 49, no. 1, pp. 100–116.

Bond, D., *Glamour in Fashion*, London: Guinness Publishing, 1992.

Bordo, S., *Unbearable Weight: Feminism, Western Culture and the Body*, Berkeley: University of California Press, 1993.

Bordwell, D., *Hollywood Glamour, 1924–1956: Selected Portraits from the Wisconsin Center for Film and Theater Research*, Introduction to Exhibition Catalogue, Elvehjem Museum of Art, University of Wisconsin: Madison, 1987.

Bowlby, R., *Just Looking: Consumer Culture in Dreiser, Gissing and Zola*, London: Methuen, 1985.

Bradford, S., *Diana*, London: Viking, 2006.

Braine, J., *Room at the Top*, London: Eyre and Spottiswoode, 1957.

Braithwaite, B., *Women's Magazines: The First 300 Years*, London: Peter Owen, 1995.

Braudy, L., *The Frenzy of Renown: Fame and Its History*, Oxford: Oxford University Press, 1986.

Breward, C., *The Culture of Fashion: A New History of Fashionable Dress*, Manchester: Manchester University Press, 1995.

Breward, C., *Fashioning London: Clothing and the Modern Metropolis*, Oxford: Berg, 2004.

British Fur Trade Yearbook, 1933, London: Hutchinson, 1933.

Brittain, V., *Chronicle of Friendship: Diary of the Thirties* (edited by A. Bishop), London: Gollancz, 1986.

Brown, Helen Gurley, *Sex and the Single Girl*, London: Frederick Mueller, 1963.

Brownmiller, S., *Femininity*, London: Paladin, 1986.

Bruzzi, S. and Gibson, P. Church (eds.), *Fashion Cultures: Theories, Explanations and Analyses*, London: Routledge, 2000.

Bryer, R., *The History of Hair: Fashion and Fantasy down the Ages*, London: Philip Wilson, 2000.

Buckley, R. and Gundle, S., 'Flash Trash: Gianni Versace and the Theory and Practice of Glamour', in Bruzzi, S. and Gibson, P. Church (eds.), *Fashion Cultures: Theories, Explanations and Analyses*, London: Routledge, 2000.

Burke, T., *London in My Time*, London: Rich and Cowan, 1934.

Buszek, M., 'War Goddess, the Varga Girls, WWII and Feminism', *N. Paradoxa*, issue 6, 1998 (http://web.ukonline.co.uk/n.paradoxa/buszek).

Byers, M., *Designing Women: The Art, Technique and Cost of Being Beautiful*, London: John Miles, 1939.

Campbell, B., *Diana, Princess of Wales: How Sexual Politics Shook the Monarchy*, London: Virago, 1998.

Campbell, C., *The Romantic Ethic and the Spirit of Modern Consumerism*, Oxford: Blackwell, 1987.

Cannadine, D., *Class in Britain*, London: Yale University Press, 1998.

Caron, S., *Alma Cogan: A Memoir*, London: Bloomsbury, 1991.

Carr, L., *Four Fabulous Faces: The Evolution and Metamorphosis of Garbo, Swanson, Crawford and Dietrich*, New Rochelle, NY: Arlington House, 1970.

Carr, L., *More Fabulous Faces*, New York: Doubleday, 1979.

Carter, A., *Nights at the Circus*, London: Chatto and Windus, 1984.

Carter, A., *Nothing Sacred: Selected Writings*, London: Virago, 1982.

Carter, A., *Shaking a Leg*, London: Chatto and Windus, 1997.

Carter, A., *Wise Children*, London: Vintage, 1991.

Carter, E., *With Tongue in Chic*, London: Michael Joseph, 1974.

Castelbajac, K. de, *The Face of the Century: 100 Years of Make-up and Style*, New York: Rizzoli, 1987.

Castle, C., *Model Girl*, Newton Abbot: David and Charles, 1977.

Castle, C., *The Duchess Who Dared: Margaret, Duchess of Argyll*, London: Pan, 1994.

Chamberlain, M., *Growing Up in Lambeth*, London: Virago, 1989.

Chapkis, W., *Beauty Secrets: Women and the Politics of Appearance*, London: Woman's Press, 1988.

Chernin, K., *Womansize: The Tyranny of Slenderness*, London: Woman's Press, 1983.

Chernin, K., *The Hungry Self: Women, Eating and Identity*, New York: Times Books, 1985.

Chierichetti, D., *Hollywood Costume Design*, London: Studio Vista, 1976.

Chitty, S., *Diary of a Fashion Model*, London: Methuen, 1958.

Claxton, E., Dolce, D. and Gabbana, G., *Hollywood: Dolce & Gabbana*, New York: Assouline, 2003.

Clayton, L., *Modelling and Beauty Care Made Simple*, London: Heinemann, 1985.

Clayton, L., *The World of Modelling; and How to Get the London Model Girl Look*, London: Harrap, 1968.

Cohen, L., 'The Horizontal Walk: Marilyn Monroe, Cinemascope and Sexuality', *Yale Journal of Criticism*, 1998, vol. 11, no. 1, pp. 265–88.

Cohen, L., '"Velvet is Very Important": Madge Garland and the Work of Fashion', *Journal of Lesbian and Gay Studies*, 2005, vol. 11, no. 3, pp. 371–90.

Collins, D., *A Nose for Money: How to Make a Million*, London: Michael Joseph, 1963.

Committee on the Age of Majority, *Report of the Committee on the Age of Majority*, Cmnd. 3342, London: HMSO, July 1967.

Cook, Hera, *The Long Sexual Revolution: English Women, Sex, and Contraception 1800–1975*, Oxford: Oxford University Press, 2004.

Corson, R., *Fashions in Make-up*, London: Peter Owen, 1972.

Coward, R., *Female Desire: Women's Sexuality Today*, London: Paladin, 1984.

Cowie, C. and Lees, S., 'Slags or Drags?', *Feminist Review*, October 1981, no. 9, pp. 17–31.

Cox, C., *Seduction: A Celebration of Sensual Style*, London: Mitchell Beazley, 2006.

Craig, M., *Ain't I a Beauty Queen? Black Women, Beauty and the Politics of Race*, Oxford: Oxford University Press, 2002.

Craik, J., *The Face of Fashion: Cultural Studies in Fashion*, London: Routledge, 1994.

Crawford, M., *The Little Princesses*, London: Transworld Publications, 1953.

Davey, R., *Fur and Fur Garments*, London: Roxburghe Press, 1896.

Davidoff, L., *The Best Circles: Society, Etiquette and the Season*, London: Croom Helm, 1973.

Davies, J., *Diana, a Cultural History: Gender, Race, Nation and the People's Princess*, Basingstoke: Palgrave, 2001.

Davis, K., *Reshaping the Female Body: The Dilemma of Cosmetic Surgery*, New York and London: Routledge, 1995.

Dawnay, J., *How I Became a Fashion Model*, London: Thomas Nelson, 1958.

de Beauvoir, S., *The Second Sex*, London: Cape, 1953.

de Courcy, A., *1939: The Last Season*, London: Orion Books, 2005.

de Grazia, V. with Furlough, E., *The Sex of Things: Gender and Consumption in Historical Perspective*, Berkeley: University of California Press, 1996.

Deeble, S., *A Girl's Guide to Glamour*, London: Ryland Peters and Small, 2005.

DelGaudio, S., *Dressing the Part: Sternberg, Dietrich and Costume*, New York: Associated University Presses, 1993.

Devlin, P., *'Vogue' Book of Fashion Photography*, London: Thames and Hudson, 1979.

Dior, C., *Dior by Dior: The Autobiography of Christian Dior*, translated by Antonia Fraser, London: V&A Publications, Weidenfeld and Nicolson, 2007.

Docker, N., *Norah: The Autobiography of Lady Docker*, London: W. H. Allen, 1969.

Dors, D., *Behind Closed Doors*, London: W. H. Allen, 1979.

Dors, D., *For Adults Only*, London: W. H. Allen, 1978.

Douglas, S., *Where the Girls Are: Growing Up Female with the Mass Media*, New York: Three Rivers Press, 1994.

Duff Gordon, Lady, *Discretions and Indiscretions*, London: Jarrolds, 1932.

Dyhouse, C., *Students: A Gendered History*, London: Routledge, 2006.

Edwards, M., *Perfume Legends: French Feminine Fragrances*, Paris: H. M. Éditions, 1996.

Ellis, A., *The Essence of Beauty; A History of Perfumes and Cosmetics*, London: Secker and Warburg, 1960.

Emberley, J., *The Cultural Politics of Fur*, Ithaca, NY and London: Cornell University Press, 1997.

Entwistle, J. and Wilson, E. (eds.), *Body Dressing*, Oxford: Berg, 2001.

Etherington-Smith, M. and Pilcher, J., *The 'It' Girls: Lucy, Lady Duff Gordon, the Couturière 'Lucile', and Elinor Glyn, Romantic Novelist*, London: Hamish Hamilton, 1986.

Ewing, E., *Fur in Dress*, London: Batsford, 1981.

Faludi, S., *Backlash: The Undeclared War against Women*, London: Chatto and Windus, 1991.

Fascinating Womanhood: A Practical Course of Lessons in the Underlying Principles by Which Women Attract Men – Leading to the Proposal and Culminating in Marriage (no author), London: Psychology Press, 1930.

Featherstone, M., *Consumer Culture and Postmodernism*, London: Sage, 1991.

Featherstone, M., Hepworth, M. and Turner, B., *The Body: Social Process and Cultural Theory*, London: Sage, 1991.

Ferguson, M., *Forever Feminine: Women's Magazines and the Cult of Femininity*, London: Heinemann, 1983.

Ferguson, M., 'The Woman's Magazine Cover Photograph', in H. Christian (ed.), *The Sociology of Journalism and the Press*, Sociological Review Monograph no. 29, University of Keele, 1980.

Finkelstein, J., *The Fashioned Self*, Cambridge: Polity 1991.

Flowers, D., *Glamour Girls*, London: L. Miller, 1947.

Fonda, J., *My Life So Far*, London: Ebury Press, 2005.

Fowler, M., *The Way She Looks Tonight: Five Women of Style*, New York: St Martin's Press, 1996.

Freedman, R., *Beauty Bound: Why Women Strive for Physical Perfection*, London: Columbus, 1988.

Friedan, B., *The Feminine Mystique*, Harmondsworth: Penguin, 1965.

Gabor, M., *The Art of the Calendar*, London: Hodder and Stoughton, 1976.

Gabor, M., *The Pin-Up: A Modest History*, London: André Deutsch, 1972.

Gaines, J. and Herzog, C., *Fabrications: Costume and the Female Body*, London: Routledge, 1990.

Gardiner, J., *Gaby Deslys: A Fatal Attraction*, London: Sidgwick and Jackson, 1986.

Gardiner, J., *Picture Post Women*, London: Collins and Brown, 1993.

Gardiner, L., *Faces, Figures and Feelings: A Cosmetic Plastic Surgeon Speaks*, London: Robert Hale, 1959.

Garland, A., *Lion's Share*, London: Michael Joseph, 1970.

Garland, M., *Fashion*, Harmondsworth: Penguin, 1962.

Gell, A., 'Magic, Perfume, Dream ...', in I. Lewis (ed.), *Symbols and Sentiments: Cross Cultural Studies in Symbolism*, London: Academic Press, 1977.

Genders, R., *A History of Scent*, London: Hamish Hamilton, 1972.

Giddens, A., *Modernity and Self-Identity: Self and Society in the Late Modern Age*, Cambridge: Polity, 1991.

Gilman, S., *Creating Beauty to Cure the Soul: Race and Psychology in the Shaping of Aesthetic Surgery*, Durham, NC: Duke University Press, 1998.

Gilman, S., *Making the Body Beautiful: A Cultural History of Aesthetic Surgery*, Chichester: Princeton University Press, 1999.

Gilman, S. L. and Xun, Z. (eds.), *Smoke: A Global History of Smoking*, London: Reaktion, 2004.

Ginsberg, S., *Reeking Havoc: The Unauthorised and Outrageous Story of Giorgio the Bestseller Fragrance*, London: Hutchinson Business Books, 1989.

Gledhill, C. and Swanson, G. (eds.), *Nationalising Femininity: Culture, Nationality and British Cinema in the Second World War*, Manchester: Manchester University Press, 1996.

Glendinning, V., *Rebecca West: A Life*, London: Weidenfeld and Nicolson, 1987

Glyn, A., *Elinor Glyn: A Biography*, London: Hutchinson, 1955.

Glyn, E., *'It' and Other Stories*, London: Duckworth, 1927.

Glyn, E., *Romantic Adventure*, London: Ivor Nicholson and Watson, 1936.

Glyn, E., *The Career of Katherine Bush*, London: Duckworth, 1917.

Graves, R. and Hodge, A., *The Long Weekend*, London: Faber, 1940.

Green, J., *All Dressed Up: The Sixties and the Counter-culture*, London: Jonathan Cape, 1998.

Greer, G., *The Female Eunuch*, London: Paladin, 1971.

Grieve, M., *Millions Made my Story*, London: Gollancz, 1964.

Gross, M., *Model*, London: Bantam Press, 1995.

Gross, M., *Model: The Ugly Business of Beautiful Women*, New York: Perennial, 2003.

Gundle, S., *Glamour: A History*, Oxford: Oxford University Press, 2008.

Gundle, S., 'Hollywood Glamour and Mass Consumption in Postwar Italy', in R. Koshar (ed.), *Histories of Leisure*, Oxford: Berg, 2002.

Gundle, S. and Castelli, C., *The Glamour System*, Basingstoke: Palgrave Macmillan, 2006.

Gunn, F., *The Artificial Face: A History of Cosmetics*, Newton Abbot: David and Charles, 1973.

Hammerton, J., *For Ladies Only? Eve's Film Review, Pathé Cinemagazine, 1921–1933*, Hastings: The Projection Box, 2001.

Handley, S., *Nylon: The Manmade Fashion Revolution*, London: Bloomsbury, 1999.

Harlow, G. (ed.), *The Nature of Diamonds*, Cambridge: Cambridge University Press in association with the American Museum of Natural History, 1998.

Harper, S., *Women in British Cinema: Mad, Bad and Dangerous to Know*, London: Continuum, 2000.

Harris, D., *Cute, Quaint, Hungry and Romantic: The Aesthetics of Consumerism*, New York: Basic Books, 2000.

Hartnell, N., *Silver and Gold*, London: Evans Bros, 1955.

Haugland, H. Kristina, *Grace Kelly: Icon of Style to Royal Bride*, New Haven: Yale University Press, 2006.

Hoggart, R., *The Uses of Literacy, Aspects of Working Class Life, with Special Reference to Publications and Entertainments*, London: Chatto and Windus, 1957.

Holland, J., Ramazanoglu, C., Sharpe, S. and Thomson, R., 'Power and Desire: The Embodiment of Female Sexuality', *Feminist Review*, 1994, no. 46, pp. 21–38.

Hollander, A., *Seeing through Clothes*, New York: Viking, 1978.

Hopkins, H., *The New Look: A Social History of the Forties and Fifties*, London: Secker and Warburg, 1964.

Horwood, C., '"Girls Who Arouse Dangerous Passions": Women and Bathing, 1900–1939', *Women's History Review*, 2000, vol. 9, no. 4, pp. 653–73.

Horwood, C., *Keeping Up Appearances: Fashion and Class Between the Wars*, Stroud: Sutton Publishing, 2005.

Hudson, W., *Osprey; or Egrets and Aigrettes*, London: Royal Society for Protection of Birds, 1894.

Hulanicki, B., *From A to Biba*, London: Hutchinson, 1983.

Hutchinson, A. S. M., *This Freedom*, London: Hodder and Stoughton, 1922.

Ironside, J., *Janey*, London: Michael Joseph, 1973.

Ironside, V., *Janey and Me: Growing Up with My Mother*, London: Harper Perennial, 2003.

Irvine, S., *The Perfume Guide*, London: Haldane Mason, 2000.

Jackson, P., Lowe, M., Miller, D. and Mort, F. (eds.), *Commercial Cultures: Economies, Practices, Spaces*, Oxford: Berg, 2000.

Jacobowitz, F. and Lippe, R., 'Empowering Glamour', *Cineaction*, 1992, vol. 26/27, pp. 2–11.

Jeffreys, S., *Beauty and Misogyny: Harmful Cultural Practices in the West*, London: Routledge, 2005.

Jellinek, P., *The Practice of Modern Perfumery*, London: Leonard Hill, 1954.

Jellinek, P., *The Psychological Basis of Perfumery*, London: Blackie, 1997.

Jephcott, P., *Girls Growing Up*, London: Faber and Faber, 1942.

Jordan, T., *Growing Up in the Fifties*, London: Macdonald, 1990.

Kennedy, W., *Birds and Their Protection*, Hertford: Stephen Austin, 1895.

Kennett, F., *History of Perfume*, London: Harrap, 1975.

King, E., *Eleanore King's Guide to Glamour*, Englewood Cliffs, NJ: Prentice Hall, 1957.

Koshar, R. (ed.), *Histories of Leisure*, Oxford: Berg, 2002.

Kuhn, A., *An Everyday Magic: Cinema and Cultural Memory*, London: I. B. Tauris, 2002.

Kuhn, A., *Dreaming of Fred and Ginger: Cinema and Cultural Memory*, New York: New York University Press, 2002.

Lakoff, R. and Scherr, R., *Face Value: The Politics of Beauty*, London: Routledge and Kegan Paul, 1984.

Langhamer, C., *Women's Leisure in England, 1920–1960*, Manchester: Manchester University Press, 2000.

Laut, A., *The Fur Trade of America*, New York: Macmillan, 1921.

LaVine, W. Robert, *In a Glamorous Fashion: The Fabulous Years of Hollywood Costume Design*, London: Allen and Unwin, 1981.

Lee, H., *Virginia Woolf*, London: Vintage, 1997.

Lee, J., *This Great Journey*, New York and Toronto: Farrar and Rinehart, 1942.

Lehmann, R., *Invitation to the Waltz*, London: Virago, 2001 (1932).

Lindsay, K., *Glamour Girl*, London: Herbert Jenkins, 1942.

Links, J., *The Book of Fur*, London: James Barrie, 1956.

Lloyd, F. (ed.), *Deconstructing Madonna*, London: Batsford, 1993.

MacCarthy, F., *Last Curtsey: The End of the Debutantes*, London: Faber and Faber, 2006.

McConathy, D. and Vreeland, D., *Hollywood Costume: Glamour! Glitter! Romance!* New York: Harry N. Abrams, 1976.

McDowell, C., *Dressed to Kill: Sex, Power and Clothes*, London: Hutchinson, 1992.

McDowell, C., *Fashion Today*, London: Phaidon, 2003.

McDowell, C., *Forties Fashion and the New Look*, London: Bloomsbury, 1997.

McDowell, C., *Hats: Status, Style and Glamour*, London: Thames and Hudson, 1992.

McDowell, C., *Shoes: Fashion and Fantasy*, London: Thames and Hudson, 1989.

MacInnes, C., *Absolute Beginners*, London: Allison and Busby, 1980 (1959).

MacInnes, C., *England, Half English: A Polyphoto of the Fifties*, Harmondsworth: Penguin, 1966.

McLaughlin, T., *The Gilded Lily*, London: Cassell, 1972.

Madonna/Sex: Photographed by Steven Meisel, London: Secker and Warburg, 1992.

Maitland, S. (ed.), *Very Heaven: Looking Back at the 1960s*, London: Virago, 1988.

Mallet, Captain Thierry, *Glimpses of the Barren Lands*, New York: Revillon Frères, 1930.

Manvell, R., *The Film and the Public*, Harmondsworth: Penguin, 1955.

Marshall, C., *Prime Time Woman: A Guide to Looking and Feeling Great All Your Life*, London: Sidgwick and Jackson, 1987.

Marshall, C., *The Cat-Walk*, London: Hutchinson, 1978.

Massey, A., *Hollywood Beyond the Screen: Design and Material Culture*, Oxford: Berg, 2000.

Matthews, J., 'They Had Such a Lot of Fun: The Women's League of Health and Beauty', *History Workshop Journal*, 1990, vol. 30, pp. 22–54.

Mayer, J. P., *British Cinemas and Their Audiences*, London: Dobson, 1948.

Melly, G., *Revolt into Style: The Pop Arts in Britain*, Harmondsworth: Penguin, 1970.

Melman, B., *Women and the Popular Imagination in the Twenties: Flappers and Nymphs*, Basingstoke: Macmillan, 1988.

Menkes, S., *How to Be a Model*, London: Sphere, 1969.

Merriam, E., *Figleaf: The Business of Being in Fashion*, Philadelphia and New York: Lippincott, 1960.

Millum, T., *Images of Woman: Advertising in Women's Magazines*, London: Chatto and Windus, 1975.

Molloy, J. T., *Women: Dress for Success*, New York: Peter H. Wyden, 1980.

Moseley, R., *Growing Up with Audrey Hepburn*, Manchester: Manchester University Press, 2002.

Moseley, R., 'Respectability Sewn Up: Dressmaking and Film Star Style in the Fifties and Sixties', *European Journal of Cultural Studies*, 2001, vol. 4, no. 4, pp. 473–90.

Mulvagh, J., *Costume Jewellery in Vogue*, London: Thames and Hudson, 1998.

Myrdal, A. and Klein, V., *Women's Two Roles*, London: Routledge and Kegan Paul, 1956.

Naudet, J. and Riva, M., *Marlene Dietrich: Photographs and Memories*, New York: Alfred A. Knopf, 2001.

Neustatter, A., *Hyenas in Petticoats: A Look at Twenty Years of Feminism*, Harmondsworth: Penguin, 1990.

Newquist, R., *Conversations with Joan Crawford*, New Jersey: Citadel Press, 1980.

Nicholson, V., *Singled Out: How Two Million Women Survived without Men after the First World War*, London: Viking, 2007.

Offer, A., *The Challenge of Affluence: Self-Control and Well-Being in the US and Britain since 1850*, Oxford: Oxford University Press, 2006.

Ollerenshaw, K., *Education for Girls*, London: Faber and Faber, 1961.

Orbach, S., *Fat is a Feminist Issue*, London: Hamlyn, 1979.

Orbach, S., *Hunger Strike: The Anorectic's Struggle as a Metaphor for Our Age*, London: Faber and Faber, 1986.

Orwell, G., *The Road to Wigan Pier*, Harmondsworth: Penguin, 1972 (1937).

Ouellette, L., 'Inventing the Cosmo Girl: Class Identity and Girl-style American Dreams', *Media, Culture and Society*, 1999, vol. 21, no. 3, pp. 359–83.

Our Animal Brothers' Guild, *Fashionable Furs: How They Are Obtained*, Bristol, 1911.

Payne, G. and Abbott, P. (eds.), *The Social Mobility of Women: Beyond Male Mobility Models*, London: Falmer Press, 1990.

Peiss, K., *Hope in a Jar: The Making of America's Beauty Culture*, New York: Henry Holt, 1998.

Pember Reeves, M., *Round about a Pound a Week*, London: G. Bell and Sons, 1913.

PEP (Political and Economic Planning), *Modern Cosmetics and Perfumery*, n.p., 1957.

Picardie, J., *My Mother's Wedding Dress: The Life and Afterlife of Clothes*, Basingstoke: Picador, 2005.

Powdermaker, H., *Hollywood the Dream Factory: An Anthropologist Looks at the Moviemakers*, Boston: Little Brown, 1950.

Priestley, J. B., *English Journey*, London: Heinemann, 1934.

Quick, H., *Catwalking: A History of the Fashion Model*, London: Hamlyn/ Reed International, 1997.

Radner, H., '"This Time's for Me": Making Up and Feminine Practice', *Cultural Studies*, 1989, vol. 3, no. 3, pp. 301–22.

Raeburn, A., *Talking to Myself*, London: Sphere, 1985.

Ragas, M. Cohen and Kozlowski, K., *Read My Lips: A Cultural History of Lipstick*, San Francisco: Chronicle, 1998.

Rappaport, E., *Shopping for Pleasure: Women in the Making of London's West End*, Princeton, NJ: Princeton University Press, 2000.

Rice-Davies, M. with Flack, S., *Mandy*, London: Sphere, 1980.

Richards, J., *The Age of the Dream Palace: Cinema and Society in Britain, 1930–1939*, London: Routledge and Kegan Paul, 1984.

Rindisbacher, H., *The Smell of Books: A Cultural Historical Study of Olfactory Perception in Literature*, Ann Arbor: University of Michigan Press, 1992.

Robertson, P., *Guilty Pleasures: Feminist Camp from Mae West to Madonna*, London: Tauris, 1996.

Robson, J., 'The Role of Clothing and Fashion in the Household Budget and Popular Culture, Britain 1919–1949', unpublished D.Phil thesis, Oxford, 1997–8.

Rodaway, A., *A London Childhood*, London: Virago, 1985.

Roddick, A., *Body and Soul*, London: Ebury Press, 1991.

Roudnitska, E., 'The Art of Perfumery', in P. Müller and D. Lamparsky (eds), *Perfumes: Art, Science and Technology*, London: Chapman Hall, 1991.

Rovin, J., *Joan Collins: The Unauthorised Biography*, New York: Bantam Books, 1985.

Rowbotham, S., *A Century of Women: The History of Women in Britain and the United States*, London: Viking, 1997.

Rowbotham, S., *Promise of a Dream: Remembering the Sixties*, London: Allen Lane, 2000.

Roye, H. (Horace Narbeth), *Perfect Womanhood: 48 Photographic Studies*, London: George Routledge, 1938.

Roye, H. (Horace Narbeth), *The English Maid*, London: George Routledge, 1939.

Roye, H. with Vala, *Stereo-Glamour Series: Transatlantic Authors for the Camera Studies Club*, London, 1958–.

Rubinstein, H., *The Art of Feminine Beauty*, London: Gollancz, 1930.

Rushton, P., *Mrs Tinne's Wardrobe: A Liverpool Lady's Clothes, 1900–1940*, Liverpool: Bluecoat Press, 2006.

Sandbrook, D., *Never Had It So Good: A History of Britain from Suez to the Beatles*, London: Little Brown, 2005.

Sandbrook, D., *White Heat: A History of Britain in the Swinging Sixties*, London: Little Brown, 2006.

Saunders, A., *Jane: A Pin-Up at War*, Barnsley: Pen & Sword, 2005.

Schickel, R., *Intimate Strangers: The Culture of Celebrity in America*, Chicago: Ivan Dee, 2000.

Schiffer, N., *The Best of Costume Jewellery*, n.p., 1990?

Schwarz, B., 'Claudia Jones and the *West Indian Gazette*: Reflections on the Emergence of Post-colonial Britain', *Twentieth-Century British History*, 2003, vol. 14, no. 3, pp. 264–85.

Scott, L., *Fresh Lipstick: Redressing Fashion and Feminism*, Basingstoke: Palgrave Macmillan, 2005.

Scott-James, A., *In the Mink*, London: Michael Joseph, 1952.

Seebohm, C., *The Man Who Was Vogue: The Life and Times of Condé Nast*, London: Weidenfeld and Nicolson, 1982.

Segal, L., *Making Trouble: Life and Politics*, London: Serpent's Tail, 2007.

Settle, A., *Clothes Line*, London: Methuen, 1937.

Sexé, M., *Two Centuries of Fur Trading, 1723–1923: The Romance of the Revillon Family*, Paris: Draeger Frères, 1923.

Sherwood, M., *Claudia Jones: A Life in Exile*, London: Lawrence and Wishart, 1999.

Shrimpton, J., *The Truth About Modelling*, London: W. H. Allen, 1964.

Silverman, D., *Selling Culture: Bloomingdale's, Diana Vreeland and the New Aristocracy of Taste in Reagan's America*, New York: Pantheon, 1986.

Skeggs, B., *Formations of Class and Gender*, London: Sage, 1997.

Skov, L., 'The Return of the Fur Coat: A Commodity Chain Perspective', *Current Sociology*, 2005, vol. 53, no. 1, pp. 9–32.

Smith, H., *Aigrettes and Birdskins: The Truth about Their Collection and Export*, London: John Bale, Sons and Danielsson, 1910.

Soland, B., *Becoming Modern: Young Women and the Reconstruction of Womanhood in the 1920s*, Princeton: Princeton University Press, 2000.

Sontag, S., *Against Interpretation*, New York: Dell Publishing, 1966.

Spark, M., *The Girls of Slender Means*, Harmondsworth: Penguin, 1966.

Sparke, P., *As Long As It's Pink: The Sexual Politics of Taste*, London: Pandora, 1995.

Spencer, D. A. and Waley, H. D., *The Cinema Today*, Oxford: Oxford University Press, 1956.

Spencer, S., *Gender, Work and Education in Britain in the 1950s*, Basingstoke: Palgrave Macmillan, 2005.

Spiegel, M., 'Hollywood loves Diamonds', in G. Harlow (ed.), *The Nature of Diamonds*, Cambridge: Cambridge University Press in association with the American Museum of Natural History, 1998.

Spring-Rice, M., *Working Class Wives: Their Health and Conditions*, Harmondsworth: Penguin, 1939.

Stacey, J., *Star Gazing: Hollywood Cinema and Female Spectatorship*, London: Routledge, 1994.

Stearns, P., *Fat History: Bodies and Beauty in the Modern West*, New York: New York University Press, 2002.

Steedman, C., *Landscape for a Good Woman: A Story of Two Lives*, London: Virago, 1986.

Steele, V., 'Anti-Fashion: The 1970s', *Fashion Theory*, 1997, vol. 1, no. 3, pp. 279–96.

Steele, V., *Fetish: Fashion, Sex and Power*, Oxford: Oxford University Press, 1996.

Steele, V., *Fifty Years of Fashion: New Look to Now*, New Haven and London: Yale University Press, 1997.

Stuart, A., *Showgirls*, London: Jonathan Cape, 1996.

Summerfield, P., *Reconstructing Women's Wartime Lives*, Manchester: Manchester University Press, 1998.

Tapert, A., *The Power of Glamour: The Women Who Defined the Magic of Stardom*, London: Aurum Press, 1999.

Taylor, L., *The Study of Dress History*, Manchester: Manchester University Press, 2002.

Tennant, E., *Girlitude*, London: Vintage, 2000.

Thorp, M., *America at the Movies*, London: Faber and Faber, 1945.

Tinkler, P., *Constructing Girlhood: Popular Magazines for Girls Growing Up in England, 1920–1950*, London: Taylor and Francis, 1995.

Tinkler, P., *Smoke Signals: Women, Smoking and Visual Culture*, Oxford: Berg, 2006.

Tobias, A., *Fire and Ice: The Story of Charles Revson, the Man Who Built the Revlon Empire*, New York: William Morrow and Co., 1976.

Trent, P., *The Image Makers: Sixty Years of Hollywood Glamour*, London: Octopus, 1973.

Turner, A., *Biba: The Biba Experience*, Suffolk: Antique Collectors' Club, n.d.

Turner, K., *I Dream of Madonna: Women's Dreams of the Goddess of Pop*, London: Thames and Hudson, 1993.

Turner, M., *The Woman's Century: A Celebration of Changing Roles 1900–2000*, London: National Archives, 2003.

Twelve Ways to Glamour (no author), London: Gladding and Frost, 1946.

Veblen, T., *The Theory of the Leisure Class*, New York: Macmillan, 1912.

Vieira, M., *Hurrell's Hollywood Portraits: The Chapman Collection*, New York: Harry N. Abrams, 1997.

Vivat Vamp! An Album of Photographs in Praise of the Vamp from Mae West to Marilyn Monroe, from Marlene Dietrich to Brigitte Bardot (introduced by Spike Milligan), London: Dennis Dobson, 1959.

Vreeland, D., *Allure*, Boston: Little Brown and Co., 1980.

Wallace, C., *Germaine Greer: Untamed Shrew*, London: Richard Cohen, 2000.

Walsh, J., *Not Like This*, London: Lawrence and Wishart, 1953.

Wandor, M. (ed.), *The Body Politic: Writings from the Women's Liberation Movement in Britain, 1969–1972*, London: Stage 1, 1972.

Watt, J., *The Penguin Book of Twentieth-century Fashion Writing*, London: Viking, 1999.

Waugh, E., *A Handful of Dust*, London: Chapman and Hall, 1934.

Weekes, D., 'Shades of Blackness: Young Black Female Constructions of Beauty', in H. Safia Mirza (ed.), *Black British Feminism: A Reader*, London: Routledge, 1997.

Weldon, F., *The Life and Loves of a She-Devil*, London: Coronet, 1983.

Westmore, E. and Westmore, B., *Beauty, Glamour and Personality*, London: Harrap, 1947.

White, C., *Women's Magazines, 1693–1968*, London: Michael Joseph, 1970.

White, N. and Griffiths, I. (eds.), *The Fashion Business: Theory, Practice, Image*, Oxford: Berg, 2000.

Williams, I.C., *Underneath a Harlem Moon: The Harlem to Paris Years of Adelaide Hall*, London: Continuum, 2002.

Williams, N., *Powder and Paint: A History of the Englishwoman's Toilet*, London: Longmans Green and Co, 1957.

Williamson, J., *Consuming Passions: The Dynamics of Popular Culture*, London: Marion Boyars, 1986.

Wilson, E., 'A Note on Glamour', *Fashion Theory*, 2007, vol. 11, issue 1, pp. 95–108.

Wilson, E., *Adorned in Dreams: Fashion and Modernity*, London: Virago, 1985.

Wilson, E., *Mirror Writing: An Autobiography*, London: Virago, 1982.

Wilson, E., *Only Halfway to Paradise: Women in Postwar Britain, 1945–1968*, London: Tavistock, 1980.

Wilson, E., *The Contradictions of Culture: Cities, Culture, Women*, London: Sage, 2001.

Wilson, E. and Taylor, L., *Through the Looking Glass: A History of Dress from 1860 to the Present Day*, London: BBC Books, 1989.

Winship, J., *Inside Women's Magazines*, London: Pandora Press, 1987.

Wolf, N., *The Beauty Myth: How Images of Beauty Are Used against Women*, London: Vintage, 1990.

Wood, J., *Aircraft Nose Art: 80 Years of Aviation Artwork*, London: Salamander, 1992.

Woodhead, L., *War Paint: Elizabeth Arden and Helena Rubinstein, Their Lives, Their Times, Their Rivalry*, London: Virago, 2004.

Wykes-Joyce, M., *Cosmetics and Adornment: Ancient and Contemporary Usage*, London: Peter Owen, 1961.

Wyndham, J., *Love Lessons*, London: Virago, 2001.

Zweiniger-Bargielowska, I. (ed.), *Women in Twentieth-Century Britain*, Harlow: Pearson Education, 2001.

Index